broken summers

HENRY ROLLINS

2.13.61 Publications, Inc.

Design: Chapple Design, www.chappledesign.com
Cover Image "Brisbane at Night": Henry Rollins
Back Cover Photo: Grove Pashley

ISBN 1-880985-75-6

2.13.61, Inc.
7510 Sunset Blvd., #602
Los Angeles, CA 90046
www.21361.com
www.henryrollins.com

Thank you: Carol Bua, Heidi May, Mitch Bury of Adams Mass.

Sorry to see you go so soon: Amy, Dee Dee, Mad Marc, Wesley

JOE COLE 4.10.61 – 12.19.91

2001

12-23-01 LA CA: My next door neighbor died. Ninety-seven years old. Concentration camp ID number tattooed on her arm. I never met her. I knew she was in there but I never saw her. Two men loaded the body into a gray van a couple of days ago.

Last night, my doorbell rings. The dead woman's granddaughter. She was emptying the place out and came by to ask if I had a Valium to spare. How Eagles Greatest Hits is that? For some reason, she told me she was four days clean of kicking a "twenty dollar a day heroin habit," and then goes into a condensed version of the story of her life. I guess she needed someone to talk to. It's dark, there's a barred iron gate between us and I'm listening but I want this to be over. She tells me that she got into dope from hanging out with a bunch of musicians and I look at the ground and pull back into the shadows. Too late. She recognizes me and that turns into another monologue. Finally she leaves after asking me if I remember her name and I confess that I don't. She reminds me and tells me next time she comes by, I'm going to invite her in.

Last night I stood out front and looked at the house. All those years that woman lived in there invisibly. Start your life in a concentration camp and finish it out in LA. A van takes your body away, the family comes to haul out your stuff and make arrangements for you and your possessions, the granddaughter hits up the next door neighbor for tranquilizers, the house goes up for sale and it's a wrap. I wondered what I was doing in my place when she died. She died small and alone with no one around. I hope she died in her sleep.

Can't wait to leave. LA is a strange place to call home. I can't do it. I drive the streets and see places I've been in the past and there's no feeling of nostalgia. It all feels rented here. It feels like a mouthful of dirt. I have no feeling of familiarity with any landmark here. I do get a slight twinge when I drive by the Fat Burger at Gardner and Santa Monica because it used to be a place called Oki Dogs, an outdoor diner. It was quite the hang out many years ago. When we were living up the street from there in 1981, Black Flag roadie Mugger and I would sometimes go there in the evening and try to scam free food. Nice girls from the Valley or girls from Orange County were always a soft touch.

Oki's is the place where I watched Big John Macias back down a cop. John was the singer of a punk band called Circle One. John was one big man, hence the name. He was really cool and his band was good. He was not, however, a man to mess with as some unlucky people found out. Legend had it that one night he bit a guy's ear off at Oki's. I don't know if it's true or not but I wouldn't put it past him.

One night John and I were at Oki's eating a plate of french-fries. It was the first food I had eaten that day so I was into it. A cop came over to the table and told us to leave. I got up to leave immediately. There was no way I was going to argue with a cop. I was standing there waiting for John to get up but he didn't. He just sat there and kept eating. John looked at me and said, "Sit down." I didn't know what to do. The cop said, "I thought I told you faggots to leave." John got up and as he rose, I watched the cop size John up. John is now standing only an inch from the cop's face, grinning. John is taller and has the same build. John tells him that he's not a faggot and he paid for his food and he's going to eat it. No one at any of the other tables are even breathing at this point. It was all of a sudden very small and quiet. I watched the cop try and glance to the street to see if he had any back up and he didn't. Then I watched the cop's face work as he weighed his options. It was obvious he didn't want to get into it with John. He pulled back and told us to hurry up and then he walked away. Everyone started laughing as the cop passed and he pretended not to hear it but we all knew that John had made him back down. That was a great moment.

John was shot and killed by a policeman in Santa Monica, CA about ten years later. Joe Cole cut out the obituary and saved it for me so I could read it when I got back from tour. Joe was dead a few months later.

Recently, I drove by a building that many years ago used to be a club called the Cathay De Grande. It's where I met Jeffrey Lee Pierce of the Gun Club. It wasn't much, a dingy, poorly lit place for bands to play. Had some real good times there though. Played there a lot. Saw the two guitar line up of Minor Threat in there and they were amazing.

Sometimes I get a twinge when I drive by the Whiskey and remember when I used to hang out in front not having the money to go in. Sometimes near the end of the night, if the place wasn't crowded, the security guys would let the people hanging out on the street in to see what was left of the show. It's how I saw Social Distortion, Agent Orange and China White. Past that, this town has been a twenty year location to store my stuff in between tours. I am ready to go. I'm always ready to go. There's nothing here for me.

12-30-01 LA CA: 11:23 p.m. Listening to King Crimson live 05-04-74 McMasters University, Hamilton, Ontario, Canada. I like bootlegs. They allow me to put my ear up to the past and listen through a hole in time. I like the idea that through all the events in the world, through all the noise, confusion and time wasting, torturous, irrelevant distraction, the signal can still be heard. You can search out the past via these recordings. It's as if the speakers of the stereo are directly plugged into the past and you're sneaking through some breach in time and amazingly you are there. All too often, contemporary music doesn't give me what I need, so I go into the past looking for the good stuff.

I read an article on U2 recently in the *LA Times*. Robert Hilburn interviewed Bono. In the beginning of the article, Hilburn says that the most recent U2 record has sold over ten million copies worldwide. He praised it as the epitome of rock or some other paid-by–the-word crap. Recently, I sat and listened to that record two times and all I heard was a well produced, tired ass band bleating away, no talent playing and corny lyrics intact. Rock? At what point does that turgid disc rock? But then again, look at what the masses are into. They line up to eat at McDonald's. They read corny drugstore books and watch Julia Roberts films. Their tastes can't be taken seriously. I fear them for sure. I fear being trapped by their mediocrity and low-level ignorance. I fear their desperation and greed but I know what to look out for and how to avoid the consequences more often than not.

Tonight is the first night where I can start focusing my thoughts on the upcoming tour. I just spent three long days working on a movie. So far, it has no title. The film is about a man searching for meaning in life, to see if there is a connection between people or if all human acts are just a bunch of random events. He becomes disgusted with psychics who prey upon the weak and take their money. He goes into psychic shops, sits down with the psychic and asks them to tell him what's on his mind. If they're psychic, they'll know, right? Basically, what's on his mind is, "I'm going to kill you, you fucking psychic piece of shit." Of course, the psychic doesn't know this and he ends up killing them. He kills a few people who have it coming. Of course, I got to be the killer. I liked the writing and the director wanted me for the part so I went for it. Work keeps me out of trouble.

Like most low budget films I've worked on, everyone was really cool and only there because they need the work. There's no room for attitude on a set like this. My wardrobe consisted of the clothes I wore to the set.

Nothing eventful. Just scene after scene shot quickly here and there. The work we did in the two psychic shops was interesting. I had never been in one of those places before. They were both pretty much alike. A crap house in a fucked up part of LA. The front room dressed up to look all mystical and shit. Wax skulls, pyramid candles, beads, pieces of cloth hanging on the walls, a filthy floor. Behind a curtain is the rest of the house. A dump with a big TV and a couch. Broken furniture, the smell of dog urine. Poor folks figuring it out in Amerika's harsh shuffle.

The second shop we worked at was owned by a Gypsy family. Mom and dad were both over three hundred pounds, son and daughter were on their way. They all sat in a Cadillac and watched us work. By the end of the shoot they were jeering at us and beeping the horn when the camera started rolling. Friendly.

I finished last night. It was a good time but I'm glad to be done. I really want to get my head around the upcoming shows. I can't say I mind the work all that much, it's the actors who are hard to be around. It's easy to work with actors who are talented because you can be intense and really do the work. It's difficult to work with people who get their lines wrong take after take or can't hit their marks, making everyone else have to figure out how to save the scene on the fly. And how about that conversation in the van on the ride back to base the other day? Two girls sitting together talking about their breast implants like they're talking about car parts for the entirety of the trip. Zzzzzzzzzzzzz.

Soon, it will be a show almost every night. There will be constant cold and hardly any days off. We'll be on a cramped bus with all the gear and it will be a test. I am preparing myself for this. I will turn forty-one on this tour.

My body is almost there, I have to work on my mind now. I will get there by the time I hit Belfast for the first show. It's a process of throwing things out of my mind. I try to keep it spare in there. It's human connections that make things difficult. I can handle a lot of information but human relationships make things difficult when on the road.

It's been a long time since I had a girlfriend. I can't imagine being in that situation again. I am not remotely interested in knowing someone intimately or being known intimately. Don't know, don't want to know. I used to care about all that, now I don't as much. Maybe I'm too old or just apathetic. Apathy—now that's an easy one! I bet I'm just a self-absorbed asshole who doesn't give a fuck about much else other than precisely what I want to do. That's the one we'll go with! A selfish pig who likes a schedule better than real life! He's in denial! Blowing it! You'll have regrets when you're old! You'll see!!

I just want to go. A tour itinerary for me just cuts through all the possible crap I can come up with. It makes any nonessential thing in my life fall away. After so many years, it's only the way I can reference how my life is going. When I am here, it's always a countdown to when I leave again. Always. There's always a tour looming.

The road is the truth. I have to prove it every night. After the show is over, the achievement is immediately erased. I have to gear up to prove it again the next night. There's nothing to fall back on. I go out there every night and stand them down. It's the only way I can justify my right to eat. When I am off the road, it's just day after day tedium. Another trip to the grocery store.

Los Angeles isn't a town you live in—just one you live through. While here, I witness, I gather information and document the facts as they happen. It's a microscopic history, easily erased, a tiny signal emitted from the great Amerikan crime scene.

Things that just happened:

1. I got an e-mail from a girl who told me that I missed a good show the other night. She said it was insane to watch Dee Dee Ramone singing 'Do the Locomotion.'

2. Most days of the week there's a man begging for money at the intersection where I turn left on to go to the office. He's a hardcore street guy who wears women's clothes. He has painted nails that are usually chipped. He wears low cut pants that expose shaved pubic stubble. Sometimes he's wearing lipstick. If I catch the red light, I stare into his eyes until the light turns green.

3. At the foodstore tonight a beautiful dreadlocked woman was ahead of me. She was buying really good food. Vegetables, fish and fruit. I thought to myself how lucky one would be to eat at her place that night. After she left, the bagger guy said to the cash register guy, "That was Whoopi Goldberg, dude." The cash register guy pretended not to hear him. The bagger guy held up my can of soup and said, "I sure could use a bowl of this right now." Put the fucking can of soup in the bag before I break your skull with it.

Only a few days away from leaving this city of whores.

12-31-01 LA CA: 4:22 p.m. Listening to a semi-legit Lou Reed CD called *American Poet.* It's got some good stuff on there. It's a live concert of his "rock band" line up from 1972. It's a little strange to hear him sing the line in Heroin "and all the dead bodies piled up in mounds," and then hear a piercing guitar solo. It's as if the rest of the band doesn't know what the song's about. It makes the song even more sick in a way.

I'm almost finished with my second pass through the CNN documentary *Cold War.* The first viewing was really interesting but it's even more fascinating the second time around. I reckon WWII and the Cold War pretty much determine who's friends with whom now. Did the Cold War really end or has it just mutated into something even more intense and life threatening? I wonder if Amerika nuked Japan only to see how the bombs worked on mass human population and to let Russia and the rest of the world know what's up.

The documentary is riveting and at times, infuriating. No one stepped up to challenge Stalin. I wonder how much countries like Amerika and England knew what he was doing to his own people.

He's the ultimate monster of history. He dressed up a third world country as a super power only to starve and kill millions in the process.

The wars in Korea and Vietnam were just ways to fight Russia without having to resort to direct confrontation and mutually assured destruction.

The segment on the Civil Rights movement was hard to sit through. I have seen every documentary I can find on the Civil Rights movement and the Black Panthers. Watching the clips of Dr. King speak never fails to move me. Hoover's FBI was such a bunch of bastards. Hoover was a nightmare. He and the government that allowed all these crimes to be perpetrated should be put on trial. I don't care if they're dead.

By the end of the Civil Rights segment last night, I was back to that angry, disgusted state that I always get in when I think about racism. At one point, I started thinking of what country I would move to. I know there's racism everywhere but the Amerikan version chokes me with rage. You would figure we'd be on to something else by now. Happy New Year.

2002

01-06-02 LA CA: 0026 hrs. Band practice commenced a few days ago and we're sounding good. We have one more bash at it in the afternoon and then nothing more until we hit it for real in Belfast. We brought some new old songs into the set, 'Disconnect' and 'Low Self Opinion.' 'Disconnect' sounds different with the boys playing it. It rocks harder. It sounds better than I remember it. I come back from practice with a headache and my body feeling pounded, we must be doing something right.

This thing always happens to me the last few days before I go back out, it varies in its level of intensity but it always happens, I get very lonely. I get nostalgic and sad. I miss women I went out with one hundred and fifteen years ago. My room looks different, it looks better than I remember the day before. I know what it is—it's weakness trying to trick me into getting soft. It's comfort trying to put lead in my shoes. Being here too long isn't good for me. I think too much. I obsess. The days pass without meaning. A week feels like a day. On the road, a day feels like a knotted rope pulled out of your guts. You have to work to make it back to your bunk at night. Sleep is the reward. I don't get that same feeling when I'm here. Sometimes before I'm about to leave, I wonder if I can still do it. I wonder if I still have the guts to take the pain every night and deliver the real thing. No way to know until I get out there and that's one of the reasons that I really need to get going.

These things happened:

1. A few days ago, I got a letter from a girl who said that she liked me and wanted to get to know me. Her letter was so brave and vulnerable. She wasn't crass, her words were well-considered and sincere. I admired her for putting herself out there like that. I told her I was-

n't good at getting to know someone or letting someone get to know me. Then I made fun of myself so perhaps she wouldn't feel embarrassed for writing me. I hope she got the hint. Being close to someone makes the road hard to take. It's better not to be attached to anyone if you travel a lot or want to get a lot done. I think about it sometimes though. How amazing would it be to have a woman concerned about me? To know a woman was thinking of me and I was thinking of her and that we meant something to each other, that level of trust—it's great when I think about it. Not as great when I have an itinerary and work to do. I'm an intellectual romantic! A woman might say that I'm just a shallow coward. I care about the schedule and the work. You don't get to do it all and you have to go without some things to get others. I think it's alright to bitch about bad luck but not about the choices you make.

2. I was driving east on Santa Monica Blvd. last Thursday afternoon and while at a red light, I stared at a man in a pink jacket and leopard print skirt. He saw me staring and blew me kisses until the light turned green. I have always admired the guys who work on that part of Santa Monica Blvd. They're so full-on. That's the real hardcore. It makes all those guys with piercings and stupid pants you see in bands these days seem completely lightweight. When you drive down Santa Monica Blvd. on a cold morning and see those guys out there, no shirt, strutting on the corner, raw, fully confrontational—it's so cool. Or when you see the she-men walking with the exaggerated hip sway, it's like they're taking the whole world on. I'm so into that. I can't imagine what that would be like to face every day as my employment but I can't see how people work at McDonald's either. What is more flat out core than a male prostitute with his dick pushing against his mini-skirt flicking his tongue at you while you wait at a red light?

3. I was driving to band practice several hours ago. Going east on Hollywood Blvd. with Mann's Chinese Theater on my left. I looked at the people on the sidewalk and it seemed that almost all of them had logos on their shirts. It reminded me of when I've been in some remote corner of the world and seen people walking around in worn

thin clothes and so often their shirts have brand name logos of things they would never come into contact with or never be able to afford if they did. When I saw those people on Hollywood Blvd., it struck me that we are refugees in our own country. We walk around with logos on our clothes, we are warm blooded billboards, advertising product to other warm blooded billboards. Working for our pimps. Amerika as one big ad for Amerika. Men going door to door spreading the good word of Nike and DKNY. Microsoft taking out ad space in the Bible. We are inhabitants of a factory so huge we can't even see it. We run in and out of the doors with product. Product as a virus. We spread it and infect others. Amerika as the groovy accessorized First World leader with a Third World lean. Wake up to your mother trying to sell you black market Duracell batteries and a Sean John factory second t-shirt. In the future, the Tooth Fairy will leave Master P brand bullets and Starbucks flavored condoms bought from Amazon.com under your pillow. No one in Amerika is out of work. We're all in advertising.

4. Every other bus stop bench has an ad for Lenny Kravitz's new album called *Lenny*. The album cover and the bus bench ads are laid out like a DKNY ad. How very crass and telling. He names the record after himself, perhaps to say, "This is the real me," and it looks like a fashion ad. Corny. I met the guy once and he was really cool to me. So what. I am at war so I'm calling it as I see it. Fuck being nice. Fuck being cool to those who don't deserve it. Fuck looking the other way. Let's go kill some vampires. No wait, you go do whatever you want. I'll kill alone. I will kill with truth. I will kill with thousands of miles traveled. I will kill with fuck you.

5. MTV wanted to interview me about something the other day and I told them to kiss my ass. Fuck MTV. Fuck *Rolling Stone.* I remember David Fricke at *Rolling Stone,* he used to be cool. Now he just kisses ass and tries to be hip. Pathetic. I'd buy a copy of *Rolling Stone* if they did an expose on the magazine's owner Jan Wenner. Dish it, girl! That I'd read for sure. Amerikan culture is weak. Amerikans eat too much. Amerikans take up too much room. Amerikans waste enough food to feed a starving country. Amerika is not as strong as it used to

be. It's just meaner and more efficient at laying down economic suppression fire. A bunch of fat morons driving around in SUV's wonder how a rag tag army of extremists was able to take out the Pentagon and the World Trade Center. Millions of television-addicted mediocre slobs wonder why people hate Amerika. So much wonderment. Britney Spears singing with Aerosmith at the Super Bowl? I don't wonder. Et tu Steve Tyler? Fuck you, Steve. All you have to do is listen to the songs on the radio and you know that Amerika is weak. If I was seeking to invade Amerika, the music would be my cue. "They're listening to Creed. We're going in. We'll take the Capitol in a day."

6. A girl wrote me a letter and I answered in a humorous way but I don't think my mirth was in her strike zone or maybe it was and she was having a good time. In any case, I went with it and this was the exchange of letters over a two day period:

A: Henry, Hi, I was wondering what kind of music you listen to. Have you ever listened to Enya, or Enigma? They are more new age I guess. But I was just curious if you get into the classics or more modern stuff. -A

H: A, now which Enya are we talking about? The New Age Enya or the other one who did that 'Take A Toke Off My Ass Pipe' 12" last year that was getting all the club play? I don't listen to either one but I know they're both mighty popular. As far as Enigma goes, I've never been able to figure them out. -Henry

A: Henry, Definitely not the ass pipe toking Enya. She is an Irish born musician. She does all the music and vocals herself. Very mellow music good to listen to when you're just chilling with a cup of tea... what do you listen to? I have always wondered if musicians listen to their own stuff. -A

H: A, I've been listening a lot to Sting and the new Kid Rock CD. It's not as amazing as his last one but still really good. He's not the same now that Joe C is gone. I am saving the new Creed CD for when I get back from church tomorrow. What is the best Enya CD to start with? -Henry

A: Henry, All of Enya's work is excellent - you can start with any of them really they are all unique in their own way. Her latest is called A Day Without Rain. Her web page is pretty good too. It is Enya.com. I like Creed's work also, hear My Sacrifice a lot on radio and sometimes overkill of a song *can turn you off of it or the group all together. Somewhat surprised to see you like Sting, I could've sworn I saw an interview once where you were ragging on him and his wife. Just please let me know if you start digging U2. And church...(you're BS'ing right?) Just didn't figure you as a regular church attendee. No offense intended. And one more while I am on a roll...do you know if you ever plan to come back to Akron Ohio for any music or Spoken Word tours? -A*

H: A, well I don't think I'll ever like U2 but Sting is really an amazing musician and the way he tackles heavy world issues and folds them into an eclectic, yet pop nuanced motif is all the more impressive. Yeah, I go to church now and then. I don't care what kind, whatever's closest, it's all pretty good to me. I still go to the Mosque now and then, not as much as I used to!

There's a church up the street from my office and it's pretty different to say the least. They once had on the sign out front, "If you're gay, or in AA, you're always welcome in The Lord's cabaret!" I thought this was pretty cool so I started checking the place out when I was in town. The minister, Louis-Farakhan Celine... He's on fire!... Psychotic! ... We worship and chew our own flesh!... You can learn a lot by checking out some of his stuff!

I don't know when I'll be getting to your city again, we were just there with the band and it was a real good time. I'll be checking out some Enya for sure. Thanks for writing. -Henry

A: Henry. Well with a sign out front like that who wouldn't feel comfortable going in? Sounds like they accept everyone without judgement, isn't that refreshing. I don't go to church and haven't for years. I am not sure I am on good terms with The Man anyway. Most religion you see now a days is so advertised and judgmental of all the others. It is hard to get a grasp on faith. I have always considered myself more of a "spiritual" person anyway rather then the stereo-typical religious person. I can go outside on a beautiful sunny day and see God. Course I think I see him when I am winning on the slot machines in Vegas too! Take Care. -A

I like LA for one thing at least. It keeps me mad. Like Iggy said in a recent interview when asked how he keeps his rage, "I work at it." How awesome is that? You have to. You have to keep seeing it clearly.

01-06-02 LA CA: 11:31 p.m. Alan Vega's flawless album *Deuce Avenue* is playing. Alan is a sore point for me. I put out several of Alan's records over the years and much to my regret, bitterness, sadness and frustration—not many people cared. Those records are so great! The one we put out in 1996, *Dujang Prang,* is so damn cool. The one we put out with Ben Vaughn and Alex Chilton playing with him, the Alan Vega Trio *Cubist Blues* is brilliant. Alex fucking Chilton! How good does a record have to be to get someone to check it out? That's just it. It can't be any good. It has to be a piece of shit to sell.

Every time I hear one of Alan's records, I want to get back into the trenches and fight for his records out there in the marketplace. I know it would be futile. I just have to tell myself not to take it personally. It's just that I believe 110% in his talent. His vision is totally unique and brilliant. Those who know, know. I have been into the guy for over twenty years now. I still have the Suicide album I bought in 1979. I played it the other night and it's still ultimate.

Today was the last day of band practice. The set is strong, perhaps our best one yet. It's a long one. It will be hard to put it up every night. It's not like there's anything else to do out there so that's that.

Everyone seems to be in good spirits and ready to hit the road. We'll leave Tuesday afternoon.

Someone Likes You Dept.: I got back here a few weeks ago and the guy who looks in on my place every few days called a few minutes after I walked in the door from Switzerland. He called to apologize. I asked him what for. He said he would tell me the whole story when he came over and he was on his way. Ok, if you want to be strange, be that way. He's not strange though. This was going to be interesting.

He comes over a little while later and I ask him what he's on about. He says he's sorry about the other night. Huh? He goes on to tell me that a few nights before he came by to check on the place and he had the lights on and was rattling around and came out of the kitchen in time to see a half-dressed woman leave my bathroom and go into my bedroom without seeing him! He thought he got my schedule wrong and I was back and in the middle of some encounter.

She scared the hell out of him. He snuck out, not wanting to startle us. I asked him if he was kidding. He looked at me like I was insane. I asked him if he was sure it was a human being who came out of the bathroom. He told the whole story over again. I was in Milan, Italy on the night in question so this raises some concerns.

Then in typical guy fashion, my next question, which I am sure will come as no surprise, "Was she hot?" He looked at me like I was nuts and then said, "Well yeah. I was happy for you."

So, I've got a stalker. I've got love in my life. I'm no bum! Hey Ma, look! I've got a gal!

My house watcher pal left and I did a perimeter check of all the windows and doors. It all looked ok. The next few nights were a little light on sleep. Just got all the new locks.

01-10-02 Belfast Northern Ireland: 7:12 p.m. Backstage such as it is. A small, cold room next to a pile of chairs. Hey, it's a gig and we'll take it. We go on in a few hours and I am looking forward to it. I have to get at least one show on the board so I can know that I am on tour.

The last twenty-some hours have been suspended in the strange, blurry syrup of jet lag. We got here yesterday afternoon and met up with Darrell, front of house sound, and Shawn who does merch. He's Mike the road manager's cousin. He sold merch on the last tour and he fit in with the tribe so we dragged him out on this stretch to endure what will be a hard patch of road for sure. We all piled into the bus and headed to some warehouse district to pick up t-shirts. We ate marginal food at a pub near the warehouse as the t-shirts were still being made. We went from there to some stretch of coastline and waited until 0330 hrs. to catch a ferry to a port near Dublin. From there we drove up here. I have been in and out of sleep all this time.

When I woke up the sun was nearly gone but there was enough of it to see the buildings on the street near the venue, just incredible. Ireland is jawdroppingly beautiful in places, a beauty that silences and humbles. In other parts, it's hard-bitten, urban and worn. Many have lived excruciatingly hard in this country. Worked too many years at too low a wage, ate and slept too little and lost much too much. I think the mixture of the beauty and the pain is what makes the Irish so tough and awesome. And they are an awesome lot, too. This venue is cold. Cold enough to where I can see my breath in this tiny dressing room that is to hold all of us. It's cold and damp, yet the staff are bouncing in and out like it's a spring day. Jim, the man who brought in the catering, reminded me that we met when I was here with the Chili Peppers. I said that ten years was a long time. He said when we meet again in thirty years—that'll be a long time. Well, ok. I can hear 'Tomorrow's Dream' by Black Sabbath playing in the venue now. It's good to be here.

It's good to finally be out of LA. The last few days were depressing. The days right up to when I leave always are. The comfort of the house, as spare as it is, somehow weakens me. I brought a small duffel bag and my backpack that holds my notebooks and computer, other than that, I have nothing else out here. I really have all I need and then some. It's this perspective that makes living off the road feel like I'm on shaky ground. I see the things I own as things that will eventually be lost, stolen, sold, or somehow destroyed. I reckon I will eventually be down to a dufflebag and a backpack anyway so it's good to exist in that space more often than not and be used to it. I think when you get used to living with minimal possessions, it's makes one's thoughts clearer. Out here, without material possessions in the way, there's nothing to fixate upon but the music and life. When I am at the house, I sometimes forget that life isn't "stuff."

Out here, my perception becomes more clear, I'm more observant and more focused than I am when off the road. Focus, intensity and discipline are key for what we're doing. Especially since we are without any cushion of popularity or other insulation. All we have is our guts and the music. We have to prove it every night from the ground up. On our level, you have your shit together, or you are so out of here. Cool.

01-11-02 Belfast N. Ireland: 0041 hrs. In the bus. We'll be leaving in an hour or so. We only have 100 miles to drive down to Dublin so there's no hurry. The show was good. It was good for a first show of the year, and it was a good show anyway. Our first shows of tours have been better than ever. I wasn't really feeling the jet lag up there. Jet lag-wise, that first show in Australia last year was a monster compared to this one. European jet lag usually gets me harder than any other but so far I feel alright.

On the way to the bus there were some people by the door who wanted to get some stuff signed. Among the small crowd was a drunk guy. The classic drunk, the drunk guy I always imitate when I try to explain the phenomenon of the ubiquitous drunk guy. Here's what he did/they always do: he shook my hand about ten times. He started in with the self-deprecating rap of how he knows that I think he's nothing but a piece of shit but despite this certain truth, he loves me anyway. Now that he's on the verge of tears, it's time for another handshake. Overwhelmed by emotion, he repeats almost word for word the rap from a minute ago as if he never said it. He tells me with heart rending sincerity that he loves me and then it's time for the hug. He hugs me hard and long and I endure it. I politely explain that I have to sign all this other stuff and deal with all these other people. I actually turn him around and show him the people so he doesn't think I'm trying to fake him out. This sets him off on a third airing of the previous rap. We shake hands again. I tell him that he should give me a minute to talk to these other people. We're shaking hands again and the rap that I have heard on many continents over decades, starts again. Finally I ask his friend to take him home. But the friend is a little wasted, very wasted actually, and he starts in with his version of the age old rap. He breaks from form and with a brilliant flash of inebriated spontaneity, informs me that he and his friend are nurses at a hospital, and their shift starts early in a few hours. I urge them to go to the hospital now and check themselves in. As if I could make a suggestion that would be of use—these are veterans, studied and righteously hammered men, drinking hard for you on a Thursday night, getting ready for a long shift at the job.

7 p.m. Backstage, waiting to do the thing. We are hours away yet but I'm still trying to wake up. Soundcheck sounded good and it should be alright tonight.

Another jet lagged day in a semi-comatose state. I wrote Philomena Lynott the other day, telling her that we were playing here but never heard back. I don't know what she's up to. It would have been good to see her. She's so great. She came to soundcheck last time we were here and we all took pictures with her. She always has a badge with her son Philip's photo on it.

We will be onstage soon enough. Time to start waking up.

01-12-02 Dublin Ireland: 0023 hrs. I don't understand why the Irish are so damn friendly. I don't mind it but I don't see where they get that spirit from. Dublin is a tough town. It's beautiful and sad and harsh and true.

I walked around before the show and took in the passing cars and street lights. People coming out of the stores, men putting their fruit and vegetable stalls away. Rotten product left on the sidewalk, kids riding skateboards through it. The smell of coal and exhaust in the air. The pubs start to fill up. I saw a woman looking into a fireplace while she drank. Was she alone, waiting for someone? She looked at me and then stared back into the flames.

The show was in the place I did two nights the last time I was here on a talking tour. I recognized it as soon as I walked in. The audience, where the hell were they last time we played here? I was ready to write Dublin off considering how they were the last time. We played here 07-03-00 and the audience just kind of stood there. They weren't throwing stuff or trying to kill us, it just seemed like they weren't interested. I figured, fine, we'll go somewhere else. But tonight, it was full-on. I don't know what that's about. In any case, they were great and I think we played well.

This is a good place to play. I would like to keep coming back. Sometimes, I wonder if it's the last time I'll play some of these places. You never know. Interest drops off, promoters don't want you, you fall away. It's down to the promoters and agents. Nothing in this business is ever for sure past knowing you're always going to be hustling. Some critics think it's down to them but those of us who do this for real know that critics have nothing to do with the workings of the machine. Most critics know enough to know that no one gives a fuck and they hate it; it's why they're so frustrated. If the promoters and the agents lose interest in you, then you don't have a gig. It's hard but at least it answers a lot of your questions in advance. It's tough out here so you have to be tough. So, be tough. Absolutes will always guide you in times of doubt. Seneca said that anything that happens in nature is the truth. Bottom line reality is always cool even when it's fucked. At least you know where it's at. I am more comfortable in stressed situations and conflict. It's where everything ends up anyway so you might as well cut out the middle part and live in the eventual.

01-12-02 Cork Ireland: 6:22 p.m. Backstage. Not as cold as the one in Belfast but close. We pulled in around dawn. I got off the bus and took pictures of gulls flying over the river we were parked next to. Soon after it started raining and it's been raining ever since.

The venue is a few blocks away from the bus but they can't get the bus any closer so load in was accomplished by taking the gear out, loading it into a van, driving it a few blocks and then unloading it and carrying it up a couple of flights of stairs into the venue.

Before soundcheck, I did a photo session for *Forbes Small Business Magazine*. Photo man insisted we shoot in the alley behind the venue in the rain. So we got soaked for awhile. Then we went inside and took photos in the ladies room which was well lit and very cool looking. The guy asks me if I'll take my shirt off. I don't want him to take his shirt off, what's the deal? I told him that the shoot is for Forbes, let's go. He shot a couple more frames and he said that was all he needed and mercifully, I was turned loose. Photos or press are the last things I want to do on tour.

So let's see, backstage has no toilet, no running water. Excellent, fantastic even. It's cold, jet lag is making it hard to stay awake, we're on in a couple of hours and most of tomorrow's day off will be spent in the bus getting to Glasgow. If it could get any better, I don't see how.

01-13-02 Cork Ireland: 0010 hrs. Now that was a show. Good audience and good sound. I was getting monitor feedback so I chucked the wedge out of the way and it cleared up, the monitor man wasn't happy about that but he should have had it together. It was going really well until the second to last song in the encore when a guy hit me on the head and it drove my face down into the mic and I chipped off part of my tooth. At the last possible moment of the set, when I said good night and nodded my head down, the same guy had his index finger out pointing at me and I perfectly skewered my left eye with it. It hurts like hell and the whole side of my head is aching from it.

People kept coming backstage after the show. They just stand there and talk. We're all in various states of undress, trying to change and they just stand there and talk away. This one lady and her boyfriend kept insisting that I kiss her. Not going to happen. Finally they left after I signed her ticket. I don't mind, I know that people only think of themselves. I do it all the time.

Before we got out of the venue we had to suffer the DJ's wrath. He was playing the worst shit. Puffy, Diddy? Sean, stick to making those lame clothes.

I'm tired and my eyes are shutting on me. It's a long drive to Glasgow.

01-14-02 Glasgow Scotland: 1100 hrs. Not much of a day off yesterday. We pulled out of the show and went up to Belfast to catch the ferry. I looked out the window as we sped through the small towns on the way. It was past 0330 hrs. and there were people still out. Outside it's raining and cold and there are people in doorways huddled together, people alone in the dark under awnings just standing around. I didn't notice any of them even look up as our ship sailed by. The town peters out quickly and then it's pitch black as if the window has been painted over. No stars, no moon, just black. Then out of nowhere, lights, a gas station with a few people standing in front of it and then the blur of closed shops and the Irish night people standing soaked in doorways and then back to black and the sound of the engine and rain hitting the glass.

We drove hours from wherever the ferry let us off and by the time we got to the hotel it was dark and the day was over.

I am a few pages away from finishing one of the more crushing books I've read in a long time. Ryszard Kapuscinski's brutal *Imperium*. It's reportage from his travels all over Russia. He goes to countless cities I've never heard of with names I can only attempt to pronounce: Yakutsk, Listvganka, Irkutsk, Vargashovska, Zalozhnaya. Names of people that have me staring at the page trying to figure out how to say them fluently as if I had to name these people in an alibi under interrogation: Miltahutdinov, Samedoglu, Ivankienko. There's names of provinces, towns, rivers, leaders, deserts, concentration camps by the hundred. I don't know at all how Kapuscinski keeps all this information together, it's absolutely mind boggling. The book details aspects of the day to day life, history and brutality millions of Russians endured under Stalin. Restriction of movement and thought is almost impossible for me to imagine. It's an overload. It's incredible what people went through in the last century. Death toll in the millions. Starvation and catastrophe that defies comprehension. I had no idea that people could be so mean. When you've been raised in an environment of relative freedom, when you're allowed to say what you want about the leadership of your country with no fear of reprisal, you figure that's just the way it is. You don't even think about your rights, it's just how you're living. Consider that millions of people existed in an environment with fear as a constant for their entire lives, who never raised their voices, never expressed themselves. What would a conversation with someone who lived this way be like? Your logical points of reference wouldn't match. You would both stare at each other in disbelief that the other one thinks the way they do.

In the book, Kapuscinski relates the story of a woman at a market who remarks to a friend that the sausage was better when the Romanians made it. She gets reported and does six years. A man makes a bust of Lenin and when he can't get it into the doorway of the building he's supposed to deliver it to, he ties a rope around the neck of the bust and while attempting to hoist it up the side of the building with a pulley, he gets arrested for hanging Lenin in effigy and does ten years.

RK remarks that even now, asking the most mundane questions scares people in some regions, as asking questions of strangers is reserved for soldiers and police. The places this man has been are so intense. I can't begin to imagine what it would be like to have all that swimming around in my mind.

I have two more books of his to read. I have been making notes about some of his references and I will attempt to secure some of these books he mentions if they're in English translation. I want to learn more about the mining community/death camps of Kolyma in Siberia and see if any of these Armenian writers he mentions are in translation. So little time, so much to explore. Or not. Some people are happy just watching TV.

I can't say that brutality on this scale is totally unknown to me. I knew that there were insane statistics of human death during Stalin's reign but I never knew exactly how all these people were dispatched. Now I know a little more. In a territory the size of Russia, you can make people just vanish. Whole languages and cultures were erased. In many parts of the Imperium, it was illegal to speak your native language.

What is there to learn from all this? Good question. One of the more burning sentiments that he works off of in his writing about Africa in his books *Another Day of Life* and *Shadow of the Sun* is that 99% of the earth's surface wants you dead and tries at all times to eliminate you. I never thought about a winter day that way. Top of the food chain my ass!

01-16-02 Kesick UK: 4:45 p.m. A day off in a small town. Before I got on the plane, I went to the magazine stand and purchased a copy of *Rosie* (Rosie O'Donnell's magazine) and a copy of *O* (Oprah Winfrey's magazine). I wanted to see what they were all about.

Perhaps I could learn something. The man who rang me up gave me a strange look.

I read both of them on the way over. Some quick stats:

Rosie Magazine February 2002 issue
Price 3.50 USD
150 pages
14 images of Rosie O'Donnell
Opening line of Rosie O'Donnell's intro page: "I just ate four Mallomars."
In this issue: Rosie talks to Susan Sarandon on the phone.

O Magazine January 2002 issue
Price 3.50 USD
179 pages
15 images of Oprah Winfrey
Opening line of Oprah Winfrey's intro page: "We're beginning a new year by exploring one of the defining values of my life: truth."
In this issue: Oprah goes to Ground Zero with Mayor Rudy Giuliani.

Neither magazine advertised any tobacco or alcohol products. Both magazines advertised pharmaceutical drugs such as Zoloft and Advair.

Personally speaking department: *O* Magazine is better reading. The articles are well written and the topic matter is more varied than *Rosie*. Rosie O'Donnell seems to have an obsession with showing everyone she loves children. It makes me think she uses this as a shield against critical scrutiny. It's hard to attack someone who loves children sooooooooo much. Both magazines have self-improvement articles. *O* more than *Rosie*. *O* has financial advice and a book and poetry section. *Rosie* has neither. Does that intimate that *O* caters to a more literate financially independent readership?

Curiosity Department: Is Rosie married? Does she have a man in her life? She has a few children. Adopted? Abducted? Is Rosie a lesbian? If so, does she have a partner? Does said partner help out with parenting or is Rosie doing it all herself? If Rosie was in an open field setting, could Ted Nugent bring her down with one arrow? Will

Purina some day market a "Rosie Chow" food product? If Rosie and Donald Rumsfeld ran at each other as hard as they could, which one would be left standing? Has Ringling Brothers ever offered her a job? Would you have the courage to kick her trough at feeding time? If a Geraldo Rivera / Rosie O'Donnell sex video were released ala Pamela Anderson / Tommy Lee, would it sell? Would you wrestle her for charity or just send in a check? I've seen a harpoon sticking out of her side in some photographs. Has she ever read Moby Dick? After she has lunged from the breakers onto the shore and dragged a seal back into the sea, does she floss?

We played in Newcastle last night. A good show. A lot of monitor feedback onstage but we played well in spite of it. The audience was great, too bad the barricade kept them so far away.

I managed to get online and received a letter telling me that Ted Demme, the man who directed our 'Disconnect' video had died. The letter had an address to get more information so I checked it out. He was playing a charity basketball game and had a heart attack. He was taken to the hospital in full cardiac arrest and died. He was 38. He was a good guy. Glad I got to work with him, sorry as hell he's gone.

I read this quote of Michael Jackson the other day in *Mojo* magazine, he was talking to reporters about wanting to set up a school on his ranch to educate children and keep his children close to him. "How can they go into society? He's Prince Michael Jackson. She's Katherine Paris Michael Jackson—it would be too difficult." Is he saying that his children won't get to leave the Jackson compound? Is MJ afraid of something? Could it be he's afraid the world will see that his children are pure Caucasian and he is in fact, not their father? If this is true, how does he plan to deal with this? He can't keep them locked up forever. Will he secretly release them into society when they reach adulthood and pay them to keep their mouths shut?

The cover of his new record *Invincible*, is an insane airbrushed picture of his face that gets stranger the longer you look at it. The craziest rumor I ever heard about him was that the father of the children is an LA cop who is an old boyfriend of the mother and he was paid to sign over on the birth certificate and he gets a sum every year to keep his mouth shut. Who the hell knows if it's true. You have to wonder if any of this stuff will ever come to light. I don't think Michael Jackson will age very well. Can you see him at sixty with that face? That'll be as core as a . . . as a . . . male prostitute on Santa Monica Blvd! Hey, Mikey!

01-18-02 Dudley UK: 1141 hrs. On the bus. Woke up a couple of hours ago. I was in my bunk asleep before we pulled out of the parking lot of last night's show in Whitehaven.

But now it's a brand new day and we're in wonderful, cosmopolitan Dudley. I checked out the upcoming shows list they had posted for this venue. Who says culture is dead? Check out what's happening in Dudley: Stairway to Zeppelin, a Led Zep tribute, A Shania Twain tribute, Teen Spirit the Nirvana tribute band will also be appearing. A one man show called "Adolph" based on Adolph Hitler will be going for a few nights, this is the one written and performed by Pip Utton, not the one man show of the same name written and performed by Sharon Stone. Does Pip hang out by the stage door signing autographs after the show? Does he sign them, "Seig Heil!! –Pip 'Der Furher' Utton." Do people ever tell him that his performance was just like being in the same room as Hitler? Makes me remember one of the greatest Iggy Pop quotes of all time. When asked what it was like to hang out with Raquel Welch (which he did, apparently, backstage at some television show) he said, "Intense! It was kinda like hangin' out with Hitler!" Well, now you know.

Later: Show over. We had a good time and played well. Minutes after we were done, people just walked into the dressing room to get their tickets signed while we were in various states of nakedness but they didn't seem all that put out by it at all. Whew!

Tonight was show #2 in a six straight run, and then onto Russia. I think I've got my jet lag beat and am starting to feel acclimated. Definitely ready to play every night. Dudley? Intense! It was kinda like hanging out with Pip Utton.

01-20-02 Nottingham UK: 3:28 p.m. Sunday. On the bus. It's been consistent at least. The weather, that is. Cold and raining every day! It's winter, that's what you get around these parts.

I went walking around near the venue hours ago to see if there was anything happening. Saturday night had happened, that's for sure. The sidewalks near the venue told the tale: Puddles of vomit, used condoms, broken beer bottles, empty champagne bottles and corks. Other than that, it's just crap weather and a bunch of people limping into the local mall theater with their kids to see *Lord Of the Rings*.

England can be tough going if you're living on the bus in weather like this. The showers backstage, if there are any, are always rickety, the rooms are low-ceilinged, damp and poorly lit. The food situation is usually dire and it's sometimes hard to get fed. If you don't approach it right, you could be mighty bummed out about the whole thing. On the other hand, it's always a good day to be breathing and rain isn't so bad. I like it out here.

We're eight shows in and holding well. The last few nights have been good but there's not been much to mention event-wise. We just get up there, hit it and leave. There's not many people after the show hanging out by the bus. It's usually raining and really cold so we just wait for the driver to wake up and head out for the next town. Been sleeping in truck stop parking lots. There's a lot of tedium in this business, a lot of time passed in gray spaces, sweating in your clothes and waiting it out.

7:23 p.m.: In the crap room waiting to get it going. I tried to fall out in my bunk but it wouldn't happen. I feel alright though and want to play. I don't know how it works out, but by the time it's about an hour or so out, there's nowhere else I'd rather be and nothing else I'd rather be doing. I don't miss anything back at my place. It's all out here for me at this point. When I'm in the bunk, I think about what it would be like not to have this. I don't know what I would do with myself.

I am looking at the grimy walls of this room and all the stupid shit these bands write. All their stupid stickers, all the idiotic insults, the drawings. I don't like meeting musicians most of the time. You see what they leave on the walls—there's nothing to talk about.

It's hard to meet people anyway, isn't it? I went to a noodle place tonight to get some food for after the show and people came in while

I was waiting because they recognized me. They were cool but it just dragged on and on. One guy wanted me to sign something but he didn't have anything to sign, he didn't have a pen and he's getting nervous and his friends are getting nervous so I took the receipt for my food and a pen off the counter, signed my name and gave it to him. Can it be over now? No. He pulls out a camera which repeatedly refuses to work, this always seems to happen. Now people in the restaurant are looking, the cooks and waiters are looking and I feel stupid and on display and if I wasn't so hungry I would have left. Eventually the camera worked and they were done with me. Whenever anyone says, "There's someone I want you to meet," I always want to say, "Do I have to?" and I feel like the little kid in the museum who wants to leave NOW.

A few days ago I got an e-mail from someone telling me they would be in LA in April for a conference and wanted to get together with me because he/she (couldn't tell from the name) was sure that we would have hours of things to talk about. I wished this person the best of luck with the conference and left it at that. Another e-mail comes in from this person with hotel details and inquiries as to what is the best time for me. Am I picking them up or are they cabbing over? Funny. Delete. What the hell is there to talk about? Everything I guess. It's just not for me to do it. My social skills have deteriorated with the passing years. The shows take more out of me as I get older. The show becomes all I think about all day. If I'm not in the dressing room at least ninety minutes before the show, I can't concentrate on anything. During this time, I don't want to talk to anyone unless they're band or crew. It's going to take me a long time to be a real human being after all this is over. Maybe I won't get there.

01-21-02 Cambridge UK: 6:22 p.m. Backstage. Much better room than last night's dungeonous, damp cube of misery. The room is warm, a first on this tour.

Living on the bus and in the back of these venues teaches you a valuable lesson in economy. I plan the days I can shave by the times I can get some hot water. A lot of the sinks backstage here have none. If there's a shortage of towels, which there usually is, I remember to take my towel from stage with me and use it for the shower after-wards, if there is one. I time my laundry out so I have some sem-blance of clean clothes as the tour goes on. I time the minutes pre-show to maximize time to think, read and write before I have to start concentrating on the show. I like living this way. I like all moments counting. I like not taking things for granted. Taking things for grant-ed is one of the backslaps of modern convenience. Convenience has dulled us. I remember when I got a phone with speed dial. I stopped remembering phone numbers. I don't want to make my brain lazy. When you see people working at cash registers just punch in the dol-lar bill amount you gave them and let the register do the rest, they're doing no math at all. They're just doing what the machine says. They could be giving out the wrong amount every time and neither the cashier or the customer would notice. No matter how I try, I cannot get this lean frame of mind when off the road. I crave it when I don't have it.

I read a bit of *Imperium* last night. The part I read detailed stories of Stalin's starvation of peasants in 1930. Someone said that they saw a man standing next to a doorway with his son hanging by the neck. The man said that his other son was hanging dead in the closet. When asked why he hanged his two sons, he said that when his wife could find food, it always went to them, now it would go to him. I have to learn more about Stalin. For the life of me, I can't understand what his campaigns of terror and torture against defenseless people was all about and why no one tried to stand up to him. I have been reading Edvard Radzinsky's book, *Stalin*. It's good but not easy for me to follow. It's just so insane to me.

I had a dream last night that I was on a train taking me to a Russian concentration camp. When I woke up, it was pitch black and I had no idea where I was. It took me a minute to figure out I was on a bus headed towards Cambridge, not some place in Siberia.

Today's weather was overcast but at least it hasn't rained yet. I used to get depressed in the UK. The weather, the crap rooms you spend hours in, the stinginess of the amenities. It's as if the venues hate you and want you out. I know, it's beer that makes them money.

Punters are beer drinkers so fuck the bands. This used to get me down. Now I don't notice it. Like Keith Richards says, "All the crap you have to deal with, how bad is it really?" I used to get depressed from loneliness. Now I don't get lonely that much or for that long. I don't have anything or anyone to miss. It makes all the work easier to focus on. I am out here to smash it up every night no matter who shows up, where we are, or how crap the venue or stage is. That's why you buy a ticket. You want to see a band kick ass and seem like they don't want to be anywhere else. So, isn't it in your best interest, if you are committed to playing music live nightly, to eliminate any obstacles that lessen your potential for absolute integrity of delivery? Presumably, you are here to play completely full-on. I am only in Cambridge for one reason. I am here to rock out in this fucked up little room in front of a few hundred people. Anything that I can do to hit it harder is a plus. This mindset makes me extremely hard to be around so since I like everyone I work with very much, I do my best to stay away from them because I know I drive them crazy.

01-22-02 Norwich UK: 7:52 p.m. Backstage. Groggy. Walked around earlier today. I guess I went in the wrong direction because all I saw was closed kebab places and taxi stands. The other guys found restaurants and other stuff.

I have been hanging around near the venue for the rest of the time. The backstage is pretty warm so it's not all that bad. This is our last show in the UK.

Yesterday it was a year ago that my friend Deirdre O'Donoghue died. I met her in 1983 when she interviewed me on her radio show on KCRW FM called *Snap*. We hung out until three in the morning after the show talking about music and were friends ever since. When I wasn't on tour, sometimes I would save enough money to take the bus from SST to her place in Santa Monica on the weekends. She always fed me, it was great. I would go to KCRW with her and hang out. We had a great time and she taught me a ton about music. She turned me onto to a lot of music I had never heard before and a lot of music I never thought I would like. She lived for music. She had a ton of dedicated listeners, her enthusiasm was contagious. Bands loved her. I used to answer her phone when I was at her place because you never knew who was going to call her: Fripp, Eno, Cale, Harold Budd. She also did the very popular radio show *Breakfast with the Beatles*. She used to get Christmas cards from George Harrison.

In 1986 she started having health problems. I was living near her and my girlfriend and I would bring stuff from her little apartment to the hospital. She never got better really and they never quite figured out what it was that she had. At times they thought it was MS, then she'd get a different opinion and it would be something else. In any case, it kicked her ass for the rest of her life and she fought it and kept doing her shows and kept her incredible spirit. In the mid-nineties she came to me for a loan for medical needs. I was happy to be able to help her out. She always used to worry about paying me back no matter how much I told her she could take all the time she wanted. Actually, I didn't care if she ever paid me back. I was happy to be able to help and felt so bad that she got dealt such a bad hand of luck. She was a trooper until the end but finally she just gave out. I did the eulogy at her memorial service. It was a hard afternoon.

I was in Vancouver last year when I got the e-mail telling me what had happened. That was tough. Right before I left on this trip, I found some of her letters. I read them and it brought her back a little. She was one of the most "up" people I have ever met.

Four people I knew died last year. I talked to two of their mothers. That was hard. Losing people like that makes me not want to know anyone. It hurts too much. I know that it's part of life but all those people died way before they should have. One was only in her mid-twenties. It's not right. Ok, have to get ready to play now.

01-24-02 Moscow Russia: 4:42 p.m. Backstage. This a different venue than the other two times I played here. This one's much bigger and more together. The PA is for real as is the gear. It makes the set up from the last two times laughable.

We got in last night with little difficulty. There was hardly anyone at the airport so the line at immigration was short. Traffic wasn't bad. The weather has been holding steady at freezing. It's not great out but not the cold I expected. On the way in from the airport the ground was covered with snow, it was blank and beautiful.

I got to my room and had a little time before we all met in the lobby to get some dinner. A small crew from MTV met us at the restaurant and I had to do a short interview. It was relatively painless but it's strange how they do things here. They have press for you to do while you eat. You are in the middle of a meal and a man sits down next to you and starts asking questions in a mutant form of English. Since he has a notepad or a Walkman, it must be an interview. You ask him if this was planned and he says yes of course. And so, your meal gets dismissed as you answer those burning questions they always have. How do I like Russia? It's great, people interview you all the time, no one knows what's going on and nothing runs on time.

I went back to my room and tried to sleep. Didn't get much, mostly tossed and turned and had strange dreams.

Woke up this morning and had to leave to do a radio interview. Press here is as tiring as it is constant. It was an interview that took much too long. After that, traffic, food in the same place we ate last night and then to the venue.

5:53 p.m.: Soundcheck and the last interview done. Man, this shit takes it out of me. I just want to play. All this other stuff is really distracting. None of these people have their thing together. The press is excruciating to sit through. Mics don't work, walkmans run out of battery power, the lady has no questions, you name it—it goes wrong. Now I'm done with all the talk and I can get ready to play. It's the only thing I came to Moscow to do and it always seems like the last thing of importance. Tonight after the show, we catch a train to St. Petersburg.

7:14 p.m.: I fell asleep on the floor for a little while but got woken up by people in the room who insisted on talking almost the whole time. There's a difference in our job requirements. Crew guys don't have to perform. They do their work, which isn't unskilled or at all easy, but they have none of the pressure that a performer does. For me, the post soundcheck nap is all important. I can understand when others don't get it. On this day, we have no place to be other than in this room until we go on. It's a small, stuffy space and it's made smaller by the constant inflow of people who do nothing but interrupt and distract. There's a woman whose job it is to maintain the backstage area. You move, she gets up. You touch something, she looks for something to do, or she just lurks, waiting to do her job. She's a very nice gal but it's a pain in the neck having her around. Promoter guy is also bothersome. They're all cool but at this point all I want to do is get into this show. Since I got here, there's been a lot of talking and nodding. I have done their bidding for today and now all I want to do is the one thing I came here for.

Nights off have become hard. I would have rather played last night even though my voice needed the rest. Pre-show distraction has become harder to tolerate. Past soundcheck, all I can think of is the set and anything in the way is the enemy. You want to play all the way or do you want to come all this way just to fuck around? The answer is clear. I am having a good time playing, that's for sure. I like the music more than ever.

01-25-02 En Route to St. Petersburg Russia: 0250 hrs. Now this is really something. I am in a sleeper car, on a train out of Moscow to St. Petersburg. The train left Moscow at 11:55 p.m. I have been told it's about an eight hour journey. I was in the diner car for awhile. Beautiful, high-ceilinged, lamp-lit, what a cool scene.

Outside my window is snow, trees, occasional lights but mostly just countryside. I cannot ride on a train and not think of the great Thomas Wolfe and his incredible writing on dark Amerika as contemplated by his character Eugene Gant as he rides the train at night. Check the beautiful train riding passages in his novel *Of Time and the River*. I have spent a lot of time on trains. I have been all over Europe and Amerika on trains. I used to do a lot of the travel for my talking shows on trains. Some of those trips were grinders. Sleeping on benches in stations, several hour waits between trains, where all you can do is get through it. I learned a lot from those trips. Sometimes when I think of those times and how much shit I've been through, it makes my bones ache.

I am too tired to stay up and think about it. The day was long and the show took it out of me big time. The show was pretty good. The acoustics in that arena were not so great though. I thought we played well enough but it's hard to connect with the audience from such a high stage with them so far away behind the barricade. At one point, some kids were getting too into it for the security and two full-on soldiers came in and took one kid away. They were big, grim men and the boy wisely gave them no resistance at all. I was sorry to see him go. After that, no one moved.

Just as I was getting used to the bad sound onstage and starting to get into the music, the show was over and I was in the shower. It seemed so short tonight. People seemed to dig it though. Some girls followed us to the train station and stood outside our car and wrote on the windows in magic marker that they missed us and it wasn't fair that they couldn't come with us. When the train pulled away from the station, they ran after it for quite a distance. When Japanese girls see you off at the train, they just stand and wave.

01-26-02 St Petersburg Russia: 0011 hrs. In my room. We're not getting many hotels on this tour. Not many days off either and that's alright, none of us care.

The first couple of hours of the train ride here were pretty good. I actually slept some and then the heater was turned on and the room became a hotbox from hell. It woke us all up. I didn't get back to sleep and just sat up for the rest of the trip. About an hour before we hit the station, the radio comes on and the woman who takes care of the car and all of us little passengers walks down the hall and punches each door to reinforce the message that it's time to get the hell up. It would be great to have her on the bus. Every morning she could walk down the aisle and punch us awake. "It must be time to get up, the old woman just punched me in the neck."

We pulled into the station around 0755 hrs. The platform was crowded. People waiting for the next train, people waiting for people getting off the train, men walking up and down asking, "Taxi?" Very packed and busy. Steam coming out of everyone's mouth, a lot of people smoking cigarettes, some soldiers, dark, temperature at about freezing. It's great to be here.

We left the station and loaded into a van. There was already lots of traffic. St. Petersburg looks a bit like Budapest, Hungary. The construction of the buildings is very Eastern Block but modern. The city seems more cosmopolitan than Moscow. Not as oppressive and impersonal.

After going to the hotel restaurant and getting some food and long stares from almost everyone in there, I went to my room and slept for at least an hour.

A few hours later, I had to go out and do a radio interview and a meet-the-fans type of thing. I did the interview in a small room packed with people.

Whenever I have done press here, be it radio, TV or print, there's always a lot of people around for things that don't take many people to do. They stand around like they're in storage. They're all very nice but it's always cramped and a lot of time gets wasted. The girl who interviewed me looked very much like a woman I dated some time ago. They could pass for sisters. It was strange to trip on that while looking at her and answering all the average "band on tour" type questions.

From there we went to a restaurant. I asked the promoter gal, who is a constant source of non-information, what we were doing at a restaurant. "Perhaps you want to get some food now?" Aren't we supposed to do that signing thing now? Oh, I see, it's going to take place in the restaurant. Too bad no one told the restaurant about this detail in our schedule.

We walk in and the poor folks in the front of the restaurant trying to eat are hemmed in by people who wanted their stuff signed, press people and two camera crews. When they all surged forward and the diners saw who was the cause of this total meal ruining nuisance, they gave me some mean looks, believe me. I looked at promoter gal and she just looked back at me with her classic blank stare. I asked her what the deal is and she just got on her cel phone to call someone who might know. Meanwhile, there's CDs and mics in my face. Walkman's under my nose, two camera crews trying to light the room and everyone talking at once. It was wacky. Then out of nowhere, Mike walks right through all of these people and says, "This is over right now, let's go." Who the hell's going to argue with such succinct and well delivered marching orders? Not I. We walked out, got into a van and went to the venue like it never happened.

The venue wasn't so bad. They weren't all that organized which is no big deal if you're organized. You just let them do what they need to and then you get the real job done and everyone's happy. We eventually got it all together even though the Russian crew seemed hellbent on getting in our crew's way when they were trying to get everything set up so we could get all the bands soundchecked. Our crew is setting up mics, their crew are moving them and every few minutes, an old woman appeared onstage with a broom and insisted on sweeping. It was a little zany but we got onstage on time.

The audience was intense. No barricade so they were all over me as soon as I got anywhere near them. Pounding my legs, hitting me on the head and grabbing my free hand. It was never antagonistic, they just wanted to say hi. I thought it was cool. We played our asses off and we had a good time and it seemed that they did too. Before I knew it, the whole thing was over. These sets are going by fast even though they're the longest ones we've ever done. It's a twenty four song set and it takes awhile to pound through it all but it goes by fast.

We hung out in the dressing room as the crew got all the gear packed. We did photos with the opening band, a good bunch of guys from St. Petersburg. It's great to meet people in music who aren't jaded and are still excited. That's how the people and the bands are here. It's a reminder of how corny and corrupted the scene is in Amerika. So many of the bands we endured on the Warped tour were so weak compared to the band that played with us tonight. These guys have crap gear and no real chance of making it out of here but they hit it with everything they had. In Amerika, no sense of irony.

What a city! Totally inspiring. Some cities are more than cities. St. Petersburg is a world. St. Petersburg doesn't have a history. St. Petersburg is history. You could live here your entire life and still be discovering the place. We were driving back to the hotel tonight and the driver points to a building and gruffly says, "October Revolution." I could drive him down Hollywood Blvd. point out the window and say, "Starbucks coming soon," but it wouldn't be the same. I've got to get back here some day.

We head to Finland in the morning.

01-26-02 Helsinki Finland: 8:08 p.m. In the hotel room, waiting to go to the venue and rock this town. Soundcheck was good.

I get sent interviews via e-mail for upcoming shows. Here's the kind of corny shit I put up with. Last thing you want to do is sit in a room and answer this idiotic time waste. Is this some kind of test of my mental strength? Am I being groomed by the Pentagon for special operations? I suffered through this virtual labyrinth of boredom, and now, so shall you.

The story goes that you jumped onstage with Black Flag and just began performing. Was it that spontaneous? Why did you do it? Although we know the end results, what was that first night like for you and the members of Black Flag?

Now, at almost 41, what drives you to be so intense onstage? What is it about touring that attracts you to these whirlwind journeys? Is there something you are still searching for? Is there something you are running from?

What happened when Joe Cole was killed? How did you escape that fate? Being there, how did that experience affect you? Does that experience still affect you now?

What attracts you to doing spoken word?

When the party's over, perhaps when you get to an age where performing musically isn't an option, or there comes a time when spoken word won't draw in the masses for you, what will you do? Do you have plans for yourself 10, 20 years from now? Does getting older, or being "your favorite aging icon" frighten you? What do you believe death is? As such, why should creativity continue when everyone is just going to die anyway?

You said once, "I don't want a wife and I don't want kids...If I met a woman of my own age and married her, I'd also be marrying her former life...It would destroy my creativity." Still true? As such, is Henry Rollins a lonely man? The tortured artist, perhaps?

What were you like as a boy, before you jumped onstage with Black Flag? Popular at all? What were your habits and hobbies?

What are your thoughts on September 11 and this new "mood" in Amerika?

How is your throat?

What are your current opinions on politics, music and culture in Amerika? Thoughts on punk, metal or Electronic music?

Finally, I encountered you last summer on the Warped Tour and attempted to approach you immediately after your set at which point you growled and stormed off only to pace intensely for several minutes beside the stage. What goes on in your mind during those moments when you are onstage that requires such downtime? What gets your blood so pumped that you can't be approached immediately after a performance?

Anyway. We left Russia and arrived here hours ago. Helsinki is freezing and beautiful and I am glad to be alive in it. I watched Clinton on the BBC a few hours ago. A great speech. I liked what he said about the possibilities of getting a lot of the bad things in the world turned around. He made solutions seem in our grasp and it was really inspiring. I don't know if he was a great president but I wonder if George W. Bush could speak for an hour, or even more than ten minutes, and get people pumped up like that. I have never seen Bush speak more than a few sentences at a time. He never connects with the material he's reading and he never connects with the audience. It's like he's in front of the mirror, rehearsing.

Check out Tony Blair. The British Prime Minister has to stand down Parliament. The opposition party goes for him hard and Blair has to have his shit together. He has to answer every question they throw at him. Everyone's hooting and hollering, it's nuts but they get it all aired out. Bush could never deliver on his feet like that, no way. I also watched Blair speak for an hour on the BBC recently and he was brilliant, concise and clear. He laid out his plans for the year. He was totally together. It was one of three speeches he had to make that day. Bush doesn't have enough vision to pull this off. Is Blair a good guy?

I don't know. I know he can put a sentence together and at least you can understand him. I have an understanding of Bush too—there's nothing to understand.

Have you noticed that no president since Kennedy has been an eloquent speaker? They could all speak, but not with the gravity and charisma of Roosevelt, Truman or even Johnson. At least when you hear old records of these speeches, these guys are coming from something. All I get from the last several presidents is soundbytes and clichéd acting jobs. Watch old footage of Reagan, he's acting. He knows where the light is, he knows how to work the camera. Because people are so used to television sitcom acting, they found Reagan engaging. He should have been in a movie about a president. He was like William Shatner with jowls. Carter wasn't a powerful speaker but easily a good man.

I watched some MTV, that's some sorry "music." These "bands" are so weak! I'm glad it's not my problem. The band Incubus is on the road, detailing their exhaustion and then they cut to the band onstage sitting on stools playing with no sweat. Come out with us for a week, it'll throw you a beating you'll never recover from. Achtung all bands, don't let this happen to you: don't let an old man like me be in better shape than you and blow you off stage. It's pitiful. Your girlfriends should deny you access. Work harder. Well adjusted people shouldn't make music.

I saw a thing on CNN a few days ago about all these rockstars going to Sacramento, CA to lobby for the SB 1246 bill which would roll back the state Labor Code that exempts record companies from a seven year limit on personal services contracts. It was hilarious to see Stevie Nicks, Sheryl Crow, Beck Hansen and Don Henley at this thing. Poor Don Henley. It's hard to feel for a guy who's sold countless millions of records and charges one hundred and fifty dollars or more for a ticket. Charge what you want but don't complain. Fat Don Henley, fat Stevie Nicks. Poor, poor, well-fed, rehabbed millionaires. They're pissed, boyyyyyyyy! Free the multi-millionaires! No more slavery! Let them break free from these corporate shackles! Stevie, can you hear your master callin'? He's sendin' a town car for you, he wants to meet you for cocaine and sushi at Matsuhisa. Don't just slouch there, trundle to the lobby! Lockdown at the Four Seasons! "Not that kind of chocolate, the other kind! Send it back, can't you see I'm being oppressed?!" I hear ya loud and clear Don, I'm right with you all the way. Sheryl, I got your back. Beck Hansen, you're on your own, perhaps L. Ron Hubbard will help you—but you other two, well, put it this way: anyone who fucks with Don and Sheryl are fucking with me so if you want to start the shit, just go ahead and see what happens.

You fucking lambs. If you had to do it on your own, you couldn't. You need a record label to baby-sit you. Fuck the labels, fuck these soft whiners. Don Henley said that musicians are basically naïve and enter into bad contracts because they don't know any better so they should get a break. That may be for some but at this point, if a contemporary musician can't figure out how to call a lawyer and get a contract straightened out, he's just a dumb fuck who should get screwed by fakes like the posers at ReamWorks. I can't think that his royalties from the Eagles Greatest Shits have treated him all that badly. The record industry is full of motherfuckers, deal with it. You deal with them as friends, you're going to get screwed. I did and I toughed it out. It's their game, so play it or don't. You all deserve each other.

All you gotta do is keep on rockin'. The only time you fuck up is when you impede your progress with useless information and comparison. I can't care who does what. I must put all my energy into what I am doing and what I have to do. There's really nothing else that matters. Focus and deliver. Nothing else needs to be done. Outside factors are to be ignored as they are nothing of importance. Critics are people with no talent who write about dummies for an audience who doesn't read so there's no use in taking them seriously. All you need to do is keep hitting it. Nothing's in your way.

01-27-02 Stockholm Sweden: 8:01 p.m. In the room on a night off. Stockholm is freezing and it's great. The quality of air here is noticeably high. On many nights in Scandinavia, I have gone out walking just for the air. Not a whole lot happening out there as it's a Sunday. I managed to get some good food in so I am alright.

We got here this morning. Not much sleep last night. Show in Helsinki was damn cool though. What a crowd. It's only the third time I've been to Finland. The other two times were festivals. I can't believe that we never hit Helsinki before. They rocked hard and so did we. Last night hurt. In the second song of the encore I was trying to figure out where the best place to puke would be. I decided that I would aim for a towel on the drum riser so there wouldn't be much to clean up. I managed to work past it and finished the show without hurling. Something was up with that show. I got backstage and rolled out my towel and had to lie down. My legs were shot. Too many nights of not enough sleep. These gigs will kill you if you don't get enough sleep.

Some girl sent a letter backstage. She wanted me to pass it on to Tony Iommi of all people. To paraphrase: "Tony, I love you, I have always loved you and always will." This amorous discourse went on for two pages. I have written some damn embarrassing letters in the name of love. The kind you reckon are not the best idea as you walk them to the mail box and then upon dropping the letter into the slot, the idea leaves not such a good idea status and proceeds right to worst possible idea status. You stare at the mailbox, wondering if it's possible to somehow wrench the letter out. Too late and now you have only a couple of days to get ready for the humiliation that is to come. Ah, the brutality of romance. Backstage antics included two girls who came in, sat down in our little room and drank beer and hard alcohol, made cel phone calls and answered my questions with murmurs. I can't help myself. In booming how y'all doing today voice, I interrogate:

"SO, ARE Y'ALL FROM AROUND HERE?"
Slight start. Indifferent murmur.
"YEAH?"
Barely perceptible nod.
"OSAMA BIN LADEN CAN PISS OVER ROOFS AND EATS CATS!"
Blank stare.
"WHILE THEY'RE STILL ALIVE!"

Nothing.

"DOES THE NAME TONY IOMMI RING A BELL?"

I sometimes wonder how long I have left in this racket. I'm just going to keep smashing it up until the parts don't work anymore. There's nothing else to do. Fuck convention, fuck tradition. Whose rules are those? Not mine. The more I focus and the more things I go without, the better I am for the shows. I am hardening as the nights go by. It takes a couple of weeks out here to get to that place. It's like regressing into a more primitive animal. The pain hurts less, I can go harder longer.

I go without things to make sure I mesh better with the work. I've made sure my off the road life is not attractive to me. The place I live is adequate but not a place I miss. That whole thing of "sleeping a night in my own bed" is not attractive to me. It's just a bed. Burn it. I couldn't have that kind of thing in my head and do what I do. I can't have anything off the road to distract me. To me, that's selling out. I get shit for some of the work I do like voiceovers and films. I get told I am selling out by getting this kind of work. I competed and beat motherfuckers out and won that work. Selling out? That's allowing girlfriend drama to fuck with your work. That's missing home more than wanting to be on the road and still going on the road. You're not being true to the work. Hey, art is supposed to wreck you. It's only for the strong. That's why I wish all these fakes would just step off. Too many bands on life support systems. They couldn't cut it where we cut it every night. I know it, you know it and you can bet those bands know it.

01-29-02 Oslo Norway: 5:36 p.m. Backstage in this basement venue. It's a different place than the venue we usually play. I think this will be the third time here with the band. I've been here a few times on my own and it was really good. As I remember, the band shows went down pretty well. This time we're at the university and it's a good venue.

Last night's show in Stockholm was a blast. I never know what to expect in Scandinavia. Sometimes the audience just stares at you and sometimes they're really into it. So far it's been great. There were a lot of people flying over the barricade last night, the security guys had their hands full but they were cool to the kids and never tried to hurt them. There was one guy who was putting up a struggle, I don't know why, the security guys were just trying to get him out of the way and back into the crowd but the guy started kicking and thrashing. As we walked off stage, there was a man who insisted on hugging each one of us as we walked by.

It gets dark so early up here this time of year. After soundcheck the last couple of shows, I've been walking around near the venue taking in the cold, checking things out. Walking around on darkened streets, looking through the windows of stores and coffee places. We are well into the tour now. It's amazing how all of a sudden, you're several shows in and you can't remember what it was like before the tour started. I'm in that small box mindset now. There's a long way to go on this run so it's best that I just concentrate on one show a night and not much else.

01-30-02 Malmo Sweden: 8:21 p.m. Backstage. Played this venue in 1987 I think. This has got to be the place. From the 1987 journal:

08-30-87 Malmo Sweden: 2:20 am. What a trip this trip can be sometimes. We play at this cool place, 3 floors, kitchen, shower, beds, stage, PA, nice people. I finish the set, they feed me this great vegetarian dinner. I get a shower, now I'm in this room on a mattress, clean, fed and tired. Crazy goddamn life, tomorrow they will probably drop the bomb. During the set, this kid hit his head and was knocked out cold. He was laid out on the floor. His friends revived him by kicking him in the balls. He finally got up. Between songs, I asked him if he was all right, he didn't answer me, he just begged me to play "Louie, Louie."

Last night was interesting. We went out there guns a'blazin' to be met by a bunch of students who drank beer and stared. One guy in the front talked to me the whole night and was mildly distracting. It didn't matter to me what they did. As long as we're playing well, I reckon that's as good as it gets. The audience pepped up a few songs in. I think the beer needed to take effect for them to loosen up.

All night long, a pretty girl stood a row back from the front, watched the band intently, and drank beer after beer. Her boyfriend tried to distract her by trying to make out with her but she wasn't interested. She was all about the beer and the music. I think it started to make the boyfriend mad. I can't count how many times I've seen that happen. The female gets into the music and the guy starts getting bent out of shape and insists on trying to make out with the girl to re-establish his status. Most of the time the girl responds distractedly and the guy covers his agitation by getting overly into the music like it was his idea anyway, or he starts laughing at us. No wonder women are so tired of us. I don't think I ever did that. Did I ever do that? Are we in Russia, Danny? No, I never did that.

Anyway, before I knew it, the show was over and we were walking off. Post show is usually quiet backstage. The opening band is usually gone and there's rarely anyone around who isn't part of the production. Last night was no exception. I talked to our promoter for awhile, a good guy named Robin. Robin is an Englishman who married a Norwegian gal. He used to tour manage The Lords of the New Church. He's got great Brian James and Stiv Bators stories. The last time I was in Oslo in 1999, it was really cold and he gave me a coat.

I went to a 7-Eleven before we left for here and got followed in by some drunk guys who were at the show. I met a guy named Thor whose right palm was cut open diagonally. The man who yelled at me all night came into the store and in a soft voice, very politely thanked me for the show and then walked out again.

Today, a semi-retarded man stood outside the venue until I came off the bus so I could sign a dirty piece of paper, he told me that he liked me in movies and that I lifted weights like Arnold Schwarzenegger. I thanked him and went inside.

Time to get ready to play.

02-01-02 Aarhus Denmark: 5:58 p.m. I have played this town a few times in my life but it was always this cool fucked up little place that I first visited in 1983 with Black Flag. I think the last time I was here was 1997. Last time the audience was grabbing my legs and putting their hands in my face. I've never figured out why it's appealing to poke the singer's eyes. Anyway, it got old fast so to put an end to it, I singled out a couple of them and started dealing on them. Kinda wacky stuff, like punching them in the face for no reason. It tripped them out and the rest of them got the message. In this business, communication skills are key. I remember the 1983 show. The opening act was our roadie's band, comprised of Black Flag members. For some reason I was told to do the front of house sound. I know nothing about how to do that now and knew even less back then. The band is playing and I start turning knobs and discover the reverb and the echo. Shit, I had the whole band echoing. Sounded really cool. No one seemed to mind and I don't think the band noticed.

Last night in Copenhagen was good. Crowd was into it and we were on. People up front were doing the headbanging thing so I couldn't get near the monitors without risking getting my head cracked. It cut down on the into it factor for me but I still had a good night up there. I reckon it's their night as well so let them do whatever the hell they want.

Woke up this morning on the bus looking out at the slate gray sky of Aarhus. Nothing happening around here so I have been reading and keeping to myself.

I have a lot of great moments out here. Last night I was walking around the pumps of a gas station, smelling the diesel and moving through the trucks. It hit me that I had all I needed out here. A show every night and my small bunk to sleep in. I have not been on a phone for over three weeks. This is optimum living to me. It's not the way I am living until I get off the road, it's real life until I have to put up with the debilitating, albeit temporary, grind of off-the-road living. It all sounds good and virtuous but let's not bullshit here, the main appeal of life out here is the low responsibility factor. I know it. It's hassle free and not real. It's a temporary break from the day-to-day of real life. It's like a vacation I guess, perhaps it's a way to not have to grow up.

02-03-02 Groningen Holland: 0201 hrs. In a hotel room at the end of a night off. The show in Aarhus was a blast. This was the best one in this town yet.

We got here several hours ago. Strange not playing on a Saturday but that's how the schedule goes.

Got to the room, watched some CNN, read for awhile and then fell out for hours. Woke up and ate and have been in the room ever since. There's not a lot to check out in this town. I have played here many times but always in a place called Vera. The show tonight is in a place I've never heard of.

I got an interesting e-mail from someone in LA who said they saw Dee Dee Ramone play the other night and Dez Cadena joined them on stage to play 'Blitzkrieg Bop.' Dez looked like "an old heavy metal guy with long black hair, straight legged black jeans and a black leather jacket."

It's interesting to get that report and also get an e-mail from Chuck Dukowski on the same day. I hear from Chuck now and then, it's cool. He's not insane, he's got a life and he survived that whole thing we were in way back there in the mist. I know that *Mojo* Magazine just ran an article about Black Flag recently. The issue was on the bus but I didn't read it. I don't have many good memories of those days. It was cool but I'm glad it's over. I know we were good and I know that Greg was a one-in-a-million talent. I heard a Black Flag song the other day and when Ginn's lead comes in, it's incredible. It sounds more amazing as time goes on. When you hear what people are playing these days and then you hear Ginn—damn. He's like Albert Ayler.

I know things. The facts keep me on my own. The highs and lows I have known have turned me inward to the point where I'll never feel anything close to normal. I don't feel isolated, I don't want in. I feel like one of those guys who gets asked, "What the hell happened out there?" and all I can respond with is a smile and a shrug. There's no confession to make, there's no truth burning to come ripping out of me. What I know keeps me out here. I will always make relationships with people an approximation of a relationship. I think that's better. I think things are more beautiful when you're on the outside. I'd rather put my trust in the seasons than people. I'd rather miss cities than people. I'd rather love animals than people. People hurt me too much to get too close to them. I know that death is part of life. I know. I know. I know. Last year was hard going in the someone-I-know-just-died department and it made me pull back more.

On the other hand, walking back from eating hours ago was an experience of simple perfection. The air was cold and so clean smelling that it was intoxicating. Men and women walking arm-in-arm passed me, people on bikes passed me. I looked in at people in their living rooms as I passed by their apartments. It's hard not to see in, the windows are huge, there's no curtains and the lights are on.

I am feeling good about these shows. I'm underweight and not eating enough but I'm playing hard as hell and my voice is hanging in there. I don't care how many people show up, I don't care how many people buy the records, I just want to play the music in a state of animal purity.

02-08-02 Barcelona Spain: 7:22 p.m. Backstage, waiting for the show. It's hours away. We played last night in Madrid and it was easily the best time I've ever had playing that city. The onstage sound was pretty bad and the monitors cut in and out all night but still it was a good time. Backstage was cold enough to see your breath, whatever. Luxury compared to watching a Julia Roberts film.

I had two days off after the show in Groningen, Holland. I went to Madrid ahead of the band and hung out and waited for the shows to resume. I didn't sleep much and by the second day I was restless and distracted. Getting back to the bus and doing soundcheck was a relief.

The days off were blank time. I walked the streets and looked at people. I walked some more. I sat in the room and watched CNN, I read back issues of the *New Yorker*. I thought old thoughts. I thought about dead people. I thought about sad things. I lay in bed with the lights off and stared into the semi-darkness. Lame. Things are better now. I'm back in line with the roar. Two days off was too much.

02-09-02 Bergara Spain: 8:24 p.m. Backstage. Going on in two hours. Every square inch of wall space here is covered with idiotic graffiti left by bands. Not a shred of sense or humor in any of it. So many musicians are morons.

Being out here makes me see how dead it is in Los Angeles. Even after twenty plus years of existing there, I still don't know my way around the city all that well. It's an unrelenting desire to somehow not take part in what I consider a temporary but compromised geographic setback. I live there but I don't. I exist there between tours. My house is an airport hotel room. I don't know anyone there besides the people I work with. I don't keep up or pursue friendships there, it's a dead city as far as I am concerned. When I am there, I merely pass time before I leave for the world again. Los Angeles is a cultural deadzone to me. The rest of the world exists outside of LA.

When I'm in Washington DC, the city I spent the first twenty years of my life in, I walk the streets and some of it comes back to me. Memories echo and landmarks fill my thoughts for days after I leave. The events I remember are at most, blurred recollections, enhanced by time and loneliness. There's a wonderful quality in the air at night in DC during the summer. The air is almost something you could fill a glass with. It's green and wet and sounds like crickets. With each breath, you weave yourself deeper and more invisibly into the night's fabric. On one of my visits there last year, I sat outside for hours one night because I didn't want to let the night go. At times there is a stillness in the air where the world seems on pause and the night and the world are completely yours. I live for these moments of grace, isolated, perfect instances. A lot of my still moments are spent thinking about walks through those nights and what there is left of a life.

The people I know there are friendly but the time and distance have taken their toll. I no longer really know these people and they no longer know me and the conversations are sometimes strained. It's what happens when you leave town for decades. They get on with their lives and you get on with yours and that's that. That's life.

The more time I spend out in the world at large, passing through these cities year after year, through exhaustion, jet lag, various degrees of internal stress and emotional vicissitudes, memories of my past and certain songs will continually ricochet in my mind. Some of the events happened so long ago, my memory of them might be fact-free. Time has reduced all of them to varying degrees of enhanced reality.

So I am here and nowhere else. The world I can see around me is vague and semi-real. I feel a stranger in it. Real life is the shore and I feel like I live underwater. I know schedules, call times, sleep broken into fragments, airports, busses, venues, hotels, exhaustion and a sense of singularity that is perhaps isolation disguised as a sense of individuality.

02-12-02 Basel Switzerland: 0012 hrs. In a hotel room on a night off. Only ten more shows in Europe. We drove about eighteen hours to get here. Not so bad. Would have rather played than put up here over night but I'll get my chance soon enough.

Been watching CNN. Iran had its 23rd annual celebration of revolution and thousands filled the streets of Tehran with their anti-Amerikan signs. Iran has reacted strongly to Bush's term "Axis of Evil" he says Iran is a part of. No wonder Iran is pissed off. Such a lame thing for Bush to say. You would think that one of his babysitters would have warned him.

We are twenty-five shows into the tour and it's feeling alright. Last night in Valencia was good. There was less tobacco smoke in the air and it was easier to keep up. The audience was good, the opening band was lame but that happens a lot. A lot of pretense but not much substance with these bands. It's not my problem. Do what you're going to do.

02-13-02 Codevilla Italy: Our bus driver says we're about 80 miles out of Milan. From walking around the venue, it seems we're nowhere. A few industrial buildings and a road are all I can see. The ground outside the venue is strewn with rubble, broken chairs, toilets and mic stands. The dressing room is a small tiled room covered completely with graffiti. It's a crazy dump in the middle of nowhere and I look forward to the show.

I turned forty-one today. A non-descript age. Like thirty-one with more gray hair and lines in the face. I was taking it in last night while onstage, thinking about the fact that it was to be my last show at forty. Since my birthday last year to last night, I've done one hundred and eighty shows.

Some prime entertainment is coming to this venue in the not too distant future. Some of the upcoming shows are as follows: Nerds: A Tribute to Motorhead, Muppet Suicide: A Tribute to Guns and Roses, In the Mode: A Tribute to Depeche Mode, Easy Cure: A Tribute to The Cure, Clive Bunker and Beggar's Farm: A Tribute to Jethro Tull and lastly, The Achtung Babies, a band who covers U2. Now how would you take out a classified for that? Needed: Hilarious front man, bass player (no talent required), drummer (no talent required), guitar player (one note required.) Please apply for BEST BAND IN THE WORLD.

So last night was cool, the best time I've had in Basel, Switzerland. At one point, people were yelling out songs they wanted to hear and I told them that if they kept that up they would hurt their voices and recommended they write down their requests on a piece of paper and send it up to the front and one of the security personnel would hand it to me. I was only kidding. But, as the night went on, pieces of paper were being placed onstage by security. What nice folks.

The tour has settled into the grind mode. It's cool but it's all about play and drive. Now matter how much sleep you get, or think you get, you are kind of beat at all times except when playing or getting ready to play. Everyone in the band and crew has that look now. It always happens. We live on the road, a lot of people shoved into a small touring bus, everything is cramped and it wears on you. But as always, spirits remain high and everyone's having a good time. I don't know of many people off the road who have a good time every day, a lot of them just get through their lives and reserve the good times for weekends or holidays. As grinding and routine as all this can sometimes get, it's still the best time I've ever had. We're in Italy, how bad can that be?

02-18-02 Salzburg Austria: 10:39 p.m. In my room on a night off. Olympics and CNN on television. Nothing happening in this town after eight.

My life is numbers. I constantly run numbers in my head. Repetitions, how much time, how many days, how many songs. I live by the numbers. I have a schedule that's all numbers. Time to do this, time to do that. Time to do nothing. Minutes before a set I will look at the clock and see that I have seven minutes to think about anything I want before I have to start thinking about the set. I like that discipline. I know it and it's mine.

Italy was great but you have to relax and not take anything but the show seriously because rarely is anything running on time or well organized. It's rare when much of what you are promised comes through, sometimes the sound is less than what they said it would be so you have to smile and rock out. Still, the shows come off and it's alright. By the last show, when we were going on almost an hour late, we all were a little over that beautiful but very silly country.

Austria, by comparison, is cold water in the face. The venue is immaculate and precisely tuned. The backstage area is sterile, the food is bland and everything runs to the minute. Last night in Graz was great. That was six shows straight and it felt fine.

02-21-02 Budapest Hungary: 4:41 p.m. Backstage. Yesterday was Zagreb, Croatia. Since Croatia has problems with Austria, something to do with Austria not allowing Croatian trucks to drive through, the Croatians are practicing a little tit-for-tat by not allowing our bus, which happens to be saddled with Austrian plates, over the border. Hours of calls and paperwork and still they will not allow the bus to go into the country so we can do the show.

The promoters drive up in vans to where the bus is parked and we load in gear and bodies and go to Zagreb.

The venue was ancient and really cool. The stage was small and the monitors were crap but I had the feeling that it was going to be a good time anyway. I am past the point where bad monitors slow me down.

The audience was great. There were these girls up front who were grabbing my arms, legs, mic cord, whatever else they could get their hands on. Finally security had to get them off me. How rockstar.

It's good to be back in Hungary. I remember the Budapest show as one of the best ones from the 1997 tour.

I don't feel ready to go back to Amerika. I am digging it out here. These days, I need time off from Amerika. I love it, it's without a doubt my favorite place but it's a hard hang these days. It's great out here. I could use some more time spent in a not-so-recently-attacked country.

Thinking of staying out makes me think of those few days I spent in Bangkok last summer. It was so cool to be "nowhere." I felt so remote and not on the planet. For a few days I was off the screen. What would a few years of that be like? What would it be like to do a temporary Rimbaud and just split?

02-22-02 Prague Czech Republic: 6:21 p.m. Backstage. Last night in Budapest was good. The singer in the opening band went out there in a pair of black shorts and nothing else. Well, ok, but just this once. We played well and it was a good time.

Tonight's our last show in Europe. It's gone fast. We have a few in Amerika, the live taping in Chicago and then back to LA. We'll be playing two nights in Chicago at the Metro. We will be taping both nights for a live album.

Tonight is sold out. Sold out venue? Us? No way! The Fall played here recently. As always, there was a good Mark E. Smith story. Apparently he flew in at the last minute and no one knew what flight or when he was arriving and the entire show was in doubt and he came into the venue and kind of walked onstage and the reports say they were great. There are Fall records I like more than others but none of them are bad. I know people would disagree with that but I can find something redeeming in any Fall record. Mark never got cute or followed a trend. They broke the mold with that guy. I wish I could see them play on this tour.

It's cold outside and there's nothing to do before the show. I fly in the morning and will have a day off in DC. I can't wait to walk the streets of my old hometown.

02-23-02 En Route to USA: Last night was great and it was a good way to end the European shows. Five more in the US and the tour is over. We also have a show a few days after the Chicago shows in LA. It's a benefit for the West Memphis Three. I figured they could use some money so we booked a show at the Troubadour and we're going to rock out. Exene's band, the Original Sinners, are also playing.

10:19 p.m. Washington DC. In the hotel. I got here hours ago and went out walking immediately. When I am in DC, I always stay at a hotel on Wisconsin Ave. and Calvert St. in my old neighborhood so I can walk around and see the sights. I look forward to this for weeks.

Tonight, I went out with my camera and took pictures everywhere I went. I walked up Wisconsin Avenue and down Quebec St. and looked at the house I lived in right after I was born. It's the last place my parents were together before they divorced. I used to go there on the weekends after my mother got custody of me. Five days a week with my mother, two with my father per the settlement. I lived there briefly with my father before my mother took me away. I was a baby but I can remember that day. My mother came busting into the house, grabbed me, ran out, jumped into a waiting car and we went tearing up the street with my father chasing after us on foot. The wheel man was my mother's friend Lillian. Pretty dramatic. I guess later on, they worked it out in court. I never asked and they never told me. I've seen the place twice since the early 70's. Once in 1988 and again tonight. It's so small. I have a lot of bad memories of the place. The neighbors on the right were cool. An elderly couple. I don't know about the wife, but the husband was always drunk, smiling and sunk deep into an easy chair. On the weekend stays with my father, I would go to their house and hang out. The husband was a friendly, quiet alcoholic. He would do tricks with coins, make his thumb come off and put it back on. I would also spend a lot of time at the Malone's house up the street. They had two kids and they were friendly. I spent as little time with my father and his new wife as possible.

I walked down Wisconsin and checked out where I used to work before I joined Black Flag. It's a pizza place now but twenty-one years ago when I worked there it was an ice cream store. Whenever I'm here, I walk in just so I can use the door which is the same one as when I worked there. I think it's cool using the same latch over two decades later. I know, a small and pointless detail but I live for this stuff. I stood inside for a moment, wandered through my memories a little while and then hit the street. I had a lot of good times in that place. From there I walked to a pharmacy that was on my paper route when I was ten. I used to go in there and buy ice cream and candy. I looked through the window and the same freezer is still there. I tripped on that for a minute and then walked around on the streets and took in the night air and retraced my old paper route. A little lonely but good. This was a great night off.

02-24-02 Washington DC: 11:10 p.m. Another great day. I met up with Ian and we went out to Rockville, MD to 1327-J Rockville Pike to visit Yesterday and Today Records and the owner, Skip Groff. Skip produced my first record, Ian's too. I have been going into his store since the late 70's. Misfits singles for three bucks. It's always great to walk into that place. So many memories. Skip was good. He told me that this is the last year for the store. The lease is up on September 30th. Twenty-five years in that place. There's no way I am not going to be in that store with Skip on that day. I promised him I would be there.

Ian and I went to Ian's mother's house for dinner. It was so great to see his family. Whenever I am there, I never want to leave but soon enough I was walking back here. I try not to allow myself to miss anything or anyone, but I miss all of them as soon as I leave the house.

Tomorrow is the first show.

02-25-02 Baltimore MA: Back to Amerika. It was funny to walk onto an Amerikan tour bus yesterday. In comparison with the European busses, the Amerikan ones are huge and over the top. The bus is a good analogy for Amerika. Like Henry Miller said, it's the Air Conditioned Nightmare.

When we got to the venue, we were right back in it. Surrounded by stores and over abundance. There's nothing like a shopping mall here. It's an assault.

Within an hour of parking the bus, the band crew were walking in and out of the bus with all the stuff: fast food, Starbucks, the wave of Amerikana. It has, in a way, a welcoming effect to me. It feels like

I'm being swept up in pair of huge, hard arteried arms. Swept up and then held tight by network television, CNN and Starbucks. It's comfort everything. High carb and well lit. Welcome back!

Coming back to Amerika always results in a bit of culture shock for me. It gets more drastic as time passes. Amerika is bigger, brighter and more desperate each time I return. As if the cure for the ill is to make it louder, boost the color, make it go faster and force the smiles up higher. It seems overdriven and clenched. I don't think it's been the land of plenty for decades and we can't get past that. The arrogance and cultural blindness that comes with being so powerful will prove to be our undoing.

02-27-02 Buffalo NY: 5:15 p.m. We played Boston last night. It was a good time as always. Not much to remark upon. A good show and a good crowd. In the room next door they were having some matinee show of punk bands. I guess they're punk bands? Sugar Cult? What are they? All the bands that played sounded the same, complete with corny ska breakdowns and pussy harmonies. These bands are weak. I imagine they'll be huge. From the sound of the audience, they have some fans. It's not my problem. I don't own the world of music and I don't have to listen to it so I reckon I'm getting off easy. I don't know what I would do if I were a responsible parent and my kid came home with a Sugar Cult record. I don't believe in hitting children. I do think I would make the kid incinerate the CD in the backyard while *Revolution of the Mind: James Brown Live at the Apollo Volume III* blared in the background. I'd be such a rotten dad. You can't say to your son, "Your musical choices are consistently lame. You are turning into a pussy plagued with no sense of humor and entry-level intellect. You are starting to become a great disappointment to myself and your mother. This will not do. As your father, it is my duty to administer the first four Ted Nugent albums, repeated applications of the Led Zep and Black Sabbath catalogs and early morning shots of Thin Lizzy. Next month, we work towards the Stooges and the Velvet Underground. By summer we will be well into the Ramones and The Germs. You bring home anymore of this bullshit music and I will not allow you to spend most of your teenage years alone in your room, sulking, perfecting your jack off technique and plotting how to kill me in my sleep. I will make you hang out in well lit rooms and actually speak to people. Don't let this horrible fate befall you, my son. Rock out before it's too late. The first showing of Animal House starts in an hour."

03-02-02 Chicago IL: 5:10 p.m. At the venue. I thought last night was good. Clif said it was good in the truck so perhaps we have something we can use. We'll see when we start mixing the tapes next week. There's still one show to go. Clif and I will be mixing this right away when we get back. It will be at least a week of mixing and constant bee lines from house to office to studio. All in the polluted misery of LA.

Last night, someone stole my shorts out of the dressing room. I don't know what the hell you would want with those but I do use them every night and it's a pain in the ass to try to find another pair. Mike and I ventured out into the snow and found a sports store where I got something I can use. It sucks that someone ripped me off but that's life. It's hard to be cool when people are just milling around backstage, taking your things.

I love this crowd. They were so into it last night and we played our asses off. Today was just hanging around, buying shorts and waiting to come here and do it all over again. Chicago is freezing and dark and walking around is really hard when the wind isn't going your way. I walked here from the hotel and damn near froze my head off.

03-03-02 Chicago IL en route to LA: Not sure of the time, definitely morning. Last night was good. I think the first night might have been a little better sonically. I heard a lot of feedback up there last night. I guess the tapes will tell the tale.

So that's it. That's the tour. What a drag that it's over. I'm not ready to get off the road. I am rarely ready to step off. I like the bus better than my house.

I sometimes wonder if I am blowing it. Do I like the road because I like it or is it because I can't deal with real life? What if this is the case? Real life is a bunch of people in traffic, divorce, boredom, compromise. I am supposed to run back to that? Call me whatever you want but it doesn't interest me at this time. The rest of the world is infinitely more interesting.

Off the road, I feel out of place. People talk and I listen but I can't relate at all. Some guy is having turbulence with his girlfriend or his shoes and it's a problem. It is? Go buy some new shoes and tell the girl to shove it. Problem solved, problem shoved. Let's go. I know what's coming. I'm going to go back to my place and it will be cool for a couple of days and then I'll see how lame it is and I'll want to throw everything out and never come back. I'll lift weights and do calisthenics to alleviate the vast amounts of pissed off that will accumulate. Good thing there's a new Slayer record to play in traffic.

03-05-02 LA CA: 11:55 p.m. What a town. Bruce Webber asked me to do a photo session for *Italian Vogue*. That's definitely a market I'm trying to break into, I need to reach that Italian-girl-who-likes-to-read-Vogue demographic big time. I thought it would be interesting so I called him and he seemed pretty cool in that wobbly arty way, replete with the distracted, mumbling speak. You know that thing where someone's talking to you but the whole time you get the feeling that they're looking for something in their pockets or playing with their hair while they're talking? Oh, he's a genius, he doesn't even know what day it is! What's with these people? Anyway, his "people" were told that I wasn't going to take my shirt off and pose out. If the guy wants to take my picture, fine but I don't want to that whole stupid pose out thing with my shirt off, I'll leave that to Brad Pitt. Been there, done that. I'm in my forties, give me a break. He communicated back through his people that me keeping my shirt on would restrict his artistic vision. Well, we wouldn't want that, now would we? I don't give a fuck about him or his fucking vision. So, he went away. Got to get out of this town. Insert the Stiff Little Fingers song 'Gotta Get Away' and play very loud.

03-06-02 LA CA: 5:45 p.m. Two days away from the benefit for the West Memphis Three. It's sold out and all the money will go to the boys defense fund. Can't wait to rock the Troubadour. I love that place. It sucks being back here but at least there's a show to look forward to.

Spent most of the day at the office wading through mail. I got a letter from Damien Echols' wife Lorri Davis. She thanked us for doing the upcoming benefit and said that Damien is hanging in there pretty well. She went on to say that she's amazed how he gets on with his life in the midst of such dire circumstances. I can't imagine. I don't know how I would hold up in prison. I wrote her back and told her that I was planning more than just the benefit to raise money and awareness of the case. I reckon the job isn't over until those guys get a new trial, otherwise, they just hang around in there. I don't know how you end up marrying a guy on Death Row™, what's the upside? I imagine it's pretty cool for Damien to have someone on the outside looking after him but I can't imagine what it's like for her.

Several weeks ago, I got a letter from a friend of a girl I knew who was killed in an accident last June. She said she had her letters and journals and she wanted to give me the letters back as well as all the journal entries that pertained to me. She sent them. The package was here when I got in. I put off opening it for a few days but today I did. There were a lot of letters from the last nine years, print outs of my e-mails to her and several pages of her journal detailing the time we spent together last April. I read as much as I could. She wrote so beautifully and clearly. She said such nice things about me. So strong and unguarded. She was supposed to fly out here and meet me a few days after I got back from tour but was killed in an accident three days before her flight. No one knew how to contact me at first so I didn't find out for a few days. It was as bad as you can imagine. I saw the police report and figured out she was killed while I was flying over Colorado on a plane from London. For three days I was cleaning the house and getting the place ready not knowing what had happened.

I'm uncomfortable when someone shows concern for me. It makes me feel weak. It makes everything I say feel forced, like I'm acting. I don't want to feel too at ease around anyone. Stress holds me together. It's a fairly safe, selfish and cowardly way to live I guess. In her journal, she describes touching me and being able to feel how wound up I was. She was one of the only women I have ever felt ok around. She found me. She got me. She's gone forever.

A few pages in, I couldn't read anymore. It made me so sad. Her writing made her absence all the more hard to take. I think about her all the time anyway but her words and her handwriting were too much for me.

I didn't feel like working anymore so I left the office hoping that movement and a change of scenery would pep me up and make me think of something else. It didn't but I'm alright. Even when I am at my worst, I don't allow myself to feel sorry for myself. It just doesn't compute with me anymore. It doesn't do me any good and it doesn't change anything. I will say this, people bring me pain. The less of them I deal with the better I feel. Any attachment has its risks. Anything from a bike to a friend. Anything that can be taken away holds power over you. I think that's why a lot of people look back at the times in their life when they had few possessions as good times. The less you have, the less you have to worry about.

The other day I was flying here from Chicago and I was talking with the flight attendants and one of them remarked that there must be so many people to call and deal with when I return from such a long trip. When I told him that there was no one besides the people at the office and management he gave me quite a look. It hit me how differently I live than most people. I'm strange. So be it.

We have a show in two days. I can't wait. I wish we were leaving for another two months of shows right afterwards. I've been here four days and I'm ready to go. The nights have been pretty good though. I have been getting in good workouts and listening to a lot of music. The frogs are back and it's great to hear them after the sun goes down. (What are they, Hyla regilla? I'll have to look that up, why do I know stuff like this?) The phone doesn't ring at all and it's quiet besides the occasional car and the stereo.

LA looks the same. Every time I come back here I do the same thing. I get in the car and go to the office and then to the grocery store. Within a few minutes of driving, I feel like I never left. Same dried out trees, endless concrete acreage, bland buildings, nose-to-tail traffic and all those LA people. When you haven't been here for awhile, the residents of LA are a trip. The young professionals on cel phones, the hipsters trying too hard, the hot looking women who know it and are working it, even in the parking lot of the grocery store. It's a city of pros, fakes, con artists and destitute losers. Oh, and there's me. Right.

Functioning in the middle of all this blanched earth and smog, I constantly think of two environments: The first is a small piece of land with a lake and no people. The other is a small, hot room in some corner of Indonesia. Either way it's a solo invisibility trip. A way to live below the radar. A living space that annihilates the one I'm in now.

Sometimes when I see what people do to each other, what they do to wildlife and the environment I'm ready to leave them to it. Like the thing that happened to Damien, Jessie and Jason, or all the folks destroyed by the Enron thing, it makes me tired just thinking about it all. Or watching the Grammys™—those bands, those people—give them what they want so they'll leave. You want an award? Here, take mine. I also think about that time last year when I disappeared into Thailand for a few days. I was nowhere and no one knew me and no one talked to me and it was hot and it stank and it was awesome. I had shows waiting for me a few days later in Europe but I felt like staying longer.

I wish I had woken up on the bus this morning. I wish there was a show tonight. Every night since I've been back here, it's been hard to sleep without the noise of the engine, my ear plugs in and my sweatshirt over my head.

I need the movement and the confrontation of an audience. Sitting here in this room, it feels like time is tenderizing me, setting me up to fall. It's that Captain Willard in his Saigon hotel room waiting for a mission thing. I'm listening to Roky Erickson sing 'Starry Eyes,' his personal favorite. "Starry Eyes, how can I get to you?" I miss that girl.

03-09-02 LA CA: 8:33 p.m. I looked on Amazon this evening to find that the Rollins Band *End of Silence* album has been re-issued in the UK with a bonus disc of tracks. I had to master disc one for the licensing company because Terry Ellis, the owner of Imago Records and the aforementioned album, lost the master tapes. He had sent a DAT of the album to the UK company and wished them luck. Luckily, I met up with the record company people in London and told them that I would handle the mastering. I added a live track to the end of the CD for a bonus, there was no more room to add more. So Terry Ellis in all his wisdom found some tapes in his closet and either gave them to the record company and they made a bonus disc or he put it together himself but I can't see him taking the time to do anything like that. There's tracks we did with the Butthole Surfers and Vernon Reid. I am sure he didn't contact either band or their respective publishers. I am sure their lawyers will be very interested. I will make sure they get the word. This is an adult and he pulls this shit? How are you supposed to work with someone who's gaming you like that? It's hard to be cool to millionaire cheapskates but you have to. Sheryl, Don, help!

So last night was supposed to be show #41 and the end of this slice of life dragged down the road. But it was not to be. The mixing board at the venue blew out and the gig was canceled with a sold out audience inside. The show was rescheduled for this coming Tuesday. I went onto the dancefloor to talk to people and try to smooth out any bumps but there weren't any. I couldn't believe how cool people were about the whole thing. It wasn't anyone's fault really. The Troubadour is a good place, the people who work there are great. I talked to people who had driven from Seattle, Arizona and Northern California. There's a lot of support for the West Memphis Three. I met Burk, Kathy and Grove, the people who run the West Memphis Three Support Group. They've been helping to get the word out about the WM3's plight for years now. Jason, Jesse and Damien are lucky to have them around.

Last night while standing with all these people, signing their tickets and explaining the deal with the mixing board and thanking them for showing up, it hit me how fortunate I am. These people are so great. They say such inspiring things. It's amazing to hear that something I do matters so much to someone. It's all I need to hear to keep going. I stayed there until they were all gone and then I left. I got back here and burned out on my own and let my thoughts settle. It's a Saturday night. No one here but me and the music. I have a good mix CD playing, the contents listed below.

01. The Damned - Channel 7 Plan 9 02. The Buzzcocks – Fiction Romance 03. The Snakes – Glo Clock 04. X Ray Spex – Artificial 05. The Cigarettes – Here They Come Again 06. The Razors – Christchild 07. Those Naughty Lumps – Iggy Pop's Jacket 08. Wire – Ex Lion Tamer 09. TV Smith – We Want the Road 10. Ruts – It Was Cold 11. King Crimson – Sleepless 12. UK Subs - Ice Age 13. Lurkers – God's Lonely Men 14. The Mob – Witch Hunt 15. Sods – Pathetic 16. Kim Salmon and the Surrealists – Intense 17. Generation X – Untouchables 18. The Fall – Mark Will Sink Us 19. Rezillos – Top of the Pops 20. Roky Erickson – I Walked with a Zombie 21. The Misfits – Halloween II 22. Manifesto - Sugar

I have been thinking about F. Scott Fitzgerald, the great Amerikan man of letters. For the last couple of nights I've been looking at a scrap book called *The Romantic Egoists.* It consists of pictures of Fitzgerald, his wife and daughter, friends, bits of their writing, newspaper articles and other odds and ends that concern them. What interests me most are the pictures taken near the end of his short life.

In most of the later photos, Fitzgerald has a smile that looks more like a pained grimace, like a guy trying to look on the bright side before the firing squad gets the command. I think he knew he was on his way out, or he had it in his mind that he was washed up. From his journal entries at this time, he seemed used up and merely existing. This contradicts the writing he was doing at the time though, the novel he was working on until his death, *The Love of the Last Tycoon*, was published posthumously, and even in its unrefined and incomplete state, it's a great read. It's as good as any of his more well-known work I think. Had he been able to finish it and get it published, I think he would have been right back in the game. At the time of his death his books weren't selling. The first run of *The Great Gatsby* hadn't sold through. Now, Gatsby sells over three hundred and fifty thousand copies a year. It's a beautiful book. Gatsby was so sad and torn apart. It's a great doomed love story. Another one of Fitzgerald's characters looking in all the wrong places to fulfil his dreams and getting slaughtered one way or another. I've read it three times and it gets better each time.

There are so many lines in Fitzgerald's work that make me stop and re-read them. As far as construction of utterly beautiful sentences and complete mastery of character development, I think Fitzgerald is one of the best. I am no learned critic, nor have I read every book but when you read Fitzgerald's short story *Winter Dreams* or read his novel *Tender is the Night* as the main character, Dick Diver, slowly falls apart, it's obvious that Fitzgerald was a genius. From what I've read, Tender tanked and got bad reviews. Fuck them, the book is awesome. Hard to take as Diver slowly self-destructs, but what a read. That one took him nine years to finish. If you read about Fitzgerald, you know that he didn't always spend a great deal of time writing.

Fitzgerald was not all that different than a lot of the more tragic characters in his stories. I will always wonder what he really wanted, as his life seems like fiction to me, like he was working off a script. He seemed to live through gestures, like he was acting in a movie about his life. He relentlessly shredded himself to pieces in his lifestyle and writing. *The Crack-Up,* a biographical series of entries detailing his crisis and dissolution, is hard reading at times—so painful and precise, such beautiful sentence structure. He must have known his dreams were empty. I imagine he wanted the respect and success that Hemingway had. I wonder what he would have thought if he knew how Hemingway died. I think at the end of the day, Fitzgerald was all about getting paid. He spent most of his career writing short stories to supplement his lifestyle and his wife's medical care while he tried to work on his novels. If he had Hemingway's continued success with sales of his novels and wasn't always hustling to get by, who knows what he may have achieved. I prefer the work of Fitzgerald to Hemingway. Both are amazing, but having read a lot of both, Hemingway's ego sometimes gets in the way of the story where

Fitzgerald at his best, seems invisible in his work. Fitzgerald was obsessed with the rich. I think he must have seen them as somehow charmed. So many of the storylines in his novels imply that money doesn't buy you anything of real value and went out of his way to illustrate that money destroyed those who had it in great abundance. Gatsby was rich and died brokenhearted and friendless. Maybe Fitzgerald should have taken his own advice.

Fitzgerald's biggest appeal to me is that he was an incurable romantic with more sentimentality than you can stand. He couldn't help but look at his past with longing. He obsessed on his days at Princeton University. He didn't even graduate! I find myself looking back often as well. I think of the town I grew up in, the streets, the people. I carry pictures of Washington DC with me on the road.

In one section of the posthumously published collection of writing, *The Crack Up,* he talks of waking up in the middle of the night in a panic, thinking he did everything wrong and that it's too late and life will soon be over and he can't get back to sleep because of the horror of it all. That never happens to me when I sleep on a tour bus but it happens at least twice a week when I'm here.

Fitzgerald died December 21st, 1940 at forty-four years of age. From what I've read he was in his girlfriend's apartment reading and suddenly got up, grabbed the mantelpiece above the fireplace and fell to the ground. By the time the ambulance came, he was dead. Occlusive coronary arteriosclerosis.

The apartment he died in is a twenty minute walk from where I am sitting. I've been there and put my hand on the mantelpiece where his was. I took photos of the mantelpiece and the floor around it. I stood in the doorway, thinking that decades ago, the dead, prematurely aged body of one of the greatest writers the world has ever known was carried out by ambulance attendants who most likely didn't even know who he was. He died in relative obscurity, haunting Hollywood bookstores, drinking, falling apart, but still able to write great material. What's the landmark near the place where F. Scott Fitzgerald died? The Virgin Megastore. Time flies on wounded wings. Time to install and utilize the next mix CD.

01. The Damned – I Believe the Impossible 02. The Adverts – Back from the Dead 03. Rowland S. Howard – Breakdown 04. The Velvetones – The Glory of Love 05. Suicide – Surrender 06. Phil Lynott – Dear Miss Lonely Hearts 07. Ennio Marricone - Lonesome Billy 08. The Crystals – And then He Kissed Me 09. The Ramones – The Return of Jackie and Judy 10. Thin Lizzy – Romeo and the Lonely Girl 11. The Platters – Smoke Gets in Your Eyes 12. Alan Vega – Cry a Sea of Tears 13. Miriam Makeba – Ha Po Zamani 14. Al Green – Old Time Lovin' 15. Dinosaur Jr. – Start Choppin' 16. Steve Miller – Serenade 17. Aerosmith – Get the Lead Out 18. Cheap Trick – Auf Weidersehen 19. Lou Reed – Real Good Time Together 20. Dr. Mix and the Re-mix – Out of the Question 21. Generation X – Night of the Cadillacs

For the last few years, I have been reading and re-reading Hemingway, Fitzgerald and Thomas Wolfe. The latter two, especially. They were all edited and befriended by the great Max Perkins at Scribner's. The brilliant biographer, A. Scott Berg wrote a tremendous book about these men and their time called *Max Perkins: Editor of Genius*. What a great read. Perkins worked with varying degrees of closeness with all three writers. From what Berg says, Hemingway needed the least assistance, Wolfe the most, due to the nature of his writing and Fitzgerald needed financial assistance and personal encouragement more than anything else and Perkins did the best he could. Reading the Berg book got me interested in Wolfe. What a turn on. I'll have to read that one again some day. Wolfe, now that's a whole universe right there. Not everyone's taste but man, he's right up my street. What writing, what a life. Twelve hour work days. The manuscript for his second book is still coming out in parts and he died almost seventy years ago.

I have a lot of musical heroes but if I could meet anyone in history, besides Martin Luther King, writers would be at the top of my list. Besides the ones I just mentioned, I include Camus, Celine, Leautreamont, Artaud, Rimbaud, Kobo Abe, Miller, Twain, Kafka (can you imagine?!) Vian, Algren, Steinbeck, Conrad, Corbett, Hamsun, Thurber, Poe, O. Henry, Musashi, Seneca, Hammet, Rumi, Capote, Dostoyevsky. Enough already! I guess I would want to meet every writer who wrote books that mattered to me. Looking back at this shortlist, I don't read many women: Susan Sontag, Ayn Rand, Joan Didion, Flannery O'Connor. I think I have read all of her stuff. I love her book of letters *The Habit of Being* the best of all. I have read books by women but not many where I've sought out all the work like with O'Connor and Didion. How many of those people do you reckon were completely mean motherfuckers? Ninety something percent easily. It's such a bad job, writing.

I have been here less than a week and depression and frustration have set in. Exhaustion as well. It takes a couple of days and then my body realizes that it is sleeping more and moving less and it breaks down. Insomnia. My voice deteriorates to a whisper for about three days, my entire body aches for about a week. Worst is the legs. They're just shot. Pressure holds me together. Every day I wake up a little more pissed off at the sameness of a life that doesn't move fast enough, that doesn't care about a schedule, that doesn't hit it. All the fucking talk. So much talk. I can take it for awhile and then I gotta go. In the morning, I get up as early as I can, drag my ass out of bed and go to the office. Not many phone calls come in but I get through the mail and work on whatever's at hand. I finish there, do whatever errands I have to do and then go back to the house. No phone calls there. I do time. I think of dead people. I think of the town I grew up in. I listen to music. I read sections of books that I like. I try to learn new words. I lift weights in the garage. Repetitions. I run the numbers in my head. I count the days I have to train for the next tour. But mostly I just do time until I can get out of here and smash it to pieces. I do enjoy the weekends of uninterrupted solitude and large quantities of loud music. I don't get lonely living and spending so much time completely by myself. For me, it's the most natural thing in the world. It was how I was raised. I spent years living amongst my parents but don't know much about them. I don't know the names of my father's siblings or how many there are. I don't know his father's name. I don't know my mother's mother's name. They never told me much about them, or perhaps they did and it didn't stick. It doesn't matter at this point. It is a waste of time to try and make it matter.

I got an e-mail from Ian the other day telling me my mother's husband had a heart attack and was in the hospital. He told me I should call my mother and even included her number in case I didn't have it. I cannot remember the last time I called that number, at least seven years. I e-mailed her and told her I was sorry and that I hoped he got better. He's a good guy. I didn't know what else to say. It made me see how unconnected to them I am. I don't have a family and don't know many people. So that's how I turned out. Everyone turns out somehow. Everyone ends up a certain way and that's it and that's you and there it is.

It's time to go. It's time to get on the bus and go. Show after show. Let's go. Let's push it hard like we were up until last week. Every night onstage I obliterate the fakes, the Terry Ellis's of the world, the corny bands. I leave no fucking doubt.

03-13-02 LA CA: 10:14 p.m. Last night we finally got to do the show at the Troubadour. I didn't know if anyone would show up again. Well, they did and it was great. We played hard and it was a good time. It was hard to come down from it. Exene's band was great! There's something lame about leaving a venue, walking to your car and driving "home." I did just that. I walked out of the venue and ten minutes later, I was back here.

The tour is over and we gave them the real thing every night. I can still remember the first night in Belfast like we just started. It's great when you have about fifteen shows behind you. You're in shape and used to the ritual and the discipline. Pre-show warm up, seven minute nap twenty minutes before you go on. The time, the numbers, always numbers, how long, how many songs, how many hours before we leave, how many hours to the next place. How many hours before soundcheck.

Time matters out there. Here, shit, it's all The Big Whatever. Out there it all matters, here, it's just another day in traffic. It's the stillness that gets to me. It's times like right now where I wish I was on the bus, on the way to the next place. It takes me weeks to be able to sleep in the bed here because it doesn't shake and pitch. Can you imagine living your life in Los Angeles? Like all the time? That's one depressing thought.

I got word from my lawyer about that silly extra disc added to the *End of Silence* package. It seems by doing that, Terry Ellis is in breach of his contract with me. If I have to abide by the contract, he does too, right? Management contacted the record company about it and they gave some weak-assed excuse as to why they put the second disc out. NMC, the corny label who put it out are basically bootleggers. The owner, Barry is just another motherfucker in the world. There's so many of them out there. He's a generic off-the-rack industry prick. He knows what he is.

So what to do? Rejoice, that's what. Rejoice. I am alive and I am listening to some good music. Life is good. Even when it doesn't seem to be, it's just a bend in the road. You want to make music? You'll have to deal with tiny motherfuckers like Terry Ellis and this Barry fuck all the time. They come with the deal. You have to know that. They have a miserable existence. They are dishonest for a living and they know it. They think they're living but they're not. It's not my problem. My skin is thick and I never stop moving. They never get me down for long.

04-14-02 LA CA: 11:11 p.m. This morning at about 0330 hrs., I was wide awake and sitting at the table. I liked the show we did for the WM3 boys and thought we could be doing more. I thought about what that would be and it always came back to a benefit record of some kind. I know how to make a record. Benefit records are usually heartfelt but rarely memorable or effective. I hit upon the idea of doing a bunch of Black Flag songs and trying to get some cool singers to come in and sing on the tracks. Black Flag is ultimate protest music and it would be cool to hear some good singers perform that stuff. I got so pumped up on the idea that I was barely able to get to sleep. I went into the office a few hours later and started making phone calls.

It looks like the wheels have been set in motion on this project. About an hour ago, I spoke to our drummer Jason about the benefit record idea to see what he thought and he was totally into it. I made some more calls and got the same response from Marcus, our bass player, and Jim our guitar player. Ok, we have a band! I think we have at least one foot planted solidly in what will most likely prove to be a long and uphill journey.

This journal will document the making of the record, a collection of Black Flag songs with (I hope) some singers of renown to be released near the end of the year to raise awareness and some much needed funds for Jessie Misskelley, Jason Baldwin and Damien Echols, otherwise known as the West Memphis Three.

If you don't know who these people are, you can go to a website, www.WM3.org and learn more about the case and check out the reading and video list and see what we're talking about.

We can do this. Tomorrow I confirm everyone's schedules and we book practice time and get into it. I can't believe I am taking this on. I don't know what it is, something tells me this is something that I should do. I can't explain it. I guess I'm mad.

There's a lot to be done. Practice time must be booked. Songs selected, CDs made of the songs for the boys to start learning, hell, I need to learn the stuff myself. It's been a long time. I have to make lyric sheets. Projections on rehearsal and studio time need to be made. We have to contact a bunch of singers, engineers, managers, agents and whoever else. I have no idea where this will take me or what this will cost or what it's going to take from me to get it all happening.

I know we can learn the songs. I know we can do good versions of them in the studio. That's the easy part. Will anyone show up to sing? That's the question. I know I should be getting commitments from the singers before I start all this but fuck it. I want to get it going. We'll get singers or we won't. If we record it, they will come!

There's already some singers I want to ask because I think there's a song that fits them perfectly. The two I keep thinking of the most are Tom Araya of Slayer singing 'Revenge' and Lemmy singing 'Thirsty and Miserable.' I can hear the songs in my head with them singing and it's incredible. I don't know how to find Lemmy and I've never met anyone in Slayer although I am quite a fan.

04-15-02 LA CA: It's late. I told Chuck Dukowski about the record and asked him if he would participate and he said he would. He wants to do 'What I See.' He wrote it. It's a good song too. So that's one song down.

This record is going to be a series of long shots, favors and markers getting called in. I don't have much in the way of markers to call in as I don't know many musicians and I have never really been in a position to help any so it's not like any singer owes me anything. I have to hope that they either know about the case or will become interested enough to want to know more and eventually participate. I reckon Black Flag songs are pretty good bait.

This record will be a nice gesture no matter what it ends up sounding like but my manager raised a good point when he said that it better be really fucking good. He's right, it's got to stand up on its own.

What if we get singers in and they're crap?! This is going to be a lot of work. Only time will tell if it's worth it. Fuck it, it's worth it. I wrote Damien and Jason and told them that I was in until they were out and I meant it.

04-17-02 LA CA: 11:50 p.m. Today was good. I was able to track down Keith's phone number. Will call him tomorrow.

Worked the phones real hard the last couple of days. Well, hard for me. I hate talking on the phone. Hate making and getting calls. Hate waiting for calls, hate playing phone tag. I can tell there's going to be a lot of that kind of thing on this record.

I nailed down practice time at Cole. I pleaded my case to Bruce Robb at Cherokee Studios and he was immediately enthusiastic and totally pumped up on having his place involved with the project. I was unable to get Clif Norrell to engineer as he'll be in Holland working. I called David Bianco to see if he wanted to engineer. He mixed *Weight*. He's a solid guy and a good engineer. He's busy too. The good ones usually are. I have some other calls I can make.

I was in Burbank earlier today hanging out with Nick Cave and the Bad Seeds. They played in town last night and were amazing as always. Nick sang great and at this point, the band is one of the best there is anywhere. Today they played on the Leno show so I went over there to hang out with them and watch them perform 'Fifteen Feet of Pure White Snow.'

Before I went over there, I called Nick at his hotel to see what he was up to as I didn't get a chance to talk to him the night before. I told him all about what we were doing and he was familiar with the case and wanted to know more so I brought the documentary *Paradise Lost II: Revelations* with me to give him.

It was great to hang out with Nick and the guys. I recommended Ryszard Kapuscinski's books and another writer, Daniil Kharms to him. Guitarist Blixa Bargeld was all over both writers and suggested some others for me to check out.

After hanging out for awhile, it was time for the band to play. I watched from the back, above the audience. They were great. I don't know what the audience thought of them. They kind of just sat there and consumed. It was cool to see the guest Dame Edna (the comedian guy who dresses up like a woman) check out the band. He/she is hilarious. No script, Dame Edna just improved off anything Jay said.

Too soon, it was time to leave. The band had to get to soundcheck for the second LA show. I waited for Nick on the bottom floor, downstairs from the band room. Dame Edna was there talking with Nick's manager when all of a sudden, Joanne Whorley came down the hall, all made up, complete with scarf on head, looking like she just walked off the set of *Laugh In*. She is intense! She walked up to Dame Edna and said she was one of her biggest fans and then did that thing where she puts her finger in her cheek and lets loose that operatic wail, just like on *Laugh In* and she kept on walking and was gone. Everyone just stood there, looking at each other in silence. I was the first one to speak. "I just had a flashback. It's 1970. I am nine years old and I'm watching *Laugh In*. That was easily the most intense thing I have seen in a month."

Nick missed it. What a sight. A large man dressed as a woman and a large woman who looks like a man dressed up as a woman. It was a memorable sight for sure. That's showbiz.

04-19-02 LA CA: 10:00 p.m. Listening to the Miles Davis *In A Silent Way* boxset. Forget it! How good can music get?

Today was productive and eventful. I nailed down the studio time and put down a fifteen thousand dollar deposit on the room. Well, I'm in now!

I wrote Lorri Davis and told her I was in motion on a large scale project for the WM3. She wrote back and thanked me. Lorri left a good job in NYC to live in Arkansas and be near Damien. Six years she's been down there. Damien may be in a bad situation but at least he's got a woman who believes in him. It's amazing to me that some-one would go that far to be with someone else. Quit their job and life and start again miles away. I can't imagine a woman doing that for me. That's a hell of a thing.

I put in a call to Keith Morris and left a message. It's so cool to hear his voice on the machine: "Keith's not here. Leave a message," and then laughter and a beep. I have a thing for voices. Keith has one of those voices. He's the real thing. Keith is still the man. It's still cool to hang out with him. I'm always a little bit of a fan around him, can't help it. We played with the Circle Jerks last summer and they were good. Keith still has it. Will he show for the record?

I should try to recruit Danzig for this. Ok, there's something to do. I'm going to write him right now.

Later. Ok, Danzig has been e-mailed. We'll see.

The band is psyched! What a relief. I couldn't do this one with-out them. No way. I think we'll rip this music.

I listened to 'Rise Above' five times in a row today. I was nearly in tears at one point, one of the greatest songs ever written.

04-20-02 LA CA: 6:28 p.m. Newsflash! Keith just called. Keith is in. You can't do this record without Keith and we've got him. We are going to rock. I told him that as far as I was concerned, without him on the record, the record has no credibility. It's true, without Keith being on this thing, it's really not the thing, is it? No.

04-22-02 LA CA: 10:31 p.m. There's a newspaper in West Memphis AR, called the *West Memphis Commercial Appeal.* A writer there wrote an article that states that the West Memphis Support Group, namely Burk, Grove and Kathy, are a "for profit" organization and makes them out to be somewhat shady characters. This is also the same newspaper who printed Jessie Miskelley's error ridden confession before the trial started and also stated that human heads were found underneath Damien's bed. Needless to say, this publication is a little south of credible. Anyway, the writer of this article, Bartholomew Sullivan (sullivan@gomemphis.com) said that I ignored the opportunity to talk to him. I don't believe I ever got that call. This guy is trying to pull me into his world of bullshit? Bring it on Bart. Now he has me to worry about.

I got his phone number and called him. All I got was his whiney voice on an answering machine. I left all my numbers and begged him to confront me. Can't wait.

On a brighter note, Ian MacKaye came into town today. The premier for the film *Dogtown* is tomorrow and we're going to it. Ian's great as always and it's super cool to have him out here in this fucked up city of whores. How amazing would it be if he showed up on this record?

04-24-02 New Hampshire: 11:33 p.m. Had to fly out of LA this morning and do a talking show. It was a cool time. I have a few talking shows this week and then back to LA.

Yesterday was pretty cool. Before the film, Ian and I went to a record store called Ameoba. Even to give it the most cursory once-over, you'll need about two hours—it's that big. We were checking out records and we ran into the man himself, Keith Morris. It was cool to see the two of them in the same place. Ian and I met Keith together in the summer of 1980 up in San Francisco. Ian's band the Teen Idles were on tour and I was out with them. We were at Target Video and the Circle Jerks were there. We didn't know who they were. Someone told us that the singer used to be in Black Flag. We walked over to him and asked if he was Keith Morris, he said he was. We were blown away to hang out with him. Even then, he was kind of a legend to us. For me, it's still the same. We're friends and all but still, I find myself a fan as well. Tony Alva was hanging out with the band at that time and we met him also. I remember Ian, Mark Sullivan and I just looking at each other, so stoked that we had met Keith Morris and fuckin' Tony Alva at the same time. Alva and Ted Nugent got me through high school. What a day.

The premier was pretty cool. It was cool to meet Shogo Kubo, one of the Z-Boys. I talked to Alva for a while. He's still got all the charisma. I was standing in that press line thing doing photos and interviews, behind Stacy Peralta. Sean Penn comes in and blows by the line with a smile and a wave. And then Alva comes in. The whole room comes alive and everyone's looking and all the press people start yelling his name and all the cameras shift direction and it's all on him and he could care less, he just walks in and takes the whole room with him. It was the damndest thing.

It was my second time seeing the film and it was better this time around. Such an amazing piece of work. Those guys were ahead of their time. I remember in high school, those guys were my heroes. What moves, what badasses. The documentary brings it all back. Ian and I shot Super-8 film of Jay Adams skating at the Big O Skatepark in Anaheim, CA in the summer of 1978 I think. It ends up being some of the only footage of Jay from that time. Ian found out that Stacy Peralta was making the documentary, and told him about our footage and Stacy wanted to see it. Ian sent it out and it ended up in the film so we got a credit at the end of the thing. We helped!

04-29-02 LA CA: After leaving daily phone messages for Bartholomew Sullivan, after getting a message left by him telling me to call him back at a different number only to get the message machine of his editor, after calling him back on the original number and getting his machine again and leaving a message for him to get brave and confront me and not pawn me off on his female editor, after all that; I finally get to talk to the whiney one himself. He says the only number he could get for me was my film agent. I remember getting the message from agent woman's assistant boy that someone at this fucked up newspaper wanted to talk to me and I told him to bring it. Nothing happened. I made Bart understand in no uncertain terms that he was always welcome to write, call or contact me anytime he wanted to confront me. Now that he has a direct line to me, I do so much hope that little bitch motherfucker will be in touch. I asked him if the boys were guilty or innocent. He said, "It's a murky case." Bart is one the writers of a hilarious book called *The Blood of Innocents,* one of those fluffy, poorly written books that come out as the dust is still settling.

Ian left today. He hung out at my place while I was on the road. It was so great having him around, I only wish I was around more of the time he was. But it was probably good for the guy to get some time to himself. He's one busy and in-demand guy back in DC. He's the best.

I got asked to be in a film version of the Empty TV show *Jack Ass.* They wanted me to drive one of their guys around in a jeep over rough terrain while he gets tattooed. Whatever. I've never seen the show. I don't give a fuck about Empty TV but I said sure, why not? I might learn something.

We shot the scene today. The guy's name is Steve-o. We are out in some kind of motorcycle riding place with washboards and hills for you to ride your bike on. I'm given a Hum-vee and we strap in and drive around. The guy is getting tattooed in the back and I'm driving over these bumps as fast as I can, around and around. The guy's arm was getting all fucked up, bleeding and swelling up. The guy can take a lot of pain, that's for sure. He'll also have one fucked up tattoo. We did that for an hour or so and then I split for band practice. I don't know when the movie will come out. They seem like ok guys. They didn't talk to me all that much.

Then the real part of the day started as soon as I got into LA. Day one of band practice.

Whoa! The boys had already been working on the music for days and were ready. I came in there expecting to get through two songs or something. I walked in and they're all set up and in position. I told them what I had just been up to and apologized for being a little late. Jim said that if I was ready they were ready. I asked them what song they wanted to work on and he said they could play about sixteen of the songs. What?! Well ok.

Before I knew it, Jim was playing the opening riff of 'Nervous Breakdown.' My entire body started tingling. I had not sung this song for about twenty years and here we are laying into it. We played the song and then we all stopped and looked at each other. I must have looked so weird to those guys. We slammed into the rest the *Nervous Breakdown* EP, right into the *Jealous Again* EP into the *Six Pack* EP and into the *Damaged* stuff. Playing 'Rise Above' was SO intense. I forgot that I had done that song so many times so many years ago and it felt like I was singing it for the first time.

The guys are laying into this stuff so hard it's frightening. Total intensity and commitment. I've never heard them play like this. We did every song we had two or three times and called it an afternoon.

It was so heavy to go back to those songs. I've been listening to them at the office every day but it's nothing like playing them. Those are some of the best songs ever written.

We go in again tomorrow and work on more songs. I know that learning this will be hard on the guys but if anyone can do it, it's them for sure. I have to think that the music will be the only easy part of this whole thing.

To get singers on this record, it's going to take a lot of calls and connections. There's no way I can do it and make the record at the same time. Also, I have no patience with these people. When I get attitude from a manager, agent or assistant, I just get too mad. Heidi May used to work at our office doing press stuff. She knows a lot of people in the music business and she doesn't mind a lot of work. On my way out to the *Jack Ass* thing, I called her, told her what we were trying to do and that I really needed her help on this project. Luckily, she had nothing going on she couldn't get out of and she'll be installing herself at the office and getting this thing rolling.

04-30-02 LA CA: 9:32 p.m. Another good day of practice. We played them all. Twenty–four songs. It sounds pretty good and it's going to get better. By the time we record, it will be 100%.

I gave Heidi a list of singers I wanted to contact and she was all over it today. Hank Williams III was one of them. The guys in the band have talked to him and say he's cool. I've heard his music, he's great. I know he sometimes wears a Black Flag shirt onstage so perhaps he will be open to it. His manager was contacted and he passed the message onto Hank that we asked him to sing 'No Values.' That's one of the great ones! He's supposed to call me tonight so I'll know more on that soon.

It's been an interesting ride being back inside these songs again. The famous Black Flag songs were written before I was in the band. I never felt all that much a member. It was hard being the 4th singer of the band. By the time I got there, they already had their thing going and I was just walking into it. I was just a fan who got to be in his favorite band.

Singing these songs again puts me back on fan status. It's great to sing them again but it's Greg and Chuck's trip. I was lucky. Right place, right time, nothing more.

Someone told me the other day that I was handed the singer spot on a silver platter. I am reminded all the time. Close. I did have to audition, there were other singers who were auditioned and I did make the cut. Knowing that I got into an established band who already had done years of hard work always made me feel somewhat on the outside of it all. If one goes to the internet, one can read that I was the reason that the band wasn't any good after a certain period. Some people didn't like the later songs, they must not check and see who was writing almost all of that material. It was a band I was in and it was a damn good one and it was a long time ago.

By the end of the band's existence I thought the whole thing was pretty negative. The audience was fucked on a lot of nights. The band was burnt. I was sad when we broke up but it was time. Singing these songs every night has been a cool way to visit the music again and sidestep the misery aspect.

The more I think about it, this might be the only worthwhile thing I ever do with having been in the band. Black Flag is ultimate music and this record will be a perfect use of Greg and Chuck's work.

There are a lot of things I miss about Black Flag. I really liked playing with Greg onstage. I think about it still. For over a decade I have had intense dreams of playing with him again. The dreams are always depressing though. One of them is that we're playing and there's hardly anyone there and we're not all that good and people are leaving between songs, I look behind me and there's no drummer. Still though, I think about what it would it be like to get out there with Greg again and do it. I miss him even though I never really knew him all that well. Playing the songs puts me in awe of Greg and Chuck all over again. Those riffs, how the hell did they come up with that stuff? All the way out in the wasteland of the beach south of the airport, there they were making this stuff. What the fuck?! I asked the guys in our band what they thought of the music composition-wise and they said that it's off the scale, totally challenging. Jason told me that 'Depression' has a five count at the top. I never knew that. I never went on the count of that song, I just always watched the drummer's left hand.

Later: Just got off the phone with Hank III. He's in Dallas, TX on a night off. He just came from seeing Slayer and said they were amazing. He knows about the case and is totally into being on the record. What a cool guy. We'll send the music to him in Nashville and he will do his part and send it all back. I can't think it's going to be this easy with every singer but it's a great start.

05-14-02 LA CA: The benefit business is a road paved with obstacles and disappointment, brush offs and attitude. We asked the guys in Blink 182 if they wanted to sing. People buy their records, we should have one of those kind of bands represented on the record. They politely declined. We asked the White Stripes guy and he did the same. I don't know what the guy sounds like but I know that girls like him and girls buy records so we asked him. At least these people got back to us, good enough. This is going to be tough. Hopefully some artists will come through. I would hate to let the boys down.

It would have been easier if we didn't ask anyone to be on this thing and just did it ourselves but I must admit, it's inspiring as hell when someone comes through. Keith called today and he's so excited about it. The first thing he always asks is if Ian MacKaye is going to sing. I put a letter in to Ian but have not heard back. It might not be his kind of thing. I didn't want to ask him when he was out here.

One way or another, we're going to make a great record. We are absolutely on a mission.

05-16-02 LA CA: 11:19 p.m. The last two days have been good. Yesterday, we had a meeting with two interesting guys, I don't know what you call them, free-lance A&R perhaps. Sean E. and Bill Fold. They came over and looked over our wish list of singers and just annihilated it. Blink 182, White Stripes—they were laughing in our faces and asking if we were trying to make one of those lame movie soundtrack CDs. They asked if we had thought of Corey of Slipknot and we told them that we had but all we had was the number of an old manager who didn't want to help. Sean said he'd put that call in. They suggested that we call Cedric from The Mars Volta who used to be the singer in At the Drive In. I never would have come up with that one. Of course they have the number. They looked over our list and the ones that they didn't rip on mercilessly, they said they could find the contact numbers for.

What a pair, these two. Their cel phones ring every few minutes. They speak in this clipped, high speed jet stream of words. Not a bunch of bullshit. These guys are focused big time. They find good bands and bring them to the right label. They seem to know everyone and everything that's going on.

We talked for a long time. I learned a lot about how things are in the music business these days. These guys have a lot of energy and it was good for me to be around it because it's been hard these last several days.

Late this afternoon, Bill calls and says that yesterday he came on board with us because he knew a little about the case and thought our record was righteous. That night he went home and watched *Paradise Lost II: Revelations* and flipped out. He said it made him furious and he saw why we are all so mad about this and is as committed as we are. He said that he's now in full time for as long as it takes. It was so great to hear him so pumped up about it. I will take anyone's interest. We need all the help we can get.

The band is sounding great and we are ready to do this. We hit the studio tomorrow, can you believe this?! Think it up, assemble the troops and hit it. This is how you do it.

05-17-02 LA CA: 11:54 p.m. First day of recording. Got there in the morning and we set up the gear in the big room as we always do. It was strange not to have Clif there to engineer but he is out of the country working on a project. Dee and Bruce Robb, two of the owners and long time engineers, volunteered to pitch in. I figured they would be great but I had never worked with them before and didn't know what to expect.

Drum sounds were up in no time and before long we were tracking. Right off the bat it sounded good and I knew that we would be ok.

We put down a few songs with Jim using a Les Paul and it sounded great. Mike had told Steve Dachroeden at St. Louis Music about the project and Steve donated his Dan Armstrong guitar and sent it out to the studio for all the participants to sign and put up as an auction item. The Dan Armstrong was the guitar that Greg Ginn used. Greg used an original with modified pick ups and no tone control, he just soldered in an on-off switch. The one Steve sent was a re-issue and had factory pickups. For the hell of it, I asked Jim if he would play a song with the Dan Armstrong to check out the sound. I think the song was 'Revenge' and when he hit it, my hair stood up. That's the sound! A Dan Armstrong re-issue with factory pickups is still a Dan Armstrong. Jim used the guitar for the rest of the day.

We played all day and into the night. Every take, live with vocals. Got eleven songs down.

I talked to Corey Slipknot. Really cool guy. Asked him to sing 'Room 13.' I think that song is perfect for his voice and how intense he is. He said he would be happy to do it and wants to fly out immediately.

Eleven down, thirteen to go. We still need singers. I will be up soon and back on the phones before I have to go to the studio.

05-18-02 LA CA: 11:38 p.m. What a day. A few hours into it, Steve DePace from Flipper and Negative Trend comes by the studio to hang out and watch Keith sing 'Nervous Breakdown.' Keith arrives shortly after, meets everyone and asks if we're ready to go. He walks into the vocal booth and we roll the tape. He explodes. The vocal is amazing. We're all fairly stunned. If this is any indication of how well the singers are going to perform, we're going to have a great record. Keith asks if he can take the mic off the stand and hold it and do another take. No problem, go ahead Keith. He rips another vocal that blows the first one away. We break into spontaneous applause. We tell him to come in. He listens back to it and asks if it's good enough. Sure Keith, it'll do. He hangs out a little longer and then leaves. Fucking Legend. He's a fucking legend. What is he, near fifty? He blows all those people out there away. He's the only singer in Black Flag you need to pay attention to if you ask me. So now this record is real. We have Keith, the genuine article.

We went back to tracking and got through the rest of the songs by night fall. It was a hard slog. Play 'Black Coffee' five times straight and get back to me. I thought my head was going to explode. I had the headphones cranked so loud that the speakers inside were starting to burn my ears.

All the music is done and one of the vocals. I don't think any of us thought that we would get through all the songs in two days. We'll listen back to it all on Monday and if there's anything that needs redoing, we'll do it.

05-20-02 LA CA: 11:50 p.m. Another good day. We listened back to the songs and decided to do 'Slip It In' again and knocked out a much better version than the one we had.

After we got that done, we started in with guitar overdubs. Mike Curtis had come into town to help out with sounds and set ups so Jim could have some options. Fuckin' Mike just comes into town on the strength of the project to help. Jim went to work big time. I don't know how this guy can put down so many guitar parts so well to songs he didn't write. He's amazing.

In the afternoon, Jim took a break and Jim from the band Pennywise came in to do a vocal on 'I Don't Care.' An old Keith-era song. Good guy, great singer. Natural talent. He did his track in a few minutes. We played him Keith's track and he was totally into it. I don't know much about his band but he seems alright. It's good to have him aboard.

The rest of the day was guitars and exhaustion.

05-21-02 LA CA: 10:50 p.m. I started on my vocals today. I tracked keeper vocals on 'Slip It In.' It was great to sing that song a few more times. We got really good takes of the songs, I think Greg Ginn will be pleased if he ever checks out the record. It was worth it to do 'Slip It In' again yesterday, the take we have now is rockin'.

Let's see, what else? We finished the rest of the guitars and put guide vocals down on 'TV Party' for all the people who will be coming in to sing on the track. That was a trip, singing with the boys and hearing multiple voices on the choruses.

'TV Party' was the song that brought me to Cherokee Studios for the first time. When the film *Repo Man* was coming out, I guess the director asked Greg if 'TV Party' could be used for the soundtrack and he said ok. Greg took the advance and we went into Cherokee and re-did the vocals on the single version of the song. We updated the TV shows from the previous version and I re-did the lead vocals.

Greg and Chuck were ahead of their time and on their own with this music. There was nothing like those songs at the time and there wasn't anything like the Black Flag ideology. The ideas behind the band were as cool as the music. The Pettibon artwork on the flyers freaked people out. Scary flyers, intense music, a volatile following and then there was Chuck and the Nietzsche/Darwin/Huxley/Chaos thing he was coming from. "What the fuck, fuck the place up!" It was intense as hell. He was a scary guy back in the day. His ideas were so raw. He would get asked a question by some interviewer and fire a question back at the guy and just shut him down. Ian MacKaye has always said that Black Flag wasn't a matter of pre or post me, it was all about pre and post Dukowski. Ginn and Dukowski were both brilliant as they were different. The dynamic between the two was intense to be around. There's a great story there—if anyone could ever figure out how to get to the bottom of it all.

05-22-02 LA CA: 10:51 p.m. Solving problems and getting it done. We had been sending promo stuff to Slayer's manager to see if Tom Araya, the band's singer and bass player, wanted to be involved but got no response. Thanks to Sean E. and Bill Fold, we get Tom's cel number. I call him, introduce myself and make my pitch. Luckily, he is familiar with the case and is enthusiastic about being involved. He agrees to sing 'Revenge.' He has to finish some tour dates and as soon as that's over, he's coming in to sing. Yeah! I told him that we had been sending his manager stuff to pass onto him. Tom said that he never heard a word. Aren't these managers a scream? Can you believe we're going to have Tom Araya on this record? Forget it, we're bulletproof now.

I talked to Cedric of The Mars Volta and asked if he would sing on 'I've Had It' and he said he is up for it. He's got a great voice. I have never heard The Mars Volta but I have heard his old band At the Drive In and they were cool.

In the studio we did more backing vocals and cleaned up some tracks. There's a ton of work left on this record. I have to stay focused. I can do it if I don't look to either side. The more people I talk to, the more distracted I get but unless I talk to a lot of people, I won't get the parts needed. I try to keep it to a minimum but there's a lot of people to talk to regarding this thing. I've been on the phone more in the last few weeks than I have in the last year it seems.

You can do a lot of stuff if you don't fuck around. I get shit from people for having no life. They say I should go out more and interact with more people. What concern am I to anyone outside of the work anyway? It's not like anyone misses me when I am on tour. It's not like anyone is at a party and wonders where I am. Come on! Do your thing. If it's not the normal thing or someone else's thing, so what? Being on a mission is good for me. I make better use of the time. Outside of pressure, deadlines and workload, I don't matter. This can make for a stressful life in a way but there's a lot of things I don't have to concern myself with. I don't wonder where my kids are, what my wife is doing or if my tone of voice is going to bum out my girlfriend. At a certain point, that kind of thing is so ordinary and been there done that. Work doesn't cause stress. It's trying to maintain the details outside of the work that causes it. So, if you want to be effective at the work and cut the stress level, then it would make sense to go without that which causes stress. Life is short. Rip it.

05-23-02 LA CA: 9:03 p.m. Today was a good bit of work. Did the lead vocals on 'TV Party.' Inger Lorre, the singer in the Nymphs, came in and did backing vocals on 'Slip It In' and she was great! The Nymphs were cool but the record *Transcendental Medication* she did recently under her own name, is way better. She's a great song writer and singer and it's really good to have her on the record. I have known her a lot of years.

There was nothing more to do after that so I went back to the office and hit the phone. I talked to Lars Rancid who has to move his vocal date. It's no problem. I am glad that he and Tim Rancid are taking part in this. Great singers, great guys. Lars enthusiasm for the project has been inspiring to me. It's hard sometimes dealing with all these details so when you get a good phone call, it means a lot. I talked to Chuck Dukowski. He's coming in next Thursday to sing 'What I See.' That's going to be great. I talked to Exene Cervenka, she's coming in on Monday to sing 'Wasted.'

We got a call from Zack Rage Against the Machine's manager. We wanted to see if he had interest in the project, I figured he'd heard about the case and had an opinion. We had tried on several occasions to get a call back from his manager and got nothing but attitude from the guy's assistant who keeps the walls of the Castle high and thick. You can't talk to him. He only talks to special people. How dare we?! Anyway, manager boy calls today and says that Zack is unavailable.

We're past it now and stopped thinking about him several days ago, like we're really going to hang around for some fucking manager to get off his ass. Get the fuck out of here. Manager boy finds out Josh and Nick from Queens of the Stone Age are on the record. He's surprised, he manages them and no one told him. How did little mice like us get to his band? What, no one is allowed to talk to "your" band? Hilarious. The arrogance of some of these people is off the scale. I am so glad that I am not in this racket full-time. I would have to be breaking the news to too many people that they are so weak. Yeah, we got your fucking band and they're coming in on Saturday to sing in an effort to make a record to help out the plight of three kids in prison. They can't wait to come in and rock out with us. Fuck you. Oh yeah, we have Nick and Josh from the Queens coming in. Cool, right?! That was one phone call. So Nick, need a lyric sheet for 'Jealous Again?' No? Already know the song by heart? See you soon! That's about how long it took to get those guys to come in. First rate band, first rate guys. I wonder what they'll say when we tell them about their manager.

The music business is chock-full of incompetent no-talents, liars and corny, elitist charlatans. I reckon anyone we asked who didn't want to be part of it didn't have what it takes to handle this music anyway so all the better.

I am on Lemmy watch at the moment. His assistant says he's just returned from tour and is steadily rising from the depths and when he surfaces, she'll ask him when he wants to come in and sing. He's going to do 'Thirsty and Miserable.' How cool is this going to be? Bringing the camera for this. We are standing by.

05-25-02 LA CA: 11: 46 p.m. Nick and Josh Queens came in to sing tonight. Nick listens to the 'Jealous Again' track once and then walks into the booth and hits it. Kills it. Asks for another pass. Out of the park, thanks, you're done. They stuck around and sang backing vocals on some of the other songs. Awesome. What cool guys. I told them about our attempts to reach them and they said they hear only a fraction of the offers they get. I understand they're in demand but their manager should at least let them know about things. I get all kinds of offers coming into my manager's office and he forwards everything to me no matter how lame it is. Anyway, we have another song in the can and it was a good day and I met two more cool people on the planet.

05-26-02 LA CA: 11:19 p.m. We waited all weekend for Lemmy to rise and rise he did today, Sunday. We got the word Saturday night that it was going down today. Our engineers Ben and Matt didn't mind coming in.

Mike and I went to Lemmy's apartment to pick him up. He came out of the lobby a little pale but holding well. We drove him to the studio.

Mike had already gone to the liquor store and purchased the largest possible bottle of Jack Daniels, some cans of Coke and a bag of ice. Upon entering the studio, Lemmy said hello to all present and proceeded as if guided by spirits, right to the Jack, Coke and ice. He made himself a drink, lit up a cigarette and asked what we were doing.

We played him the track with my guide vocal. He listened carefully and looked down at the lyric sheet, "Can I change a few words?" He changed a word here and there, took his drink and went into the room. He did about three takes after a couple of false starts. By the last take he had it down and ripped it with feeling.

We comped the vocal and listened. Easily one of his best performances ever. We hung out and took pictures and then I took Lemmy back to his place.

We got there and I thanked him and said goodbye. He asked me to come up to his place and check out his collection. I had seen pictures of his place before and kind of knew what I was in for. Kind of.

Lemmy lives in a small one bedroom apartment that's packed with history books, videos and the most WWII artifacts I have ever seen. Daggers, plaques, medals, all the stuff you can find. It's not that he's a Nazi, he's just big on the history and he collects this stuff.

He told me to be careful of my feet. I looked down and saw that there was so much stuff on the floor that you had to follow these paths of narrow carpet to get around. Not trash but books, videos, more WWII stuff. The center of command seems to be the couch and a coffee table where there were pads of paper, books, cigarettes, a remote and lots of other stuff piled up. Liquor bottles on either side of where his feet would be. You get the idea that he spends a lot of time in that spot.

The walls are lined with ceremonial daggers, there's hundreds of them in perfect rows. The bed is covered with books and videos, it doesn't look like he sleeps there. I wonder if he just kicks it on the couch. Hanging on the wall are gold and platinum records from Hawkwind all the way to Motorhead.

He pulls out a crazy looking dagger from its sheath. The blade is well worn and inlaid with patterns that look like Arabic. It's easily one hundred years old. He hands it to me and asks me what I think of it. I tell him it's amazing. He says that it's a gift. Whoa! Pretty damn cool.

We go back out to the front room and he asks me to listen to something. His music source seems to be a boom box with stacks of CDs on top. He files through the CDs and picks out one, it's Motorhead playing 'Rockaway Beach' by the Ramones. It's for that Ramones tribute album that's either out or coming out. He puts it on. He starts playing air bass and rocking out. He's so full-on, the real thing. There I am, standing with Lemmy in his pad, we are rockin'. He plays a few different bands, and every time we listen to something, he starts rockin' out. I feel so lightweight next to him.

We get done with that and he goes looking for a notepad that has something on it that he wants me to read. He can't find it. We both look around and take in the place. It's literally piles of stuff, things in stacks. It's years of stuff put down between tours. I know the scenario so well. You get off the road for a little while, long enough to do your laundry and leave again, sometimes long enough to do your laundry, get a girlfriend, lose the girlfriend and leave again. Your place ends up with piles of receipts, coins, unlistened to CDs, half-read magazines and your hobbies and obsessions scattered all over. His place is like that with attitude. He asks me, "What's your place look like?" I tell him, "Dust free, double wrapped in plastic, alphabetical order." He says, "In a way, I admire that and in a way I don't." He then gestures to the place and says, "It's like . . ." and I say, "It's like the sea." "Yeah!" he says. I say, "It takes away . . ." "And it gives back!" he finishes. He tells me about how he lost a piece of luggage in the place for about a year and then one day it kind of came to the surface and it was fascinating to see this time capsule that had been in his place the whole time. It is quite piled up in there. It's not dirty, it's just intensely lived in, or lived in intensely, a couple of months a year. It says that the occupant is living life and not busy with the idea of living life. Big difference.

Lemmy shows me some written work, some good lyrics and assorted other stuff. One sheet of paper has "Tick-Tick-Tick- Tick-Tick-Tick- Tick-Tick-Tick- Tick-Tick-Tick- Tick-Tick-Tick- Tick-Tick-Tick- Tick-Tick-Tick- Tick-Tick-Tick- Tick-Tick-Tick- Tick-Tick-Tick- Tick-Tick- Tick-Tick-Tick- Tick-Tick-Tick- Tick-Tick-Tick- Tick-Tick-Tick- Tick-Tick- Tick-Tick-Tick- Tick-Tick-Tick- Tick-Tick-Tick . . . " and then some kind of sound spelled out phonetically at the end. He looks at me, shrugs and says, "There wasn't much on that morning."

He lent me an interesting book on WWII and loaned me a book called *Totalitarian Art* by Igor Golomstock. It will fit well into the stuff I am reading about Stalin and the Cold War right now.

I hung out awhile longer and then I had to go. Cool to hang out with the man. What a great time.

05-27-02 LA CA: 10:46 p.m. Another good day. I called Kira several days ago and asked her if she wanted to come in and do some vocals and she said sure and right on time she shows up. I had not seen her in about eleven years. She looks great. We played her rough mixes of some of the tracks we had done and she thought they sounded good. She put some great vocals on 'Annihilate This Week.' It was really good to see her again. She was on some of the most intense of the Black Flag tours and she never complained. One tough chick. Good player too. When you tour and live like we did, it's all very intense and you end up knowing more about the people you're with than you want to. That was the situation with all of us in that band at the time. There simply wasn't enough room to get away from the others. We traveled shoulder to shoulder. Nothing says it better than familiarity breeds contempt and a couple of years in, oh man. To a certain extent, it's the kind of thing you can look back on and laugh at. Well, you laugh and check for cracked ribs. She's the real thing. It's good to see someone after that many years still holding up and keeping track of the plot. There's so many casualties in this business that you're actually surprised when you hear someone's doing alright, that they're not broke, addicted or dead. There's a lot of that amongst the Black Flag alum's. Some of these guys—whoa.

Exene came in to sing 'Wasted.' She said she wanted to do it as a duet with me! She sang it slightly higher than she would have and I went in after her and sang along with her vocal and it sounded pretty good. We have her covered on both solo and duet vocals, we'll do mixes on both and see what sounds better. Pretty cool, a duet with Exene Cervenka. Lucky me.

I needed a day like this in the studio. Good people doing good stuff. This record has been a lot of work. I go from the studio back to the house, try to get a work out in and if I have any energy left, I read the pre-release copy of Mara Leveritt's book on the WM3 case called *Devil's Knot*. It's well written but depressing due to the subject matter. There's a part that deals with the "confession" of Jessie Misskelley that's heartbreaking. The hardest part of this whole thing has been the emotional load. Not so much what we're doing but why we are doing it.

This kind of day-to-day wear is destabilizing. It makes me lonely. I get lonely like anyone else I guess but I don't know what to do about it. How lame. I guess at the end of one of these days of studio, after so many phone calls and all the wheeling and dealing, I want someone to tell me I am doing good. But there's only the work to do and the mission to accomplish, the rest is that hand holding bullshit which just weakens resolve. I need some more of those Bart Sullivan fucks to inspire me. Confrontation is completely inspiring. Defiance is fuel. Aggression is gospel.

05-30-02 LA CA: 11:16 p.m. Chuck Dukowski came in today to do his vocals on 'What I See.' As far as I know, he never did that song with any of his other bands so besides singing it in the shower or something, this would be his first time singing it for real.

When he first came in, I think he was a little nervous but he cooled out when he got in the room and started powering through some takes. He really gave it the big one. It's cool to hear him sing. He sings like he plays bass: intense, chaotic, flat out. There were moments when it seemed like he forgot he was supposed to sing but he seemed to get through ok and it hit me that this was his way of timing and it's nuts but it totally works. He got through his takes quickly. He listened to rough mixes of some of the other songs and said that the music was great. The band guys were there and it was great for them to hear that from the man himself.

Keith was supposed to come down and hang out as he and Chuck hadn't seen each other for a long time but he couldn't make it so we called him on the phone. It was so cool to listen to Chuck talk to Keith. Chuck said that he hadn't talked to Keith in over a decade.

So that was the last day in the studio. We will be back to track some more vocals here and there but that was the bulk of it. Now it's more phone calls and office-bound aggravation.

06-05-02 LA CA: I got this from the *LA Times*:

> *Dee Dee Ramone, a founding member of punk pioneers the Ramones, died Wednesday night in his Hollywood home, according to a spokesperson for the LA County Coroner's office. The bassist was 50. Ramone was found unresponsive by his wife at approximately 8:40 p.m. PT. She then called the Los Angeles Police Department, and LA City Fire Department paramedics pronounced him dead at the scene.*

That's half of the Ramones gone. Hard to take.

Later: Rest of the day spent at the office, working on stuff and listening to the Ramones. They are such a part of my life. Hard to think about Dee Dee being gone. He was the first Ramone I met. It was hard when Joey died, hard on anyone who knew him or was even just a fan but at least you had a moment to brace yourself, you knew it was coming. With Dee Dee, like so much of his life, it was so broken off jagged. His band was doing great, he was selling his artwork, he had another book coming out. On the outside, it looks like things were going great so why was he shooting dope? It's so sad.

06-13-02 LA CA: 11:54 p.m. Spent the entire evening here alone, tripping on Dee Dee Ramone off and on. I cut out the obituary from the *LA Times* and listened to the first Ramones album. I read several pages from his autobiography. I haven't read that one in years.

In the summer of 1993 I was living in NYC. We were writing material for what became the Rollins Band *Weight* album. One afternoon I was standing with Richard Butler from the Psychedelic Furs on St. Marks and Dee Dee walks by. I say hi to him and he comes over and tells me about the autobiography he's working on and asked if I would read it and perhaps help him get it published.

I told him that I would definitely read it. We agreed to meet the next day at the Chelsea Hotel where he was staying.

The next day I troop over there and for the first time, walk into the famous Chelsea. I go up to Dee Dee's door and knock. He lets me in and I check out the room. There's a mattress on the floor. A box of assorted clothes. A small box of cassettes, a boom box that looks broken, a guitar, a rifle and a few other things. We sit on the floor and he gives me the manuscript and gives me a few additional pages that he just wrote. I quickly scanned the first couple of pages and it's obvious from the start that his writing is pretty cool and it's going to be an interesting book.

I asked him some questions about the book and I am being very matter-of-fact, how many words, what periods of his life does it cover, etc. He doesn't answer directly but goes into this strange metaphysical spaced out rant that I had to just hang out and listen to while I nodded politely.

From there he started talking about his upcoming divorce and how soon he will have to move down the hall to a smaller room that doesn't have a bathroom in it because he won't be able to afford the one he's in now. I looked around the room, it was small and dingy. He has to move out of this one? What's the other one like?

He asked me if I would come to a meeting he's supposed to have with a literary agent. He doesn't know what to do or what to say and is scared to go and wants to cancel. I tell him that I will go with him and he has nothing to worry about and I ask him when it is so I can arrange my schedule. He tells me it's in about twenty minutes and we have to go NOW.

We hit the street and start walking. He's wearing this intense leopard skin shirt and tells me that he's nervous about walking outside because he thinks someone might want to get him. It's not like he's standing out too much.

The closer we get to the office building where we are to meet some lady (that's all I've been told), Dee Dee gets increasingly nervous to where I think he's going to freak out on me.

Finally we get to this building and Dee Dee wants to bolt. I have to almost sweet talk him into the building. Originally I thought I was going to Dee Dee's place to pick up a manuscript, take it back to the place I was living and read it. Now this.

We go in to a reception area and I tell him to sit down, I give him a magazine to read and tell him that I'll take care of everything else. I go up to the receptionist and tell her that I have Dee Dee Ramone here for his meeting. Luckily for me, she knows who the meeting is with and tells us to wait.

Shortly thereafter, we're brought into an office and we meet this very nice young woman whose name I forget now but she was really cool. Dee Dee is now reduced to this insane nervous grin and says nothing. The woman kind of gets that Dee Dee is extremely ill-suited to this environment so she and I just talk about Dee Dee and his book like he's not even in the room and all of a sudden I am acting as his rep, telling her when I think he could have the book done and approximately how many words it's going to be. I am totally winging it but when I look back at Dee Dee, he's nodding yes.

She gets a lot of basic points down and I gently bring Dee Dee into the conversation. He immediately starts in on the same spacey rap about dragons and dreams he's been having. Nothing at all about the book. Now this woman and I are both nodding politely.

Finally the meeting is over and I tell Dee Dee to wait out in the reception area for me. With Dee Dee out of the room for a minute I tell her more about how the book could be pitched and where it could go. She's not all that familiar with The Ramones, she doesn't know me at all and I think she thought the both of us were nuts. I give her the brief history of Punk Rock and how important The Ramones and Dee Dee are to it and that The Ramones started a revolution and they're the reason so many bands play the way they do from Nirvana to Motley Crue. I tell her that the book will do well with Ramones fans all over the world. I can tell she's just politely bearing with me so I stop, thank her on Dee Dee's behalf and take my leave.

I walked Dee Dee back to the Chelsea and we agreed to talk soon. I went back to my room and read his book all the way through. It was really good. Brutal and harsh but real. He's not pulling any punches or trying to make himself look particularly good. It's very readable.

Dee Dee had given me a floppy disc of the manuscript and I start working on the typos as I re-read and make notes.

Dee Dee and I speak almost every night on the phone. He says some really insane shit to me during these conversations. One night he calls me and tells me that he can't go outside and get anything to eat because the police are waiting outside to kill him. I have to slowly talk him off the ceiling and convince him that no one will kill him and it's alright to go outside. I offer to go up there and wait for him in the lobby and take him out to eat. He says that he thinks he'll be alright.

One night he calls and tells me that we have to get on a plane that night and get to Berlin before he gets assassinated by the police. It's really heavy stuff. I talk him down again and things are cool.

The band and I are working by day at Michael Gira's practice place on new songs and by night I am inputting journal entries for *Get in the Van* and working on *Solipsist*. I take breaks from that and work on Dee Dee's book.

There's a stretch of about three days where I don't talk to him. I think it was over a weekend. I return from band practice on Monday to a blinking message machine. Dee Dee has left a message talking all this crazy shit about how he doesn't want me to help him with his book, "I spit in your fucking face." What is this all about?!

I saved the way-less-typos-than-before manuscript to his floppy and sent it to his accountant. I put in a letter to Dee Dee that now that he's talking that way to me, he better run when he sees me as I will be going right for him. I would have too. He made me mad then. That's the last I saw of him for a few years. I ran into him at a book release thing we had for one of our artists. He was nervous about coming to the thing but I talked to him and told him everything was cool and we shook hands and patched it up. During the period of time I didn't see him, I told this story to Iggy's lighting guy Bubbles, who used to work with the Ramones and he told me that kind of thing happened all the time with Dee Dee and not to pay it any mind. He had some insane stories about being on tour with the Ramones. It gave me a better understanding of Dee Dee. I'm sorry he's gone. What a great songwriter. He's one of the groundfloor corner-stone guys. How more real does it get than the Ramones? It doesn't.

The last several days have been office stuff. Layout and design, getting photos, getting managers to return phone calls, getting release forms signed. We are waiting for Clif to finish mixing a project and then we will pick up the last few vocals and mix the album. I am not burnt on the project but I am wanting to get it done so I can start getting the plan for release together.

A highpoint of the last several days has been the inclusion of Iggy Pop doing 'Fix Me.' This is huge. Iggy Pop doing a Black Flag song? Come on! I called him and pled my case and he said he'd think about it after he heard the track and read up on the case. I sent him a whole package on the thing with the original version of the song and our version as well. He called me a few days later and left a message saying he'd do it. I think that's the coolest phone message I ever got. I hit the playback button and out comes that lower than low voice. I played it over and over. So we have Iggy Pop on our record. We are so cool.

07-02-02 LA CA: 11:10 p.m. The day started with a bang. Jim Pennywise has doubts as to the innocence of the boys and wants to pull his track. His reasons are that after seeing the two documentaries, he's not 100% sure of the WM3's innocence. He said that Jessie did confess and Mark Byers did pass a lie detector test. He also added that he has two kids and feels really bad but has to take his name off the project. I have no problem with this, my problem is that he had the videos for several weeks and didn't look at them until late in the game after he had done is vocal. Some people might call that pretty weak.

Strange. I saw him last night at the *Rockline* radio show and he was all smiles. He signed the guitar we had up for auction and all seemed to be well. This morning is a different story.

Pennywise guy called and suggested the singer in AFI. I heard that record the other day. You've got to be kidding. What the fuck is the problem with you people? I read in the paper all about the bidding war to get AFI. How insane and full of shit is the major label industry? Who will win the "war?"

So, we have one less song. I feel bad about it. I don't understand why you say yes to do something before you check it out.

Later in the day I got a letter from Pennywise boy and he seemed sincerely bummed out about the whole thing. I read the first few lines and deleted it. I don't care. I have nothing to say about any of it to him. Do what you think is right and move on.

I got back to the house and got a call from Sean E. He called to tell me that Empty TV just ran a pretty big thing on our record and named a few people who were on it and also added that we didn't have a label for the release.

We do, actually. It's great that the Big Empty saw fit to run a piece on the record without even getting the facts straight. It's not like they called me to get the story, they just have to have it so they can have it. Well, fuck me then. Let's just understand the gang of pricks we're dealing with here.

Sean E. gave me his take on the Pennywise guy thing. He was totally unfazed by Pennywise guy's departure. He reckons that we have a great record with what we've got. Who cares about Pennywise guy and his problems, it's no big deal. I asked him if he thought we should bother to get another singer on the song and he said hell no, just mix the last two songs on Friday and walk away until mastering. That's what we'll do.

I think it's good that Pennywise guy fell off. I have to think at this point, if you're not on the record, you weren't supposed to be. Who needs lightweights? Who cares about this guy when you can work with guys like Corey Slipknot and Casey Chaos from Amen? Now that motherfucker Casey, he can hit it! He came in on a moment's notice with one phone call and destroyed 'Depression.' One of the best vocals on the whole record, easily the best that song ever got sung. It's performances like that and stand up people like him and Corey that make the Pennywise guy's departure a non-issue. Lose the lightweights—we're at war.

I like the conflict. I really do. I like struggle. It keeps me honest and alert. It's incentive to keep going.

David Lee Roth is on tour which means he's doing interviews which means there's an abundance of killer quotes.

From the *LA Times* 06/22/02:

". . . *Art is struggle. I love the struggle more than ever before. It's about dangerous waves of consequence. If there's no conflict I seem to create it, doc. Once something is stabilized, go bigger. We aren't innocents but we are abroad.*"

Yeah! I need to read stuff like that. It's so easy to feel whipped by all this shit. Whipped and fucked up by the every day, the idiots in traffic, people who don't come through, people who lie and let their weakness dictate their actions.

I don't think it's a good idea to be a psycho at all times but I think it's a good idea to always keep a certain amount of rage cruising through the system. Rage and intensity keep the mind pure and the direction clear, keeps the blood thin and the heart strong.

For a 24 hour period, there was talk of our band opening for David Lee Roth and Hagar. One of their managers thought it would be a good idea and put it through to us. I know their audience would have killed us on sight and I knew the offer didn't stand a chance but it was cool to think about it for a night. I contemplated the training that I would undergo for a tour with David Lee. There's no way it wouldn't be competition every night, flat out. We know each other well enough to know that it would be totally intense. That training regimen would be religious. It would be awesome and painful. He is one hard driving motherfucker. Love him or hate him, he's going for it every night. Lose that in this business and you're dead.

They try to take the wind out of your sails all the time. The thing to do is respond with at least twice what they throw at you. It fucks them up and shuts them down. Don't take shit from these fuckheads.

07-03-02 LA CA: 11:50 p.m. Listening to Wire's *Chairs Missing* album and punching in the facts. Today was a good day. We got Iggy's vocals in and the Ryan Adams version of 'Nervous Breakdown' as promised by his manager. How cool is that? Ryan hears about the project from Keith Morris and asks if he can donate his own version of 'Nervous Breakdown' and does it with no bullshit. Right on Ryan Adams.

Several nights ago, I had this great idea—Get Chuck D. from Public Enemy to start the record. Give him a line to say in that amazing voice of his as 'Rise Above' starts. His voice is one of the greatest sounds I've ever heard. In my mind, I kept hearing Chuck say, "West Memphis Arkansas . . . Get ready to go worldwide . . . Let's get it on!" as 'Rise Above' starts. Right after he says "Let's get it on!" the guitar kicks in and it suddenly becomes more than a song, it immediately becomes a classic track because Chuck brings the band in. Yeah!

I got Chuck's e-mail address and wrote him about what we were doing and what I wanted him to do, etc. The next day I get a letter back. He says of course he'll do it. And he did. He sent in a CDR of himself doing the line about twenty four times with different approaches. How cool is that?!!! And since I sing on that track, I can say that I am on a track with Chuck D. and I would be telling the truth. I can now wade into traffic and get knocked into the phone lines.

We mix 'Fix Me' with Iggy's vocal and 'Rise Above' on Friday. Saving the greatest for last. I wish it was Friday right now.

07-06-02 LA CA: 11:44 p.m. We walked out of the mix about 24 hours ago. I was too tired and burnt out to write anything about it when I got back here. I got up early and went to the office and made a CDR of the sequence I think is best. I sat and listened to it all the way through and it's amazing. The beginning of 'Rise Above' with Chuck D. calling the band in is so inspiring, I had to play his part about six times before I could let the song play on.

I got back here a few hours after that and fell into a deep depression. I sometimes get this way after finishing a record. We hit this thing nonstop for ten weeks. Came up with the idea sitting in the chair I am sitting in right now and just did it. We crossed the finish line with it last night and damn, it's good.

That's not the part that's hard to take. I have been so involved with what it takes to make a good record that now and then I forget what the record is for and when I think of three boys in prison and three more in the ground, it makes me sick why we're making the record. It's a good record but the cause is so grim and hard to deal with. But, what are you going to do when you see something that's wrong? You can't fix everything but this was too hard to ignore. It's rough going though.

I must admit, dealing with everything at the level of intensity I have been for this duration of time without a break from it has taken a toll on me. I have been losing weight and sleep and have been feeling pretty low. I know we have done a good thing. It's just hard sometimes. The more I feel like this, the more isolated and angry I get.

What is it when you feel so incredibly lonely but the thought of being with someone makes you even more bummed out? What the fuck is that?

Fuck it. Just keep going. In a few days I head off to England for five weeks of work on a TV show. Amerika, England, I might as well be anywhere. It doesn't matter. I just want to go to work.

Rise Above: 24 Black Flag Songs to Benefit the West Memphis Three was released on Tuesday October 8th. The release seemed almost discreet as if it was a secret to be kept. I thought it would be quite well received. It was where people knew about it but in most places, it was filed away into immediate obscurity. Some record chains in the southern parts of Amerika wouldn't stock it because of what it had to do with. It's much easier to deal with crack smoking multi-platinum divas than a benefit record I guess. One would be ill-advised to underestimate people's apathy and their lack of will to confront. I know the record wipes the floor with anything that came out this year and that's good enough for me. You've heard bands griping about the record company they're dealing with and how frustrated they are. Well, let's just say that there's nothing new about that one. You do what you can and despair that it wasn't all it could have been.

11-26-02 LA CA: 11:10 p.m. We are booked to play songs off *Rise Above* at Ameoba Records on December 3rd. They have a lot of room and a stage. Today was the first day of practice. It was a little rusty but almost there. We'll hit it again tomorrow and it will be happening. Two days after the instore we're going to play in San Diego at a small venue but I imagine we'll draw alright and raise some money for the guys.

The shows were booked several days ago so I have been preparing myself. A lot of chin ups and abdominal work. The shows are going to be hard but I know I can do it.

Since the shows got booked, they have been on my mind constantly. I can't wait to hit those songs live but I can't betray them so I have to be on it. Body hurts from the first day of practice, it's a good caning.

11-27-02 LA CA: 11:33 p.m. Another day of practice and it was better than yesterday. Keith Morris and Chuck Dukowski are coming in to sing on Friday. Chuck will be doing 'What I See' and I don't know what Keith will be doing yet. He can pick the songs he wants to do, it doesn't matter, anything he goes for will be great.

The other day Keith told me that Greg is mad that I used the Black Flag logo on the cover of the *Rise Above* record. What was I supposed to use, a peace symbol? Right before the record came out, I got two copies sent to me. I sent one to Ginn and the other to Ian MacKaye. I was so excited to hear what Greg thought of it. I never heard anything back from him. What Keith told me was the first thing I heard. I put a picture of the Dan Armstrong guitar we used on the record on the cover. He doesn't like it. I get Iggy Pop to sing one of his songs and he has nothing to say about that but he's mad that I used the logo.

Keith also said that Greg Ginn wants to do some Black Flag shows with all the singers except for me of course. I don't care about that kind of thing. He doesn't like me and I can live with that. I see now that there's no being friends with the guy so it's one less thing to have to think about. I have to think that the shows would draw but whether they would be any good is something else. There's no way he would be wanting to do these shows if we hadn't done the record.

11-29-02 LA CA: 10:38 p.m. Today was one for the books. Chuck came in and worked out on 'What I See' several times and it got better and better and by the time he was done, it was happening. As Chuck was leaving, Keith came in. I don't know when the last time they were actually in the same room together. It was so cool to see the two of them hanging out. I don't know if I had seen those two together for well over fifteen years. They were glad to see each other and that was cool.

Chuck left and Keith determined he was going to sing 'Nervous Breakdown,' 'Fix Me,' 'Wasted' and 'Gimmie Gimmie.' Keith doesn't fuck around. I asked him if he wanted to go for it and he said he was ready. We just handed him the mic and the boys started playing. He hit those songs like it was the last day of his life. It was so inspiring. He's like Iggy. He just has it. He doesn't have to prepare, he doesn't have to get into any kind of mood—it's just on tap. He's such a natural it makes you jealous. When he sang 'Gimmie Gimmie,' it was so full on. That's his song.

12-04-02 LA CA: 11:47 p.m. Last night was the instore at Ameoba. I got there at five thirty for a seven o'clock stage. Backstage, Chuck and the boys were there hanging out. I went downstairs for a minute and ran into Casey Chaos, it was great to see him. On the way back I ran into Joe Nolte from The Last. I hadn't seen that guy since 1980-something. I figured Chuck would want to see him so I dragged him backstage and he hung out for awhile, it was great to see the two of them together.

Around ten minutes before stage time, Keith comes in. He's into it, he's ready. He drinks some water and all of a sudden we're walking down the stairs. The place is beyond packed. The band walks out to tremendous applause. Keith walks out and the place goes off. He says a few words about the reason we're all here and then Jim lays into 'Nervous Breakdown.' People freak out. Keith is ripping the songs apart, just incredible. In no time the drums are hammering away at 'Gimmie Gimmie' and there's that voice. When you hear Keith do that song, it's an overload. I start to cry but pull it back. It's so powerful and moving. I focus myself and sing the first verse of 'Rise Above' because I think I'm going to go out there and forget the whole thing. 'Gimmie Gimmie' comes to an end and I am walking up the steps and Keith is handing me the mic. Jason starts in with the drums on 'Rise Above.' Jim hits the riff and the place roars. Easily one of the best songs ever written. People are singing along as if their lives depend on it. We come out of that and Jim takes us right into 'Thirsty and Miserable.' It's flying by like a dream. We go song to song. Everyone's singing along. 'Six Pack' is incredible. 'Revenge' is insane. People love that one. We get down to 'Police Story' and rip through it. It's Chuck's turn to sing 'What I See.' I hand him the mic. People see him and freak out. He rips the song and all of a sudden I'm back out there and we're doing 'Depression.' We rip through 'I've Had It' and now it's time for the National Anthem. The song that separates the men from the boys. 'My War.' I gave it all I had. Before I knew it, we were walking back to the dressing room. People flew from all over Amerika to see this. A couple of hundred people turned away from the door and over a thousand inside to hear Greg and Chuck's music. I wish Greg could have seen this thing go down. What a night.

Thursday is San Diego. We have three shows booked for mid-December: Ventura, LA and Pomona. We'll be playing the Whisky in LA on 12-18-02. Eleven years to the night Joe Cole and I walked out of that place and drove back to Venice. He was dead a few hours later. I know on that night I will be looking, as I always do, at the spot Joe and I were standing laughing at Courtney Love and her band Hole before we split. I remember Cobain was there that night. He was walking around kind of nervous like he was an animal not used to being around people, skittish. How much would Joe Cole have dug this thing?!

There's a lot of dead people in my Black Flag memories: Mad Marc Rude just died in prison. Joe, Louie OD'd, Bobbi Brat had cancer, John Circle One shot by a cop, Ed Danke OD'd, D. Boon in a car accident, Deirdre O'Donoghue of an unknown illness, Suzan Carson, who took so many pictures of the band, died of cancer, Hatchman of Shell Shock shot himself. People in bands we played with like Will Shatter of Flipper, Dee Dee Ramone, Joey Ramone. I'm sure I can think of more but what's the point? I have all the Minutemen records but can't play them because it makes me miss D. Boon too much. I hear that voice come in and I can't take it. Those records sit year after year unplayed. It's hard to think of him. I miss him horribly. When I sing Black Flag songs, I think of some of those people and the brutality of those days and the effect it has had on me. It leaves you with something. A lot of it you can absolutely live without.

So, we have a show tomorrow. It's going to be a lot harder than the instore.

12-06-02 LA CA: 4:23 p.m. The show last night was a good time. I didn't know how we were going to do but we rocked it. We took off for San Diego at 7 p.m. We hit stage around 11 p.m. The place was packed and people were into it. There was one guy up front who was so typical of the old days. His type was at so many shows back in the 80's. The funny guy who's not taking it all that seriously and knows that the band and all the people around him are a bit lame. He spent the entire evening yelling out for a song that he knew we weren't going to play to be annoying. What he didn't count on, because I guess he hasn't been in front of intense shit before, was that what you give out, you also get back. Several songs in I gave him a little punch to the head to straighten him out. Not what I wanted to do, I would have preferred to give him a shot he'd remember for a week but you can't be too hard on these bitches. They just don't know. Besides that minor distraction, we had a great time. We made the drive back in no time and I walked into my place around 0330 hrs. Can't wait to play the other shows knowing that we can do it. Mack said it best last night in the dressing room after the show, "Too bad we're not playing tomorrow night."

On December 17, 18 and 19 we played Ventura, Los Angeles and Pomona. The highpoint was the Los Angeles show at the Whisky. Keith went out and started the set and lit the place up. I went out after him and we hit it hard. Kira came out for vocals on 'Annihilate This Week.' When she walked onstage, people flipped out. No one was expecting it. What a great night. From the four shows, we ended up making ten thousand dollars which we sent to the West Memphis Three Defense Fund. It was a good way to end the year.

2003

04-30-03: On an airplane to Brisbane Australia: 12:24 p.m. I got an e-mail from Mike today. We are confirmed for summer tour dates to benefit the West Memphis Three.

Late last year after we did the shows in southern California, we talked about perhaps doing some more shows since we had such a good time playing the music. A few months ago, road manager Mike Curtis (a man who figures greatly in this story) and I started kicking around the idea of taking this thing out on the road to properly promote the record, boost record sales, raise further awareness and to rock the nation.

We pitched the idea to the boys in the band and Jim wrote back on their behalf, "You know what I say . . . Let's do it!" So, with the band in place, we went to the agents to see if there were dates we could get in Amerika or anywhere else.

The agent pitched it to the Amerikan promoters who were, for the most part, lukewarm about our idea but we were able to get some shows anyway. I am grateful that we could get any. I don't think there's much interest in the music we make but at this point it only makes sense to go on. It's like when the general says to his troops, "We're surrounded and outnumbered. Attack!" So, we have some shows, a lot of them actually. It's going to be great.

We're in countdown mode. Thirty-two days until the first show. Before then, I have to finish the remaining six shows here in Australia, do all the press possible, get myself and the band in shape and walk out the door.

This will be extremely hard. This is one of the tests I knew was waiting for me. I remember thinking years ago that I would come to the point where youth was gone and it was all down to guts and confrontation. It's here. There's no doubt that we will have something to prove. People will say that we're doing this for all kinds of reasons other than the real reason. There will be snide comments from the soft-bodied press fakes and even from some fans. The delivery can't be half-assed. It has to be relentless and fucking intense. We proved we can do it but now we have to do it night after night, week after week. That's the test. There's no way I am failing this music and looking like some hack.

Later. In the hotel. A fairly punishing workout of cable, calisthenics and running behind me. Nutrition intake will be targeted, high protein, low carbohydrate. The joy of push-ups and more push-ups. In anticipation of this tour, I have been training hard so I would be ready to up it to what I will have to do until the tour starts. Now I'm ready to take the training to the next level.

05-01-03 Goldcoast Australia: 6:25 p.m. Backstage. Drove down here from Brisbane a little while ago. We wanted to do Australian dates on the *Rise Above* tour but it looks like there won't be enough money to break even on such a venture. They are working on it but it's not looking good. Too bad we're not a bigger band but that's the way it is. One of the ways you stay around in this business is to work extremely hard and never, and I cannot overstate this, never overestimate your market value. Those who do so run the risk of getting caught out there. I would like to think that I've kept that to a minimum.

It's rough, in the entertainment business, you live and die by the numbers. It's constant comparisons to the time before. Ticket counts, record sales, guarantees, etc. One must separate the figures from the feelings. You always have high hopes. Any band, at the end of the day, just wants people to dig what they do. When you've worked so hard for so many years and given so completely onstage night after night, it can be heartbreaking when less people come to see you than the time before. You have to have a thick skin and a strong heart for the constant barrage of facts and figures that are rarely complimentary for long.

Soon I will be onstage. I have been out on this tour a pretty long time but I don't feel it all that much. It started on January 07 of this year and tonight is show #84. I'm feeling good up there every night and having a good time with the audience but I am also thinking about the tour that's coming up directly after this. I will spend my days getting my head around the upcoming band shows and my evenings concentrating on delivering on these last few shows here.

Another good workout today. Ran hard. Wanted to do more abdominal work but they hurt too much from yesterday's battering. I looked in the mirror and noticed that my unshaven face has a lot of gray. There's very little sand in the hour glass. You are not as old as you feel. You are as old as it says on your passport. Train harder.

05-02-03 Brisbane Australia: 6:37 p.m. Backstage at the Tivoli. I've done a lot of shows in this place. I'm here for two nights. For workout today all I did was run. The rest of me is too sore to do anything else. The running is good. It gives me the long range mental toughness I will need for these shows.

As the years go on, I become less and less welcome in the music world. I become more square as it gets more round. I have to be stronger every time I go out. The sliding scale is against me. The current gets stronger as I get older and my stamina decreases. Talk about conflict, this is all the conflict a boy could want. Have to get ready to hit stage.

05-03-03 Brisbane Australia: 3:04 p.m. In the hotel room. Encouraging news from Mike. He reports that word has been getting out about the tour and people are getting back to him and they're very excited. Promoters always talk but we'll see how real it is when it's time for them to put up their money. That's the only way to know how much they care about anything.

7:01 p.m.: Another sold out night here in Brisbane. I am looking forward to the show. Had another good workout today. I am looking forward to the move to Melbourne tomorrow. I have been in the same room for four days now.

I think about being back in LA for the pre-tour work and I am looking forward to getting that done and getting back out on the road. I say bring it on. I've been moving hard since January when this tour started and it will be hard to be in one place day after day but it will be eventful and full of work. I can't wait to get back into the practice room and play those songs. We had our first practice for these songs on April 29th of last year and here we are a year later hitting it again.

05-04-03 Melbourne Australia: 11:31 p.m. In the hotel room. Flew in here for the day off. I worked out hard again. It's great finishing off these workouts with a run. It beats the hell out of me but nothing like what the shows are going to do—that'll be a beating.

I hung out tonight with my old pal Mick Geyer. I have known him for many years. Mick and I have been having one long conversation since I met him in 1989. Every once in awhile, we are in the same place and the conversation that never ends picks up again. Tonight it was four hours. There was a momentary interruption when a few drunks came up to tell me who I was and to inform me I have a lot of gray hair but besides the distraction by these common fuck ups, it was the usual.

Mick is Australian. The last time I saw him, about seventeen months ago, was in Italy. He was living in Switzerland at the time and took the train to see our show in Milan. Before he left, he gave me a piece of paper with the name Ryszard Kapuscinski written on it and suggested I read his books. The next time I went online, I ordered all his books and read them one after another and damn, what incredible stuff. Devastating. Looking forward to reading *Imperium* again. Reading that one sent me off on a tear that has taken in Robert Conquest's *Kolyma: The Arctic Death Camps* and Janusz Bardach's *Man Is Wolf to Man: Surviving the Gulag.* I have sourced and followed up every recommendation Mick has passed onto me. Checked every record, book and film he suggested, if I could find them, and never once have I been let down. Some of the references he's given me are now some of my favorite artists. He once lent me a copy of Nelson

Algren's *Never Come Morning*. What a read. That lead to me reading Algren's *Man with the Golden Arm, Walk on the Wild Side, The Neon Wilderness, Somebody in Boots*. Great stuff. Especially *Somebody in Boots*.

Tonight's conversation sweep took in Bush, Rumsfeld, Stalin, Proust, Nabokov, Cave, Kapuscinski, Kharms, Fante, Hamsun, Miller, Kafka, Dostoyevsky, The Fall, Fellini and a good chunk that I can't remember right now. It resumes at 4:30 tomorrow afternoon.

Besides the three shows I have coming up, which I am looking forward to, all my thoughts are on these band shows. How will they be received? What will the perception be? We have a great chance to help the WM3 out with the money we can raise. The DNA testing is their last shot I think. Otherwise, the case stays right were it is with Jessie and Jason in for life and Damien on Death Row. The money we will hopefully raise could make the difference. I have a feeling I'm going to take a ton of shit from a lot of people about this tour but it's worth it. I don't know what else to do for them and I can't do nothing, so here we are and here it is.

I already know that some of the press types will say that I am looking to cash in on past glory or something. I'll have to deal with the low blows and the cheap shots, I know they will come. These guys are such a weak and wretched bunch. It's Greg Ginn and Chuck Dukowski's music, we're just going to go out and play it for a few weeks. It has to be really good or we're screwed.

Having all this on my mind puts me in an even more isolated space than I usually occupy. At this point, it's just down to determination. I feel it in the workouts. I feel so solo when I hit the gym, like the last man at some outpost. This is going to be some life defining shit coming up. I have to stick to the workouts and the music. Can't think of anything else. When I think of those three guys in prison, living in a world I can't even begin to imagine, it gets me inspired to hit it. It's for them.

Fuck it. Train. Train harder. Attitude? I'm bringing more than you can handle.

05-05-03 Melbourne Australia: 11:14 p.m. In the hotel room. Today was pretty good. I felt good at the gym today and I saw a great movie with Mick tonight. *The Russian Ark,* directed by Aleksandr Sokurov. Shot in the Hermitage in St. Petersburg Russia, the entire film was done in one, unedited take with a steadicam. It's basically a strange trip through the art museum with time changes and it takes you through these immense rooms and scenes and never stops moving, it was really something. I can't see many people digging this film. Actually, the more I think about it, the more amazing it is to me. One shot! How the hell did they do that? I went online and found out that they rehearsed on and off for a couple of years and since it's a real museum, they couldn't close the whole place down for long so they had one day to do the film. Apparently there's a few thousand extras in it. I knew that ballroom scene was big but I didn't know it was that big. Not at all surprised that Mick picked this one out. He's the source.

I am glad the two days off are over. It was good to see Mick but I really want to get back to the shows, even though there's only three of them left. Two days off makes me nervous. It's a good thing I had those workouts to keep me even.

Body is in a lot of pain but it's one of those "the more it hurts now, the less it will hurt in the game" situations. There are a few levels of pain to go before I'll be operating at optimum. The first one is the intensified workouts, the next one is workouts combined with band practice and then the last and hardest one is the leap to the live shows. It doesn't matter how hard I have trained before tours, the first few shows are brutal and they hurt more the older I get. It keeps me very well aware of my limitations. It was intense when I first noticed my stamina decreasing because of age. You come to some intense conclusions. "I can't do that anymore" is a hard one to swallow. I have done this kind of training many times before so it's just saying hello to old friends.

05-06-03 Monash Uni. Caufield Australia: 6:40 p.m. Backstage. This is a suburb of Melbourne I guess. It will be a cool show. It's a great looking hall. Too sore to hit the gym today.

11:40 p.m. Show done and back in the room. A good show. Watched some band videos on TV when I got back here. People really like this shit? It's so weak. I wouldn't have been into this crap even when I was the "right" age. A nation of soft youth with domination and fear in their immediate future. If you come out of the chute and your first taste of rock music is this shit, unless you encounter some divine intervention, you're fucked for life. These people aren't in bands, they're models with musical instruments as accessories. They wear their music like a handbag.

05-07-03 Melbourne Australia: 6:30 p.m. Backstage. Today was a blur. Out of the hotel to a radio station to do an interview. Back to the hotel to change up and go to the gym and then run back to the hotel, change up and go to the venue to do another interview and then back out to eat and then back again to the venue for soundcheck and now it's almost show time. This is the hardest show of the Australian tour. The Melbourne crowd is great but this is a hard venue and I want to get onstage and do this show, waiting to do it is hard as hell. I think I'll have a good show but I want to get it happening and be done with this waiting around. J Mascis and Kim Salmon are hopefully showing up tonight. J is out here doing shows on his own. I wish I could see a few of those. I think I have every record he's done and for me, there's not a bad one to be had. Let's go already.

05-08-03 En Route to Sydney Australia: 1133 hrs. On the plane. Last night was really cool. I had a good time up there and the audience was fantastic. I'm happy I pulled it off. There's nothing like a good crowd. They were totally into it. It's sometimes hard to have an objective that has such constant potential to fail. So, when all goes well, I forget that it was that way the night before and wonder what it'll be like the next night.

J Mascis and Kim came backstage after the show and hung out for a little while. Kim gave me his new CD but I had already bought it so I asked him to give it to J, which he did. Those two guys should know about each other's stuff I think.

After they left, I went outside and signed stuff for the people waiting. After that, Mick and I went to a coffee place and resumed the conversation until about 0130 hrs. I was falling off from the workout and the show so we parted ways. It's always great to see him. Hopefully I'll see him again soon.

More good e-mail from Mike. The US dates are solid and the European dates are filling in nicely. Relieved I'll be out again in a little more than three weeks. I don't miss anything in LA and knowing that I'll be right back out will make the time there easy to deal with.

My legs are hammered from the workouts and the running but it's all for the best. In a week or so they will be able to take it and when it's show time, I'll be able to take the beating. I found out years ago that the stronger your legs and lower back are, the more energy you can play with.

I have one more show tonight and this thing is over. After I walk offstage, there will be no distractions, only the songs and the shows. I look forward to immersing myself completely. It's the only way I am going to be able to handle the beating this tour is going to throw me.

05-09-03 Sydney Australia: 2:18 p.m. On the plane, waiting to take off. Last night was the last night of the tour. It was a good show and a good way to end the thing. I didn't stick around to meet anyone. I walked out the side door with the mic in my hand and got into the car and we took off. I didn't want to talk to people after the show, as much as I like them, I didn't want to dwell with people at the end of the tour because I know it would make me feel sad later so I just left. Got to the hotel, packed my stuff, got some sleep and here I am.

So, what is there to say after 89 shows? That's how you do that. I had a great time. I will never be able to thank these people enough for showing up. I know I will feel withdrawals tonight in LA. I'll want to be with them, onstage, doing the thing. Well, soon enough.

I will get to the office today in the early afternoon. I will knock out all the work I can there, get some food for the weekend and then hole up. I'll need a couple of days to cool out before I can deal with people. I think press starts Monday.

05-09-03 LA CA: 10:09 p.m. Yesterday kept going and going. Went from the airport to the office and started working. I was pretty burnt but got some things done.

I got the press release from the PR company and made some fixes and sent it back. I usually write it myself, I learned that from Perry Farrell but I didn't have time so I had to let them do it. This is the thing that all the press types will be sent:

Rollins Band Announces 24 U.S. Dates in Support of The WM3

Rollins Band and special guests will soon begin a summer tour to raise funds and awareness for the West Memphis Three, a group of teenagers (Damien Echols, Jessie Misskelley and Jason Baldwin) who were charged and sentenced for the brutal murders of three young boys (James M. Moore, Steven E. Branch and Christopher M. Byers.) A crime many believe they did not commit.

In December of 2002, Rollins Band played 5 dates in Southern California for the WM3 cause (with special guest appearances by Keith Morris, Chuck Dukowski, and Kira Roessler.) This was the first time since 1986 that Rollins had performed Black Flag songs live. Now, nine months later, that historic moment will again be captured as Keith Morris (the original singer of Black Flag) and other surprise musical guests will join Rollins on his 24-city tour.

Rollins became interested in the West Memphis Three case after seeing the HBO broadcast of "Paradise Lost I & II." After meeting with the West Memphis Three Support Group located in Los Angeles and learning more about the case, Henry wanted to help bring awareness to the plight of Damien, Jessie and Jason. He rallied together a number of today's most respected artists (such as Chuck D, Lemmy, Corey Taylor, Tom Araya, Iggy Pop, Mike Patton, Ice T, Exene Cervenka and Ryan Adams amongst others) to record the benefit album Rise Above: Twenty-Four Black Songs to Benefit the West Memphis Three released on Sanctuary Records in October of 2002.

The album was recorded with a Dan Armstrong guitar (the same kind of guitar Black Flag founder Greg Ginn used for many years). After recording, the guitar was signed by the Rollins Band, as well as most of the guest artists on the album and was then auctioned off to raise funds for the West Memphis Three.

The guitar (purchased by Rollins' tour manager Mike Curtis) has now been brought back and will be raffled off at the end of the summer tour. All attendees of the WM3 shows will have the opportunity to win a rare guitar signed by an array of legends by purchasing a one-dollar raffle ticket at the show venues, all monies going to the WM3 Defense Fund.

Tour dates are listed below, all proceeds raised from the tour will go to the WM3 Defense Fund. The money raised will have a profound effect on the case as the funds will go to DNA testing on evidence collected at the time of the murders but has until now, gone untested.

For more information on the case, please visit the website: WM3.org. This is a one time only tour and shouldn't be missed.

I went through the mail and then went and got some groceries and tried to work more but was getting too tired to concentrate. I went back to the house and cleaned and that woke me up. I fell out really early and got up this morning at 0330 hrs and went back to the office and have been working all day. I got in a good lift and had soup and salad for lunch and dinner. Since it's Saturday, there was no phone or e-mail on the tour dates or anything else. There's more to note here but I can't keep my eyes open.

05-10-03 LA CA: 10:09 p.m. A package from Lorri Davis was here when I got back. Inside was a book Damien had given her to pass on to me, Italo Calvino's *Invisible Cities*. Damien had it in his cell for eight years. It's intense turning the pages and trying to imagine where it was just days ago. I've never read Calvino, I don't know much about him but Damien said in his letter that this book has really stayed with him. I wonder how many times he's read it. I've always wondered how incarcerated people deal with time. An hour for Damien is sixty minutes just like it is for me, but there's no way we could make a comparison. Two completely different head spaces. Since he's been in, Damien's become a Buddhist. I guess you don't know how to deal with a place like where he's at until you have to.

Damien's all coffee portrait of Bhodi Dharma.

L to R: Marcus, Henry, Chuck, Jim, Jason
Cherokee Studios, LA CA

Henry and Kira 05-27-02 Cherokee Studios, LA CA

L to R: Jim, Engineer Matt, Lemmy, Henry, Jason, Engineer
Ben, Marcus 05-26-02 Cherokee Studios, LA CA

Henry and Tom Araya 06-18-02 Cherokee Studios, LA CA

Photo: Henry Rollins

Keith, Jason 11-29-02 Cole Rehearsal Studios, LA CA

Photo: Grove Pashley

Henry, Chuck, Keith 12-03-02 Ameoba Records, LA CA

Photo: Henry Rollins

Keith, Ian 06-12-03 9:30 Club, Washington DC

Photo: Brian Blumeyer

Jello picks winning ticket.
07-01-03 The Fillmore, San Francisco CA

Keith

Jesse & Darrell en route. 07-02-03 LAX

Photo: Henry Rollins

Mike and Darrell with Grapes.
The Astoria, London UK 07-10-03

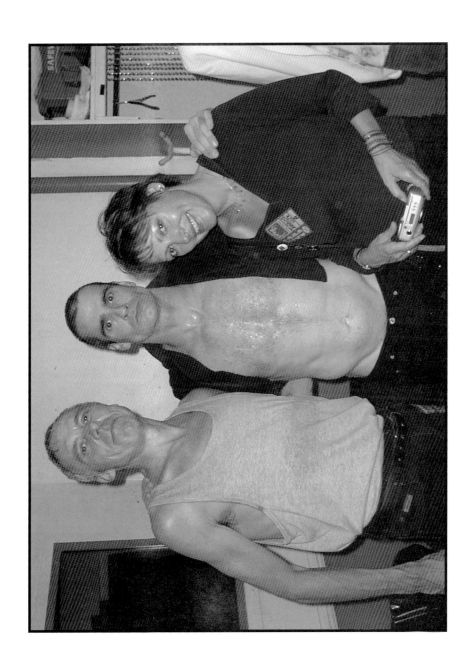

TV Smith, Henry, Gaye Advert.
The Astoria, London UK 07-10-03

Brian with Black Eye, Nottingham UK 07-12-03

Yesterday & Today Records, Rockville MD 02-24-02

Ian, Skip, Henry. Yesterday & Today Records,
Rockville MD 09-30-02

He knows things I'll never know. Talk about wisdom that comes with a price. Sometimes when I'm on a long flight, I will think to myself that in twelve hours, I'll still be in this seat and there's nothing to do but do the time. I can't imagine doing that every day. Damien has never been to a rock show.

05-11-03 LA CA: 11:09 p.m. It's been hard to come off the tour. It happens every time. I get back here and it's the constant waging of war with depression and unrest. I managed to get some sleep last night and was up at 0700 hrs and back at the desk.

Answered mail for about four hours until I found myself getting impatient with it so I moved onto other work. Later on, I got in a good workout and some reading.

I miss the shows. I miss the audience. I wish I was back on tour. I don't care about this place at all. I don't mind access to my books and being able to listen to a record that I have not heard in awhile but past that, let's go. I don't know what the fuck I am going to do when all this is over. I workout to get ready to confront audiences and myself. I don't know how I will be able to hold myself together without that pressure to deliver.

It always gets me when I come back from these things. I am so lucky to have that audience. They are an unbelievably cool bunch. They keep showing up! Every night when I walk off the stage, I wonder if I gave them enough. Sometimes it keeps me from sleeping. Sometimes I want to call them all up and drag them back into the building and tell them more. I wanted to do that in Brisbane. Time to sleep for a few hours and then start back in on the mail.

05-12-03 LA CA: 3:41 p.m. I've been at the desk since about 0500 hrs. and I can no longer concentrate on anything. Made the first draft of the newsletter and sent it over to Carol to have her look it over and then to Mike to look at it and then to Burk Sauls at the WM3 Support Group for him to go through it to make sure that I am not out of line or incorrect with any of the information.

Tonight is leg workout and hopefully some reading. I recently read an interesting book by Scott Donaldson called *Hemingway vs. Fitzgerald: The Rise and Fall of a Literary Friendship*. It was F. Scott who told his editor at Scribner's, Max Perkins, about Hemingway and it was that introduction that brought him to the company. Both of their stories are fairly tragic on their own but when they are synched up and compared and you read the letters going between Fitzgerald, Hemingway and Perkins, the dynamic makes for interesting reading. Now I want to read Matthew J. Bruccoli's version of the study called *Fitzgerald and Hemingway: A Dangerous Friendship* and I have been trying to crack it open for the last two nights but have been unable to stay awake. Bruccoli is the foremost Fitzgerald scholar. His biography on Fitzgerald, *Some Sort of Epic Grandeur: The Life of F. Scott Fitzgerald* is ultimate but he just revised and added a bunch to it so I bought it again, knowing I will have to eventually re-read it. People like me will always live alone. Thankfully there's frozen food.

05-13-03 LA CA: 0702 hrs. Back at it. Last night was a failure. I went from the office to the grocery store and stopped for gas on the way to the house. As I was about to get in the car, a large car with its top down rolled by me and the man driving said, "I love ya, man. Love the spoken word." I said thanks and then he rolled up his sleeve to show me a tattoo that said "ROLLINS" in bold Helvetica outline like on the Life Time album of ours. It took up his whole forearm. I forgot what I said, something like "Damn!" and then he just smiled and pulled out into traffic and was gone.

Right before I was going to head into the garage to hit the legs, I figured I would lie down on the couch for a second to let the protein shake I just had assimilate and woke up three hours later. Went from there to the bed and slept another seven hours. Guess I needed it. Woke up and went into the garage and hit the weights and then came here.

Got an e-mail from management that says Greg Ginn called him and left a message. I don't know if the two of them spoke but I bet it's going to be dramatic. So it starts! The drama! What ya came for! We'll see how that one pans out as the day goes on. I predict there will be a lot of this. Welcome to baggage claim! Have no life? Hop on the carousel!

I got word from Mike yesterday that it looks like we are go for Australia. The tour will end there on July 26 in Sydney if all goes as planned.

1:14 p.m.: Just got off the phone with Lorri Davis. I went through the newsletter with her and got the DNA stuff right and now we can send it out and get this thing going. Here's the newsletter.

Monday May 12, 2003 0609 hrs.

Good morning or whenever this reaches you. I have been back from the tour for a couple of days and there's a few things I wanted to tell you.

All those shows: There were eighty-nine dates on the tour this year. I just wanted to thank you profusely for coming to the shows. I had a great time and am hugely moved by your attendance, energy and enthusiasm. I know perfectly well, without an audience, I have no show, no job, nothing. To walk out there every night and see you is incredibly inspiring and gratifying and there's no possible way I will ever be able to thank you enough.

With things being the way they are in the world, it's not easy touring and being onstage nightly. It's not easy no matter what anyone's doing. There's a lot of distressing, depressing, infuriating and frustrating information to deal with daily, and it keeps on coming. But in spite of it all we somehow keep jamming. I make mention of this because the single thing that has been keeping my spirits up in this time has been the shows and seeing you out there. So, again and again: thank you.

When I walked offstage the other night after the show and got into the car my heart sank. It was hard to believe that I had just finished all those shows. I don't remember the plane ride back here. The last two days have been a blur of cleaning, assorted work and short periods of sleep. So again, thanks and I hope you had a good time at the shows.

And now for this: OK. This is a pretty massive undertaking but we're going for it. You remember the Rise Above: 24 Black Songs to Benefit the West Memphis Three album that we did last year. We did some shows at the end of last year with that material. Thanks to the generosity of the audi-

ences, we were able to send the West Memphis Three Defense Fund ten thousand dollars.

We had a great time playing those songs live and the audience was into it too so we have decided to take it worldwide. We will be doing several dates starting on June 01. There's a solid month in Amerika for sure and the dates are being booked as I write this. From there we go to Europe and as it looks now, Australia will be included.

For the US shows, none other than the man himself, Mr. Keith Morris, the original singer in Black Flag the leader of the Circle Jerks will be joining us. When you hear him sing these songs—whoa. We did an instore appearance last year with Keith starting the set out and when Keith and the boys went into 'Gimmie Gimmie,' I damn nearly wept. Keith did all but one of the shows with us last year and he was amazing.

So, there's a ton to be done to pull this off. The first show is in less than three weeks. We will be ready with the music, the boys are amped and ready to hit the rehearsal room. We will be learning songs that are not featured on the record. Last year we were playing 'Can't Decide,' 'Clocked In' and 'Don't Care' and they sounded great. I have to think we'll be learning some more songs for the tour.

The hard part is getting all the details hammered out. There's a lot of press to be done and countless other things. Road manager Mike Curtis has been working his ass off getting things together. This week the press release goes out and we'll see if any of the press types want to write about it. This is for us to obsess and worry about and we'll do what it takes.

Here's what I need from you. I need you to show up to these shows. Flat out. All the money we make goes to the West Memphis Three Defense Fund and right now things are at a very interesting place in the case. DNA evidence from the case that the defense never had the budget to test the first time around is now being tested. Now we're onto something. But, this testing isn't cheap and that's where the money is going.

I need you to show up at the show. I need you to tell a friend. That's what I need. I need these shows packed out and the house rockin'. From our side of things, I want to make this absolutely clear: We are not going to be casually shuffling through these songs like it's some oldies show and you'll be kind of into it because everyone's hearts were in the right place. We are *a trained assault unit. We are going to fuck you up with this music. This is not a Black Flag reunion. Greg Ginn and Chuck Dukowski wrote some of the best songs ever and we are hell bent on rendering them as best we can. If we didn't know for sure that the set was bomb proof, we wouldn't be out all summer wasting everyone's time. This is a one time, one time only tour. We're not looking to cross over to some new audience by playing someone else's music or cash in on some dubious claim to fame. We didn't write any of these songs. On this tour, we are a cover band. I should add that when I say cover, I mean you better take cover when we hit stage because we're not fucking around. I think I have made myself clear on this point.*

Hey you know what? The DNA evidence might come back inconclusive and none of this will have made a difference. This was a botched case from the beginning. Damien Echols, Jason Baldwin and Jessie Misskelley didn't get a fair day in court and that's not right and if you're down with this program then you're standing up for justice. They've been hanging out in prison for ten years and all you have to do is come to the show and have a great time as you know you will and you will have made a huge difference to three people who have absolutely no recourse now other than to depend on the will of good people to do the right thing. And that would be you, right? Please join us this summer.

Please don't respond to this letter. The next two and a half weeks will be very busy and there's no time to answer any questions. There's nothing to ask on this one. Anyone who has their own WM3 Group in their town, make some fliers for the show and get the word out. For dates, locations and other information for these shows, please go to our website. If you don't see your city, don't write us about it. Right now there's no time to answer any questions. Myself and the staff here are going to be wall-to-wall on this thing until the band heads out so please understand. Any shows that come in will be posted immediately. Get ready to rock.

For anyone who received this newsletter and are not aware of what I have been talking about, please go to WM3.org for more information.

Thank you. --Henry Rollins

So that's that. Deborah, who's lining up the press for the tour says that the Memphis press people are not dealing with her and we can't get any advance press for our show there. I think they don't want to make waves. Cowards with no balls. Hey, look in the mirror, you're a disgrace to your profession. A lot of people in that part of Amerika think the boys are guilty and don't want to hear otherwise. I remember doing press with newspapers from around there last year and they weren't all that friendly. No problem. I can be much worse. There will be a lot of this kind of thing happening on this tour. *The West Memphis Commercial Appeal,* now there's a real classy newspaper. I was hoping to talk to Bart Sullivan. I thought we could have a little chat but I guess that won't happen. I dig confrontation. It's addictive. Sometimes it's all you want to do. Weld the game face to your skull. No need to take it off.

9:34 p.m. One of the press agents told me that the *Commercial Appeal* (a newspaper in Memphis, TN) won't return phone calls. Their cousin newspaper, the *West Memphis Commercial Appeal* is the Arkansas newspaper that printed all that hilarious shit about human heads being found underneath Damien's bed. I talked to the Memphis version when the record came out I think. I was pretty full-on confrontational with the guy. They don't like me. I don't like them. You fucking pussies. See you in June. Fuck you.

Amerika's a hostile place. Amerika's playing catch up and it's out of breath. By the time they figured out that all that fast food and other crap was bad for your health, it was too late. Ronald McDonald was already in the home and he would never hurt you and you were already hooked so why stop a good thing? You're allowed to be an ignorant piece of shit in this country and someone will always be there to carry you. I meet fuck ups all the time. Divorced, substance abusers, two kids by two mothers, collecting unemployment and somehow driving a new SUV. They are pigs running wild and they are allowed to live. They are carried. Amerika spits in your face and charges you double and tells you to be proud. I love Amerika but it's hard to be proud of a place run by cowards who are afraid to tell the people the bottom line. They won't tell them to use less gas, they just get more oil.

Bush tries to sell the lie that Amerika's so bent out of shape and endangered by Saddam Hussein and his weapons of mass destruction, that there's no other choice but to go into Iraq for a little regime change. Amerika is so broken up about the plight of the Iraqis that they will spend billions of dollars to liberate them when Amerika allows millions of lives inside its own borders to twist in the wind. It's so see-through. You make your point by accusing the UN of being a soon-to-be-irrelevant organization. Amerika fools no one. No wonder so many countries hate Amerika. Amerika better find that smoking Iraqi gun soon. Dr. Germ, Baghdad Bob, what a joke. People are getting killed and you're showing faces of Iraqis on playing cards like it's some game? It's hard to take.

05-14-03 LA CA: 1118 hrs. At the office. Messenger just brought the final cut of the 'Rise Above' video, complete with the Chuck D intro. The video starts out with Chuck D right down the barrel of the lens. What a shot, what a man. Modi had a hard time tracking Mr. D down but she did it and what a video! The footage was shot at two of the shows we did last December and it's full-on audience frenzy. Hopefully we can put it on our website and some cable stations will play it so people can get the idea of the thing.

8:08 p.m.: Post workout food. All the abdominal work I am doing will payoff onstage but right now it hurts like a motherfucker.

Sent out the newsletter a few hours ago, the one where I asked people not to reply to it, there's no questions to ask me that you can't get answered from the WM3 website, but still the letters come in. De ja vu. I remember this shit from the Flag days. The fucking whining. Is it an age thing? I get these letters, this guy doesn't like the venue, another one has a problem that we're playing this town instead of THAT town. I remember being astonished by how many people in this "hardcore" movement were such a bunch of whining living-with-their-mom bitches.

Your country put your fellow countrymen in the line of fire so people could drive SUV's and you're complaining to me about some intersection you don't like? Does this guy have any idea of the beating this music is going to throw him? This isn't the fodder you've been lulled into a state of narcotica with on TV. This is the real shit that will be rendered by people who can actually play their instruments and are in shape to do it. Fuck it, maybe some of you people shouldn't come. Shit was way more raw back then. No one in a band was a fucking sex symbol, people weren't "nice" and everything hurt.

05-15-03 LA CA: 6:19 p.m. Another blah day at the office grinds to an end and now I'm here alone. Been back almost a week. I can't believe I'll be going back to Australia again this year. I wonder if anyone will show up.

I start the first of the interviews tomorrow and I am interested, well, not all that interested, in seeing how they will deal with me.

More mail about the newsletter. Can our band open? I'll be a little short on funds, I know it's a benefit but could I get free tickets? It's not about me this tour, so I answer all the questions again and again like they're kids. Now that I've been back here a few days and dealing with all this again, I remember the hole all this puts me in. I want to do it, the tour—all of it, it's just that it's hard stuff to deal with and there's a lot of negativity that goes along with all this and it's rough going. Been on this trail for about a year. Carrying all that Black Flag baggage. Baggage! Stuck in my head! Caused by . . . YOU! It's all Baggage! Baggage!!

05-16-03 LA CA: 10:57 p.m. Whoa, up late. Today was the start of the press and it was pretty good. They were into the tour and no one gave me shit about the case or anything. I don't mind doing press and I can get along with most of these interviewers but sometimes they need a smack and if you were to think any of these people were your friends, you would be doing yourself a disservice. So, I'm cool when they are and when they aren't, I do the best I can seeing that they always have the last word. So far, so good.

In the afternoon, I got a call from management and it looks like we will be playing in Japan after Australia. At this point, the tour will end in Tokyo.

The training has been good and the diet has been intense but I'm getting the results I want. I am doing a lot of calisthenics and a lot of reps. Tonight as a reward, I went and got myself a frozen yogurt.

June Carter just died. I feel bad for Johnny Cash. I met them a few years ago after seeing them play in LA. They were very friendly. When I introduced myself to June Carter, she said, "I know who you are, honey. I've seen you on TV." I never know if that's a good thing or not. She was really great that night. Watching them do 'Jackson' together was worth the whole show.

Death makes me tired. I know too many dead people. I ran into a lawyer guy I know at the yogurt place tonight. He reminded me that he had called me last year to tell me that my old accountant had died. I got an e-mail today from someone who told me that they just saw Dennis Cole on television on some lame Hollywood thing. It was the show he wanted me to do with him a few weeks ago while I was in Australia. I think he's trying to get his non-career off the ground and he can't do it on his own and has to have a pity party and use his dead son. Anyway, the guy who wrote the letter said that Dennis Cole was saying that there were Nazi books found at our house like I'm a Nazi or something. Yes there were Dennis Cole, and they all belonged to your son. Ha ha. They were some Time-Life history books on World War II. I think Joe also had a copy of Hitler's book. I remember he said he tried to read it and said it sucked and couldn't get into it. I think he found them at a bookstore we went to in Dallas on the 1986 Flag tour. I remember the detective telling me that they found the books, like he was onto something. I remember asking him if they were on the bookshelf with all the other books in the house, he said, "yes" and I just looked at him knowing that we both knew there was nothing to talk about. Poor Dennis Cole. I am sorry you lost your son. It's not my fault you're a has-been. I remember a few things about you: Your twenty-something year old girlfriends, your substance abuse problems, you couldn't get work as an actor, you couldn't make it to your son's funeral and how you turned your son's memorial service into a thing about you as you stood there getting congratulated for your loss by your insane AA friends. Such a handsome man though, what a face. What a . . . star.

There's so many motherfuckers out there. It's hard to be cool to people sometimes. It's hard to care what happens to any of them. You're an alcoholic and you have to take it one day at a time and go to AA and sit in a circle with a bunch of other fuck ups and say, "Hi my name is . . . " and talk about the fact that you can't get away from a bottle of liquid. On my good days I feel bad about that and on other days I just wish you would hurry up and step off. It's hard to be cool to some of these people. It's hard to be cool to a loser like Dennis Cole. I feel bad for him because he's weak and he fucked his life up and lost his son.

I'm all for confrontation. You got something to say, say it. None of these people are a problem. They're weak. When they do it on their own time, fine. When they do it on mine, that's something else. It's hard not to give them what they need.

05-17-03 LA CA: 7:51 p.m. Been reading a book called *The Best Democracy Money Can Buy* by Greg Palast. It's pretty damn interesting. It details all kinds of bullshit perpetrated on the Amerikan people by the government and big business. After reading about Jeb Bush and the underhanded antics he employed in Florida to get his brother elected, I was pissed! If this is true, then how come none of the Democrats brought them to justice? Is this the real truth or just this guy going off? Can you get away with something this crass while everyone's watching? It's more hard core than Michael Moore's book *Stupid White Men*, which is a pretty good read but this Palast guy's intense! His facts are well backed up. His background has background. Sure makes me wonder if we know all we need to know about the Bush family.

Workout today was arms, abdominals, push-ups, finishing with pull-ups with a forty-five pound weight. It's great when it's over. Vegetarian pasta soup and salad for dinner and that's it. Body feeling good. In two weeks I will have better abdominal strength and band practice will tell me what else I need to work on.

No one calls here except crank calls and telemarketers so I don't have a great deal of distraction. Listened to El Guapo's *Fake French* LP and it was great. Now listening to *The Crack* LP by the Ruts. A regular Saturday night ritual. The singer, Malcom Owen, died of a heroin overdose on July 14th, 1980, he was twenty-six. I listen to The Ruts all the time. Ever since I first heard them, I reckoned they were one of the best bands I ever heard. Their songs get better with time. To think Malcom Owen would be about forty-nine now. That's incredible. They hardly got a chance to do anything. One album, some singles and some assorted tracks here and there and then he was gone. There are no bad Ruts songs. The stuff they were doing right before Malcom died, songs like 'Staring at the Rude Boys' and 'West One' are incredible. I listen to The Ruts and The Damned almost every weekend when I'm here. Can't wait to get out there and play.

05-18-03 LA CA: 9:51 p.m. The end of the weekend. Good shoulder workout and more reading into the Greg Palast book. I am useless between tours. There's nothing here. Let's go.

05-19-03 LA CA: 1145 hrs. Put a call in to Keith to see what songs he wants to sing and am waiting to hear back. Band practice starts in a couple of days and then we are out of here.

Ari Fleischer, the White House press secretary, is stepping down. I liked that guy, he was fast. He said he wanted a more relaxed pace and to spend more time with his family. I can't blame the guy. Spinning the antics of the rip roarin' drunk duo Bush/Cheney would take its toll on anyone. What a grim job.

05-20-03 LA CA: 2:51 p.m. This just in from the press agent. Tim Spencer of Rock 103 in Memphis states: "Okay I'll have that Son of a Bitch on - I'd love to. I'll open up the phones and see how he likes talking to the parents of the three boys that the WM3 Murderers slaughtered just a few miles from the studio." I told the press agent to line it up.

To Tim Spencer:

Mr. Spencer. We are not dealing in shadows or any gray areas here. We are raising money for DNA evidence testing on behalf of Jessie Misskelley, Damien Echols and Jason Baldwin. We're not looking for a get out of jail free card. We're raising funds to contribute to the expenses incurred by this testing of previously untested DNA evidence in this case. Our pursuit is for facts and that's it. It doesn't matter how I feel about the case. Feelings don't count here. Only facts matter and that's all we're after. To pursue this end doesn't make me in any way an advocate of harm to children or for those who harm them. You know this. If you are convinced of the WM3's guilt then you won't have a problem with some evidence being tested, because if conclusive results are derived, it will only point to the ones presently incarcerated, thus anchoring your position in absolute truth. This is lab work done by lab technicians who have no stake in the outcome.

I am sure you and perhaps many of your listeners wouldn't believe me when I tell you how badly I feel about what happened to those children. Even after the loss of people close to me I cannot even begin to imagine the daily hell their parents live in. I look forward to being on your show.

In truth,

Henry Rollins

I asked the press agent to send that to the guy and she did. I'll talk to the guy for sure. Bring it. The show day in Memphis will be a little rough. So, train harder.

05-21-03 LA CA: 2:54 p.m.: Another round of interviews done. The interviewers were all pretty cool and were supportive of what we're doing. I just tell them that we're all about the evidence being processed as that really is the bottom line here. Anything I have to add isn't really of any consequence as it's just me thinking out loud. So, with that being the iron bar keeping the back straight, I can proceed rather smoothly.

Putting the practice set together. Keith wants to do eight songs and he phoned them in yesterday. I have a set made which I will try out first before he gets there and then we'll see how he likes it. Mike gets here in a few hours and I have to do press early in the morning for this song I did on a Waylon Jennings tribute album called *Lonesome Ornery and Mean.* I don't know much about Waylon Jennings. I did the song because I was told it would be a good idea to give back as so many people came through for us when we did the *Rise Above* record. For some reason, the critic types like what I did and the record company who put out the record asked if I would do some press and I said ok. The workout awaits. Holy shit, ten days out. Countdown has started.

05-22-03 LA CA: 10:40 p.m. Today was long and strange. Was at the office bright and early doing press for the WJ record. I did a bunch of radio interviews and they were all really cool.

After that I worked on things with Mike as he is out here now. He wanted to see the 'Rise Above' video so I went to the house to get it and when I was walking through the living room I saw a man out in the back trying to pry his way into one of the windows of my house. He was working so intently that he didn't see or hear me. I froze as I thought of what to do. I was moving towards the phone when he saw me.

He's on the back porch, I'm inside. I notice he's wearing rubber gloves. Late twenties, early thirties, medium build black male. He says hello and asked if my door buzzer was working. Huh? We're having a conversation? He comes towards the door and I'm just watching his hands to see if he goes for a weapon. We have this surreal conversation with a glass door between us. To paraphrase:

Me: What the hell are you doing?

Him: Does your door buzzer work?

Me: What are you doing?

Him: Your neighbor said to ring the buzzer. (He starts checking his watch, like he's gotta be somewhere. I guess he has a long list of houses to rip off and can't fall behind?)

Me: What are you doing at my window? You're breaking in, that's what you're doing!

Him: No I'm not.

Me: Then what are you doing. What could you possibly be doing?

Him: Let me in, let's talk. I don't have a gun. Be a man!

Me: Be a man?! How about I call the cops and we see your I.D. and we work it out with them?

Him: Why?!

Me: Because you're breaking into my house.

Him: No, I . . .

Me: Then what are you doing?

Him: I work for the cable company!

Me: Of course you do, which company?!

Him: Uhhhh. . . .

Me: You don't know who you work for?!

Him: Do you want me to leave the same way I came in?

Me: Sure.

He bolts. As I'm calling the cops, I watch him running down the hill. I call the dispatch and tell them my address, I describe the guy to a T and then call Mike who's working at the office. I tell him what happened and to look out onto the street and see if he can see the guy. Mike is walking on Hollywood Blvd. with his cel phone, he sees the guy running to the bottom of the hill and onto the Blvd. He starts to jog after him! I tell him to keep his phone line open. I call the cops back and describe Mike and give them his phone number. They call Mike and now they have a police chopper after the guy. I can hear it. Mike's telling them where he's going and follows the guy until he disappears into an apartment building.

The cops come by my place and I tell them what happened and he seems to fit the description of a man who made a woman walk to an ATM and get him money. They take their report and leave. I go back to the office with Mike who got a ride up the hill by one of the three cop cars that have descended onto my place. I went from there back to here and looked at the damage the guy did. He tried the back door and then one window and then the one that I caught him at. Fuck these people.

I went to band practice and it was great to see the guys and great to play the songs and we ripped it. I had a good time when I could forget what had just happened. Didn't sound like the first day of practice. It sounds like we're already there. All the rest of the practices will allow us to come out full-on when we hit on June 01.

05-23-03 LA CA: 10:40 p.m. At the office today, I got a package from Damien via Lorri. Inside was a painting of a Zen Monk named Bhodi Dharma. In the letter, Damien said he painted it entirely with coffee! He said the backing is made from a legal tablet, the plastic cover is saran wrap from a dinner tray and the borders were made from a page of a magazine. Too much! I don't know anything about Bhodi Dharma but here's what Damien says about him in his letter:

" . . . He was a Zen monk from China, the founder of the Shao Lin Temple, and the inventor of Kung-fu. Back in the day everyone wanted to learn from him, but he would only accept you if you could show him how serious you were. So, one student chopped off his own arm with a sword to show how determined he was. For that, Bhodi Dharma accepted him. Pretty intense, eh?"

He said that he followed my example and has started keeping a journal of everything from his dreams to the weather. That will be a trip to read when he's out of there. It will be a different man on a different planet reading about someone else.

An article in *Variety,* says that Michael Pitt and Jacob Reynolds will star in a feature film called *West Memphis Three*. It's budgeted at under ten million dollars and it's tentatively shooting in Texas and Arkansas in the fall of this year. Writer-producer Curt Johnson is in discussions with William H. Macy and Edie Falco for roles. Then the article said this, "Musician and author Henry Rollins originally brought the story to the attention of Johnson, who produced this year's Oscar-winning documentary short 'Thoth'." I don't remember doing that but what the hell.

Band practice was good again. The set will be about an hour. Keith will be doing about fifteen minutes and I will be doing the rest. I have not timed out the encore as yet.

05-24-03 LA CA: 11:41 p.m.: Saturday. Finger print man came by at 0905 hrs. this morning and said the burglar/cable guy left no prints. I didn't think he would find anything.

Another good day at band practice. I watched Keith hit his part of the set twice. He's such an inspiration to watch. He's still got it. Totally intense, the voice sounds great. He's a natural. He doesn't have to turn anything on, he just walks in with it. Some people have it.

During his sets, I did 50 rep sets of pushups and sit ups and was able to really hammer them out with the music playing so loud. Calisthenics hurt but they're the best if you can stay with them. For the last several months I have been doing hard abdominal work, the hardest I have ever done in my life and now I can feel strength in that area like never before. Took awhile. The running I've been doing has been paying off at practice big time. A few songs in I stabilize and from there, I just rip it.

So from here on in, there's nothing to do but settle deeper and deeper into it. Think about less, focus more on diet, sleep, the songs and the shows the shows the shows. Come June 01, that's all there is to know.

In *Thus Spoke Zarathustra,* Nietzsche advised the warrior to favor the short peace over the long and to make his peace a means to new wars. That's the thing keeping my stitching in at this point.

05-25-03 LA CA: 11:41 p.m.: Sunday. No band practice. Good shoulder workout. Preliminary pack. A lot of reading of *Fast Food Nation* by Eric Schlosser. Pretty mindblowing. Amerika got bought out by Amerikans, got hacked up, farmed out, marketed, packaged and sold back at a higher price. We have fucked ourselves up harder than any foreign invader could have. We are obese and depressed. We eat bad food by the ton. The 101st Airborne Division should have bombed the Enron offices. Amerika is a greater threat to Amerikans than Iraq could ever hope to be. I hate the idea that I have to watch my ass in my own country.

05–26–03 LA CA: 2:10 p.m.: Monday. At the office. Band practice is at six and then I think Greg Ginn is playing a show at the Dragonfly and none of us know what that will be about but we might go check it out.

I went out earlier today to a dentist appointment that was not to be, I guess the lady got the day wrong but the appointment had me on the road all over today. LA is so fucked up. It's filthy and the streets of Hollywood are littered with homeless. It's a leper scratching running sores. Every time I drive by the old Landmark hotel on Franklin, where Janis Joplin's body was wheeled out in October of 1970, it makes me see the evil and tragic polluted bullshit of this place. Her voice always made me feel close to her. I remember listening to her version of 'Summertime' on the *Joplin in Concert* album when I was very young and how I wished she was my mother. I drove by the place today twice. Every time I do, I always imagine the gurney coming out the front doors. She overdosed on heroin and died in room #105. She'd be around sixty now. It's hard to imagine any of those dead-so-young rockers like her or Hendrix or Morrison at that age. I just can't see it.

Gotta get out of this town. Leaving in a few days, but past that, I gotta get out of this place. I have no nostalgia for LA at all. I leave here for months and come back and I don't feel anything. It's like when you go to pick up your rental car at the airport, the Hertz place is familiar but you feel nothing for it.

Here, it's thousands of idiots driving in cars and trucks they don't need, clogging the lanes, on the phone. This morning, perhaps in celebration of whatever holiday it is today, jets flew over the house. Sounded like the sky was being torn. It was incredible. I put on a CD from the *Music of Islam* boxset and listened to the music mixed with the jet scream to see if I could imagine what it was like in Baghdad a few weeks ago.

Amerika got Amerikans hooked on the bad stuff. Amerikans are running sickened by the toxin, driven by the poison injected into their systems by the brand names that told them they were their friends. The brand names were lying. Not friends. Not one. Not ever. I see it all over but it glares at me so obscenely here in Los Angeles.

05-27-03 LA CA: 1149 hrs. At the office. I detect a subtle shift in attitude from my Memphis, TN DJ Tim Spencer. This just in:

> *Mr. Rollins,*
> *You are right. If I'm convinced of their guilt then I should have no problem with DNA testing. And I don't. In fact, I sincerely hope it happens regardless of the outcome. But my experience with the people involved with the WM3 movement has been extremely negative and certainly hasn't shown WM3 followers to be interested in facts. More like a bunch of rabid, self-righteous holy-rollers who condemn you to hellfire and damnation because you listen to metal. How's THAT for ironic?*
> *Somehow my name was mentioned on a discussion board a few years ago along with some comment I made on the air. I was deluged with hateful email because I disagreed with the premise that the WM3 are innocent. When I attempted to respond, I was ridiculed. It was clear that nobody in that little flame-fest was interested in facts, only in their agenda and their "feelings."*
> *At any rate, I think it will make for some interesting radio. I hope you're able to make it.*
> *Tim Spencer*

Perhaps this will be something worth doing instead of something merely worth enduring after all. This morning we got an e-mail from someone in an organization called Symbionese Liberation Productions in Memphis, TN. They want to film the show for us. I can't think how a production company calling themselves Symbionese Liberation Productions running around our show with cameras will be helpful on that day. I dig the name though.

11:37 p.m.: Another good day at practice. We learned 'Damaged I' and the awesome Dukowski song 'Modern Man.' They sound great. I hadn't sung either one of those in about twenty years. From there I went into the garage and worked out on legs and now I am dead.

05-28-03 LA CA: 4:21 p.m. There's no power at the practice place. It was set for 3 p.m. We're standing by.

News in from Mike. Forty-one tickets sold in Memphis TN, now there's a shut out for ya! He says that ticket sales are doing just ok not great in a lot of areas. I called management to see what was up with the 'Rise Above' video and he said that it's been serviced by Sanctuary Records, the label that put out *Rise Above*. It doesn't seem like they are all that interested in the record or the tour which makes it ever so hard on us. Management put in a letter today, basically begging for help and telling them that they have not been all that into the record or the whole thing even though they were the label who wanted to do the record. Apparently people at the label got back to him and want to help out. It will be a hard tour but the music will be good. Too bad there won't be as many people as we had hoped for. I think it's going to be hard year for touring all around. I have heard that everyone's ticket sales are down, the bus company we use are having cancellations left and right. Also, it's not like there are that many people who want to see us play under any circumstances anyway and I can handle that, but you would figure some people would rise to the challenge.

Management just called and said that he called Sanctuary and shook things up and hopefully they'll do something. Apparently, they lost money on the *Rise Above* record and don't want to do much more with it. I can see their point but I can't understand how you can manage to lose money on such a good record with all those cool singers—unless you do what Sanctuary does all the time, which is put out tons of stuff so they don't really give anything all that much attention. We brought that record in SO cheap. So many people worked for free or at a discount. It's disheartening but it's also the way it is with labels. It's the beginning of the end for them, you see how they act. When they cave in, it will only be from the weight of their greed and arrogance. The funny thing is that they don't see it. It's definitely time to do records at home and sell them to your friends and not bother with the lightweights.

No band practice tonight. So, a depressing day of negativity and apathy comes to a close here at the office and now it's time to go to the garage and workout and then microwave the identical dinner I had last night. Viva la Causa!

05-29-03 LA CA: Meet the press!

1000 - Blanquita Cullum from Newsbeat, Radio Amerika in Washington, DC.
1030 - Nicole Crowley from The Downtown in Washington, DC.
1100 - Mike Miliard from The Boston Phoenix in Boston, MA.
1130 - Matt Sebastian from The Daily Camera in Denver, CO.
1200 - Adam Smith from The Boston Herald in Boston, MA.
1230 - David Moore from Q Note Magazine in Charlotte, NC.
1300 - Anastasia Pantsios from The Cleveland Plain Dealer in Cleveland, OH.
1330 - Jim Sullivan from The Boston Globe in Boston, MA.

11:41 p.m. Today was better than yesterday. I did all the press including a phone interview in Ft. Worth. All the interviews were really cool and I am surprised how positive they all were.

I managed to get in contact with Iann Robinson of MTV News. I found him on his cel phone. I told him what we were doing and what we needed. He said he could get our tour dates posted on their website for sure. He said he was going to make some moves and see what he could get happening and get back to me as soon as he could. I gave him Mike's number to call. What a cool guy. I can't believe I am going to MTV for help. I can't stand them but fuck it. I am in no position to be choosy, we need all the help we can get. Iann's totally cool and I know he'll do the best he can. MTV, how gross. It's all about the cause, maaaaaaaaaaan!

Band practice was good today. I was a little scattered from the four and a half hours of interviews but I woke up a couple of songs in. We are ready. The shows are going to be fine and I am done being off the road and I want my damn bunk back.

The positive press response makes me feel better than yesterday. I don't like depending on these people but we need their help. This has been a pretty depressing and exhausting time here. Pretty much everything having to do with the WM3 is draining. Worth it but hard on me.

05–30–03 LA CA: 10:50 p.m. Iann Robinson, what a man. He set up an interview for MTV News so Mike and I headed out to Santa Monica bright and early, went into the MTV building and did it. This will help the tour big time. Iann's a good guy, he turned that right around and got it happening. How he pulled all that off in a little more than half a day, I'll never know. From there, back to the office and then here. Good workout, small dinner and now just walking back and forth anticipating deployment. Sick of the waiting. The last couple of days are always the worst.

05–31–03 LA CA: 11:51 p.m. On the bus. We hit the road at 8 p.m. This is the same bus I did all the US talking shows on. I spent three months on this one. We're all on and we are on the way. It was so great to walk on and see everyone here. You think it up and you do it. Who knows what's coming?

It's such a relief being back on the bus. I like the bus better than my room. I like my bunk better than my bed. I'd rather be moving. Soon we'll be at a truck stop and hours after that, we'll wake up in the desert with the first show waiting. It's so cool to be sitting up front here and see Keith right across from me. Fucking Keith Morris is on tour with us. How much cooler can it possibly get? As Jim Wilson always says: Let's do it!

06–01–03 Tempe AZ: 1000 hrs. We're in a parking lot next to a Guitar Center, waiting for them to open. Darrell, our soundman, Jesse our t-shirt seller and Mike hiked over to the local Walmart across the road and picked up a grill and lawn furniture. I came to the back of the trailer to find them lounging in these damn chairs.

I made a trip to the Walmart to check in with my Amerika. There they were. Mulleted and super-wide, staggering down the aisles. I went back outside and walked through the endless and empty parking lot of the stores all glued together for at least three city blocks. The temperature was already blazing hot and I could smell the abrupt, unwelcoming stench of the Burger King from a block away. It's the smell you don't register when you're in the place. It's the toxic blow back of the beast. When you smell that, you can't believe someone is going to eat the product—but they do. Millions of pounds of this crap uploaded into their systems every year. So many Amerikans are in bad shape. They bring it on themselves. They line up in cars to eat this stuff.

Soon, we'll be headed to the venue where we will sit all day and wait to load in.

06-02-03 Tempe AZ: 0106 hrs. In the parking lot waiting on Tim the bus driver to take us to Texas. The guys hit stage at 10:30 p.m. Keith went out there and the place exploded. I was backstage pacing. This being the first show, I felt bad about sending them all out there without me being out in front in case there was any flak, but from the sound of the band and the audience, it was clear that it was going down great. There's no question that Keith can hold his own. Soon enough it was time for me to go out there and hit it. After all these days of preparation, I was on and singing 'Rise Above.' What a fast set. Twenty-seven songs went by like no time at all. We encored with 'Modern Man' and 'Damaged I' and it was a great night. It felt like it lasted only twenty minutes.

I went out and met the line of people, signed their tickets and whatever else they had. Did my best to get the drunk girl dealt with and gone. Drunks are hard to deal with in situations like this. You have to treat them like children and they take up a lot of time.

So, finally we're on tour and life is good again.

10:04 p.m. El Paso TX: A day off is coming to a close. Today was phone interviews, reading, shoulder workout and a run. Early in the morning I have to do the phone interview with the guy in Memphis, TN. I am not bothered by this guy and he can say what he wants. We are doing a good thing and there's bound to be some resistance to it. Apparently there were people calling the venue last night giving them shit for having the show because it's "contributing to the welfare of child murderers." After the show, the venue owners sent a poster backstage for all of us to sign. They were so happy to have the show there and dug what we were doing for the WM3. It's great to get any encouragement at this point.

06-03-03 Fort Worth TX: 5:05 p.m. On the bus. I set up the weights in the shade next to the venue and Mike and I did some shoulders. The opening band is called Zug Island. They have all kinds merchandise set up at the booth. They have their logo on every garment known to man. We have like three things. We look made of tin and tape in comparison. Nice merchandise and pretty girlfriends don't get you through the show. It's only the show that matters. It's so great to finally be out here. The only thing is proving it every night and doing everything possible to realize that end. Every calorie, every waking moment—all of it can be focused on the show. I live for that. To be in a situation where you can devote so much to so little. It teaches you things. So many corny bands with no focus. I saw it on that lame Warped tour. The show they were there to perform was the formality they had to get through so they could get back to their normal, lounging bullshit. Either live for it or fuck off.

I did the interview with Tim Spencer. He was totally cool. He let me say my piece and the whole thing was like most other interviews I do except Tim Spencer was more on top of things than most of these other people, so it was good. I thought it was going to be one of those idiotic, high volume pissing contests which you never win and just waste your time. Pam Hobbs, mother of Steven Branch, one of the murdered boys, called in and we spoke briefly. It was hard to understand her due to the connection but she seemed pretty cool. I would like to meet her in person. That one's over with but we still have the Memphis show which might include some drama. Isn't the show enough? Why does there have to be corny street theater? Amerika needs a doctor. Ok, so let's go to Memphis.

06-04-03 Memphis TN: 5:33 p.m. In the bus. Today has been interesting so far. I did an interview for Fox 13 News and just did another for a local station. They were cool to me and allowed me to speak freely. One of the interviewers said that Pam Hobbs will be protesting in front of the show and asked if I would talk to her and I said I would but I wasn't going to be part of some corny TV bullshit. He asked me, "Who said we were planning on filming it?" That means nothing to me. That means you weren't planning on doing it but if the opportunity came up, then what the hell. I can't go for that kind of thing. I'll talk to her, of course but not like that. Television interviewers are so strange. They're a different breed, right down to their clothes. The men are foppish and the women are robotic. When they ask you a question, you can see their dismay if your response is longer than a sentence because they're already thinking about the edit and how they will make an easily digestible sound byte out of what you said. If you do enough of this stuff, you can learn to get your point across and make it work into their format. You speak in bytes. I learned it from reading David Lee Roth interviews and saw it first hand when I interviewed him years ago. He's the best.

It sounds good onstage. Soundcheck went well and I'm looking forward to the show. Got in a good leg workout. Now we wait. Supafuzz will be playing with us tonight. What a great band. It's good to have them on this one.

Last night was good for the most part. Great crowd. Keith killed them and I held my own. The response of people to what we're doing, the fact that they know they are part of it, makes it more than just going to a show. I have been surprised nightly at how responsive people are to the actual issues of the WM3. It's more than just another tour to them. Just when I thought they were flatline apathetic . . .

HENRY ROLLINS
152

Anyway, we did the show and it was cool and I walked out of the venue to the bus and I saw security guys in a circle around someone on the ground. It was a girl who was having difficulty breathing. I remembered her from the front row and that she got passed over the barricade at some point. I sat down next to her and held her hand. She was having a hard time and kept apologizing for having this problem. I tried to get her to calm down and she did for a little while but then she started freaking out again. Finally the ambulance came and I left her to them and went to the bus to change out of my clothes. I signed things for the people in line outside the bus and eventually met the girl who ended up being ok. She apologized several times for freaking out and I told her that it was cool. Soon after that, we hit the road.

6:15 p.m.: A few minutes ago there was a hard knock at the bus door. This pissed me off so I threw the door open and there was another news crew from a local channel. Seeing that it was a small robot interview woman and her camera guy, I assumed it was he who had knocked on the door with such force. I said, "You knocking on my fucking door? Are you a cop?" It shook them both a little. Good. Off balance is good. Robot woman timidly asked me if I would do an interview. Sure, ya hack, I'd be glad to! Thankfully it was brief. I hate these kind of interviews, they're more like depositions but they come with the territory I guess. Mike just came in and said that Pam Hobbs is out in front of the venue getting her time with the cameras. It will be good to get onstage and get some music going. The drama aspect of all this is a bore.

06–05–03 Atlanta GA: 6:22 p.m. In the parking lot of the venue. Yesterday was long and strange. I was hanging out alone near the bus to get some air. A man came up to me and told me about how he lost his driver's license by making an illegal u-turn. I asked if he was drunk at the time. He said yes but only four beers. Oh.

At that time, Pam Hobbs and a large group of people came to talk to me. I shook her hand, told her I was glad to finally meet her and told her what we were trying to accomplish with these shows and she was really cool about it. I told her that we weren't trying to upset her or challenge her in any way, we were just helping some people get some facts. She was cool with that. I didn't know what to expect but was eager to talk to her and at least have a chance to tell her what we're about.

A man named Shawn Wheeler was with her. Mr. Wheeler talked for about eighty minutes fairly nonstop about all the proof that shows the WM3 to be guilty. He was obsessed with the case and had some interesting things to say. Weeks before when I told Burk Sauls of the WM3 Support Group that we were going to be playing in Memphis, he warned me about a bad news guy I might meet at the show. I forgot his name but remembered Burk said he worked for the phone company. I asked Mr. Wheeler what he did for a living and he told me that he works for the phone company. Hello! Anyway, I stood next to Pam and we listened endlessly to him say things like "Sometimes you have to look past the DNA evidence and really get down in the dirt to find the truth." He also had proof that Damien Echols was into the occult with a history of blood drinking and furthermore, anyone who is interviewed in prison and when asked what's the worst part about being there replies, "the food," is obviously guilty. As he kept talking, his references and theories got more and more out there. There was a woman with him who gave me her e-mail and website address. Mr. Wheeler didn't give me an e-mail address. I wondered if perhaps he didn't have one on account of what Burk Sauls and Kathy Bakken had told me. He also told me that Kathy tried to get him fired. The woman gave me the address of a website where you can get Mr. Wheeler's side of the story, midsouthjustice.org.

I remember Burk and Kathy telling me some intense stuff about Shawn Wheeler. A shortlist of the highlights:

1. He's still on the internet but uses many assumed names. There are many reasons for his troubles.

2. He threatened in a public message board that he was going to send Anthrax to Burk Sauls. That got him in a lot of trouble.

3. He sent a threatening postcard to a woman who disagreed with his views and made some veiled threats about his "Smith and

Wesson." He mailed it from the state she was living in thus evoking some sort of 'crossing state lines' infraction. That one got him a nice FBI file.

4. He harassed a female DJ in Memphis, accusing her of having a disposable camera of his with his "work" on it, so often that finally, after many nasty letters to the radio station and their legal counsel, the station let her go. She went to the FBI and it was added to the many other complaints that have been filed against this guy.

I paid close attention to what he was saying. I nodded and ah-ha'd throughout the lecture. His rap was difficult to follow at times, he uses a lot names and he only stops talking to inhale. At one point, I started getting dizzy and I realized I hadn't eaten in awhile and after the leg workout I had done, I had better get something in me before the show. Right around that time, Sean's lecture wrapped up and I shook all their hands, signed autographs for some of them (!) and again told Pam Hobbs how sorry I was about what had happened to her son and that we in no way meant to cause her any upset and she told me she knew that and thanked me. I don't understand how you could get on with your life after losing your child that way.

It was funny to watch the camera man from the local station who interviewed me before try to position himself at a few different angles to hopefully catch some wild action shots of Pam and I boxing or something. He kept having to put the camera down on the ground and pick it back up again as it was heavy on his poor vulture shoulder. Eventually he packed up and left. Aren't these people a stitch?

I thought Pam was kind of sad. She gave me a brochure for her organization called M.O.M.M.Y., Inc. (Mothers of Murdered & Missing Youngsters). She told me that they're hoping to become a tax exempt organization this year. I read the brochure and it says they're a non-profit organization. I wonder how they get financing, what they have done and how they do their accounting. The brochure had typos in it and when I went online to look her organization up, I couldn't find anything except organizations with similar names.

Soon enough it was show time. What a great crowd they were. Totally into it. They stayed with it the whole time. I got groped by teenaged girls any time I got near the edge of the stage. I guess I am some kind of boy scout because I didn't think girls that age acted like that. Hey, young girls grope middle-aged men all the time, where have you been?! Supafuzz was really cool. Now there's a band who can play. Finally, a band who knows what a rhythm section is supposed to do.

There ended up being a good sized crowd and that meant a lot as all the local ticket vendors had received threats and didn't sell many advance tickets to the show. One way or the other, people showed up.

I talked to two guys after the show from West Memphis, AR who had gone to school with Damien. I asked what their impression was of Damien and what they thought about what happened to him. They said he didn't kill anyone, that he was just another kid on the block who hung out in basements listening to music with the rest of them. They added that Chief Inspector Gary Gitchell has made quite a reputation for himself from this case. Interesting. I talked to another guy who said he lived two doors down from Jason Baldwin. I asked him what he thought of the whole thing and he basically said that Jason was cool and the whole thing was bullshit. It's interesting to hear these opinions. It's not like these people ever get interviewed, especially not in a case like this, they only get ridiculed. I asked a few people about Pam Hobbs and no one had anything but mean things to say. I don't know what to believe. It's all talk, isn't it? I don't even want to imagine what they say about me.

Lorri Davis was at the show. She's very happy about what we're doing. She thanked us and started crying a little. She gave me some books of Damien's. They had been in his cell for a while. He can't have much stuff in there. He reads a book and has to get it out of his cell before he can have another one. She started crying again when she left. I can't imagine what it's like to be married to someone who's in prison. If I had a girlfriend and missed her while I was out here, it would be too hard. I have found it's better to be single if you live on the road, long distance relationships don't seem to work.

I like that town a lot but I was happy when we pulled out of there. So now, we're in Atlanta and the mighty Supafuzz is playing with us again. I did an interview with a fellow at a local station earlier and he asked me when the *Rise Above* record was going to come out! There's a Sanctuary Records rep. who lives and works in this town coming to the show tonight. I will ask him what his job is, or what he thinks his job is. This is the shit I'm talking about. How would you deal with this guy? Would you be cool? Would you ask him why the DJ who is inclined to talk about the record and potentially play tracks from it, is asking me when the record's coming out when it's been out for about eight months?! Can you see why someone would want to go to a record company office and put their foot up someone's ass? You're out here, working hard and that's the back up you get? What a drag to have to deal with some of the people in this crappy business. A little while ago, I did an interview with a guy in Florida named Drew and he was all over the record, the tour, the whole thing. Really cool guy. Earlier this morning I did an interview with Bubba the Love Sponge down in Florida. He's very cool and is very behind what we're doing. He and I have been pals for over six years now. He allowed me to talk about the whole thing and said he'd keep telling his listeners about the shows we have coming up in Florida. He's always been cool like that. It's great that no matter how many people in this business are lame, there's a few who come through, guys like Bubba who give you the time of day and a chance. It keeps the rivets from popping. It's a good thing I fear incarceration and litigation. If I didn't, I'd be broke and in jail but the string of ears used as evidence against me in court would make for good conversation.

I tried that site address Shawn Wheeler's friend gave me and got nothing. (Found out later there's a website http://pub17.ezboard. com/bmurderincorporated where you can read about what an idiot I am and that I talk too much. The chatroom posts were very concerned about whether I am affiliated with the WM3.org people. One posting said that I am not concerned with Jessie Misskelley, only with Damien and Jason. There was also concern that I think DNA evidence is a panacea. I don't understand what these people are afraid of with this DNA testing. If they think the boys are guilty, then you can't even be made to care about DNA testing, right? At one point, I said something like this wouldn't happen in LA and someone came back with you bet it would. The *LA Times* would run an article like the *West Memphis Commercial Appeal* did about finding human heads underneath Damien Echols bed without verifying it? Bet they wouldn't! *The New York Times*? Doubtful. Some serious intellect-flexing going on here! Check out this website so you can get all sides of the story.)

06-06-03 Tampa FL: 6:11 p.m. On the bus outside the venue. Mike and I did deadlifts in the parking lot earlier today. It's hot and intense out here, wanted to puke after I was done. Last night was another good show. A lot of people showed up and they were into it. They sure do drink a lot of alcohol. After the show I signed all the stuff people brought up and so many of them were stewed.

A little while ago, I was standing outside reading and a police officer rolled up and we got to talking. He was familiar with the case and said there were real basic procedural errors made. He said "don't move the body" is Crime Scene 101 common sense and he was shocked that they had even touched the bodies before forensics could get there. He thinks the boys were railroaded and added that he was glad about what we were doing. It's only an opinion but it was interesting coming from a cop.

06-07-03 Boynton Bch. FL: 5:40 p.m. Last night was another good show. Nothing to note past we played well and the audience was great. I talked to some of the opening band guys and they were really cool and donated the profits from their merchandise sales to the WM3. That's been happening a lot on this tour. Some of the bands donated their merch. money and some have even donated their pay. Very cool and it keeps the morale up around here. After the show last night there were again, a lot of drunk people wandering around near the bus. Everyone was cool though. One guy did that thing where he has to keep shaking your hand after everything he says. He must have shook my hand a dozen times. Everyone was laughing about it. He kept telling me that we would see each other again. I kept saying ok and he kept shaking my hand. That drunk thing, just wandering around fucked up. I think it would take a lot of trust to be that out of control and walk around and not fear getting taken advantage of. Perhaps I'm too paranoid but I reckon it's a disadvantaged position to be in. You can't protect yourself, you can't protect your woman, you're just something for a cop to drag to jail. Drunks are dangerous and boring. Commandment #11: THOU SHALT NOT BORE.

I was wondering if there would be any mental changes derived by playing these songs nightly. It definitely makes the workouts better, which makes the shows better. It's such zero bullshit music. It's amazing to me that the songs don't sound dated at all. It's not like they sound "80's" or anything and it's not like they can't hang with what is seen as intense music today. Quite the opposite is true. You wonder why no one has been able to come close to the Black Flag songs. And no one has if you think about it. There's a lot of bands who have tried to write some go crazy shit and there's been a lot of good songs but nothing does it like Black Flag. It's pretty incredible when you think about it. I wonder what Greg's take on the songs are. I wonder if he just thinks they're some songs he wrote and it was just a band he had or if he sees that it's some of the most essential music ever written.

06-08-03 Orlando FL: 11:27 p.m. In a hotel room. The last of a night off. I wish we had played tonight instead. I put in a six and a quarter mile run earlier and that pounded me pretty hard but I liked it.

I watched a show on television tonight about forced confessions. Interesting viewing considering the nature of Jessie Misskelley's "confession." One of the cases discussed on the show was the Stephanie Crowe murder case.

On the morning of January 21st, 1998 in North Escondido, California, a 12 year-old girl named Stephanie Crowe was found in her bedroom dead. She had been stabbed nine times. A few weeks later, the police fingered her 14 year-old brother Michael and two of his friends as the killers, saying that the motive was jealousy and a "morbid fascination with violent role-playing video games." They grilled these kids really hard. The documentary showed some of the footage of Michael being interrogated. He's exhausted, they had kept him up for hours, and eventually he just kind of caves in and tells them what they want to hear. They had him write a letter to his dead sister and in it he tells her that the police are trying to make him say that he killed her and he doesn't know why. How insane would it be to write a letter to your murdered sister? So, they have their killer—a 14 year-old brother from down the hall. Convenient. If you push hard enough you can get the square peg in the round hole. The whole thing stinks. Finally justice prevailed when they brought in a man named Richard Raymond Tuite who had been seen in the neighborhood looking in windows near the time of the murder. He had Stephanie Crowe's blood on his shirt. Charges against Michael and his friends were dropped. Next time someone says "the guy confessed," don't think that the whole thing is necessarily over and done with. Nothing like a coerced confession is there?

I remember how those pricks treated me while I was being questioned about Joe Cole's murder. They made a reference to "strawberries," a street term for the intense crack whores that worked in the alley behind the house we were living in. "The neighbors say they've seen strawberries entering your house on numerous occasions. So, we know that. Do you think that any of them could have told these guys to rob you?" Huh?! I told them that there were never any whores in the house and that I knew they were full of shit. I them asked which neighbor said that. Let's go to their house right now. Of course the fuckers had no answer. Then they asked me about the dealer they knew we were getting our drugs from. Yeah, right. I asked them what this drug dealer's name was. "Uhh, Greg." "Greg?!," I shot back. "Greg?! Greg the drug dealer?! Let's go talk to Greg the drug dealer! Let's go right now." They backed off. Then I went off on them. I told them they were full of shit and they were wasting time and asked them if any of the neighbors had told them about the human sacrifices we were having in the backyard because when we were cooking the bodies, all the neighbors came over with their plates. Then they backed off even more. I had nothing to hide and they knew it but still they tried their bullshit. At one point, one of them said, "By the end of this, we'll know more about you than you do." I told them to look up Black Flag in their files and check out all the times we told Chief Darrel Gates to go fuck himself and how we called the cops on their bullshit so many times it's not even funny and about all the corny stakeouts they used to do at SST and I promised to get them some 'Police Story' stickers that I had in a box somewhere so they could know even more. I never got a chance to give them the stickers and it's a damn shame, too. Ever seen one of those? Don't ask. You fucking cops wonder why people don't like you? Don't.

Watched Condoleezza Rice on *Meet the Press* talking pure bullshit spin trying to justify the White House's actions in Iraq even though they haven't found a damn thing. You fuckers better find something. You wonder why some people hate your guts? I don't wonder why some hate mine. Fuck you. Fuck your boss. What a bunch of cowards you all turned out to be. Sending a bunch of soldiers out into that shit hole to get shot up for what? She won't answer anything without giving herself a backdoor to get herself and her president out. It's incredible to listen to a forward rolling, propagandist spin. She's so good at it. They better find those weapons of mass destruction or they better plant some. What's going to happen to Amerika with another four years of these monsters?

I'm so happy about what we're doing for the WM3. It's great working every day for the welfare of someone else. It's like a vacation from myself. I can't wait to hit stage here tomorrow night.

06-09-03 Orlando FL: 11:25 p.m. Another show at the House of Blues, the venue I always tell myself never again when I walk out of it. I thought we played really well. They have good monitors and we could hear ourselves at least. A lot of the places on this tour will have less than perfect sound and lights. We're at the bottom of the food chain. You adjust. You remember the way it sounded many years ago when you were on your way up. It sounds about the same on your way down. If you can hang with that, you'll be alright. If you have an ego trip about it, you'll kick your own ass every night. I'm just happy to still be able to play every night after so many years. I'm not all that picky about where it happens. Great audience tonight. They're very friendly here. We got in a good workout on the loading dock. The heat was brutal and the smell of the dumpsters wasn't all that fantastic but we stuck it out.

There's never any drama at a House of Blues show. It's a very antiseptic environment. When you have performed at several of them as I have, you see that they bought all the art at once and they're all set up the same and it's all very corporate and well thought out. I know I take an extreme stance on things sometimes but I have always had a problem with the House of Blues because of the art work on the walls and the corny sheet metal siding all over the outside. It's racist to me. It's embarrassing to be in there sometimes. It's always white people at the soundboard and lights and obsequious non-whites running around doing everything else. If you looked at the art and didn't know better, you would think that the art form of the Afrikan Amerikan is to scrawl like an eight year-old in a very affected manner. I say something about it every time I am up on one of their stages. I don't think I'll be in a HOB again. I don't think I'll be in a lot of these places again. I think we're headed for the next smaller venue. I can see the dim lights of Obscurity up ahead.

06-10-03 Savannah GA: 8:00 p.m. I'm across the street from the hotel on this night off. I am looking at the river and the huge boats passing by. All the sidewalks around here have these amazing shade trees. It was too hot to go out and do much of anything today. I ran six miles in the gym and it didn't feel like it was enough but knowing I have a leg workout and six shows straight starting tomorrow night, it was enough. The South is so beautiful. The smell of the trees and the night air are perfect. It reminds me of summer nights in DC. Summer can be pretty oppressive with the heat and moisture but I like it. That kind of weather makes for good work. It boils your brain and keeps you from sleeping much and that always makes things interesting, for awhile at least.

06-11-03 Charlotte NC: 6:53 p.m. On the bus in the parking lot. Great to be done with the day off. That run I did yesterday had me pretty sore today but I'm feeling better now. We've been doing work-outs almost every day in the heat and it takes it out of you but it's a great way to train hard. I have to do it to get through what's coming up. Having other people in the crew to workout with is a plus, it always seems that someone is on the bench doing something.

Late aftershow wrap up: That was a good time. I always have a good time in this place. I always get letters when we are going to play here, people don't like the place much because I guess the sound isn't all that good or the hall doesn't sound all that good. I think it sounds good enough and the audience is always into it. Played hard and really got off on the music.

The aftershow drunk-a-thon was not to be missed. What a treat! There were the drunk skinheads lurking around and there were the two drunk women who no matter how polite you are, only think of themselves and don't leave you alone even when you're trying to sign someone's something. Finally some guy, (her pimp?!), brought one of them over and told me to look at her breasts, "They're real, Henry." She said something like here look at these and as she was taking her top off I turned away, signed someone's CD, shook their hand and walked to the bus without looking back. Drunks are such a bore. It's a Wednesday night and there they are getting loaded. What are these people thinking? One guy told me that this is the last show he gets to see before he has to go back to prison for another year or something. How would you be able to do anything with that hanging over your head?

06-12-03 Washington DC: 11:53 p.m. On the bus and leaving town. Tonight was great. We got to the venue in the afternoon. Neil Fallon from Clutch came down to soundcheck and sang 'American Waste' so he could do it with us in the encore. Q and Not U, the opening band came in and soundchecked and sounded great. I listen to their records a lot and was happy to have them on the bill. The two albums they have out right now are *No Kill No Beep Beep* and *Different Damage*. There's a cool single as well. I think they're a great band. I hardly ever get to see the bands I want to so this is a treat. Their albums are on Dischord. I think Dischord is putting out some of their best stuff ever now. The new El Guapo record *Fake French* is great, even better than their last one *Super/System* which I thought was brilliant. Also, the band The Black Eyes just put out their first album on Dischord and it's my favorite record of the year so far. I saw them here last summer and they were awesome. Someone wrote me a little while ago and told me we were playing opposite the Black Eyes tonight and she asked which show she should go to. I told her I would go see the Black Eyes.

Ian came down to the venue later on. He gave me a copy of the Minor Threat First Demo single that just came out. There's a picture of me with the band on the back cover and another picture of me with the band from the recording sessions on the inside. I was lucky to have been there. I sang on a couple of songs in that session. I get to be on a Minor Threat record? Pretty cool. Those were some great times. Some serious music history was made during that time. I was lucky to have been there and lucky to know Ian as long as I have. He's the greatest living person I know. He gets more impressive as he goes, too. Sometimes when I'm in the old neighborhood, I walk down the alley behind his mother's house and stand in the spot where I met him in 1975 or something. There's been a lot of great periods of music in DC and I think it's the start of another one with these new bands putting out such amazing records. It was incredible to be in the music scene back then. Getting to see the first ever Minor Threat and Teen Idles shows—are you kidding?! Early Bad Brains, the Enzymes, the Untouchables—what great shows! Watching the Bad Brains practice in Nathan Strajcek's basement on the Teen Idles gear? Teen Idles band practice? Minor Threat practice in Lyle Preslar's basement? Beyond cool. I was lucky. The one thing I did get right in those days was knowing that these were good times and there was not a second to be taken for granted. It was also cool seeing our local bands open for national and international touring acts and either hang in there with them or blow them offstage. Minor Threat wiping the stage with the Damned was a high point. The boxset that Dischord put out a while ago gives you a pretty good overview of the bands and gives you an indication of what was happening. There's also a cool picture book worth checking out called *Banned in DC* that has a lot of the great Susie Josephson and Lucian Perkins photos.

Ian and I are sitting backstage and he asks what song there is for him to sing. I have to say I was surprised. I didn't think he would be interested in getting onstage with us. I didn't even think to ask, so when he just came out with that, it totally surprised me. I thought about it for a second and said that we could walk out there together and sing 'Rise Above,' I would sing the verses and he would sing the choruses. He said ok. Whoa! I wanted to go buy a ticket myself.

Guy Picciotto came backstage to say hello, always great to see him. He's an amazing musician. Some of my favorite lyrics were written by Guy. He's another one of those guys who doesn't lose any speed as he goes. Rare.

Q and not U played and they were great, even better than their records.

It's time for us to hit it. Keith and the band go out there and start playing and people are totally into it. I watch Keith from the side of the stage. The guy never holds back. Not even at soundcheck. He was killin' it up there.

Keith came offstage after singing 'Gimmie Gimmie' and the band went into 'Rise Above' and Ian and I walked out there and picked up the mics, the place went off, like off off. It was so cool. It sounded great. That made the tour for me. After that, if I can get through all the shows in one piece, I'll be happy. To be onstage with Ian was the best.

The rest of the set was good and the place was packed out and people were totally into it. Neil Fallon totally killed 'American Waste,' people dug it. That guy's got a sledgehammer voice. Another good night in DC.

06-13-03 Norfolk VA: 11:49 p.m. That was a good crowd. Even though it rained on and off all day, the place was packed with about a thousand people when we hit stage. We played hard and I think people had a good time. After the show I met people near the bus and they were cool, the drunk girl was tiring but aren't drunks always annoying? They never get it. They just talk and talk and then repeat themselves. This girl was in classic drunk mode but thankfully she ran out of gas and wandered off. We got in a good shoulder workout and ate some good sushi across the street but past that, it was just another night on tour.

06-14-03 NYC NY: 6:17 p.m. Backstage, waiting for the thing to begin. I hung out with Harley from the Cro-Mags/Stimulators earlier today. He came by to drop off his new CD. I remember seeing the Stimulators play in this very venue in late '79 or early '80. I think they were opening for the Cramps. I drove up with HR and Earl from the Bad Brains. The Cramps were great. Lux grabbed the curtains and started swinging and they came out of the ceiling along with large hunks of plaster and dust. Part way through the show, the band had some kind of fight or problem with something and they all stormed off but soon returned and handed out roses to people in the front row. After the show, HR went backstage and I waited on the dance floor. He came out with a signed slick of the *Songs the Lord Taught Us* LP as well as one of Nick Knox's sticks and gave them to me. I still have them.

That night I bought a copy of the Stimulators single from the guitar player, Denise Mercedes. She was selling them on the stairs near the entrance. I met Harley that night. Interesting to run into him again in this place after so many years. It was good to see him. He has a kid now, he showed me some pictures. He's really into being a dad and is all about being the provider. It's good to see that guy on a steady path. Many of his friends are incarcerated or dead. Harley's been there and done that. From Sid and Nancy to violent episodes that would peel the paint off your car. He's still making music, I'm still playing that single.

I don't know why it occurs to me now but I have been thinking of this a lot. There's a very ambitious ad campaign in print and on television to win the hearts and minds of Amerikans and sell them Humvees or Hummers as they call them. The television ad I've seen is offensive. I hate it when these idiots get me going but this one pulled my chain. It's the ad where the smirking pretty woman is driving her Hummer with a semi-industrial loop of music playing in the background. The loop has an annoying, almost taunting vibe to it like they know they're pissing you off a little but eventually you'll have to admit that this gas draining piece of shit is something you need. Whenever I see a Hummer on the street now, it just makes me mad. There's always that asshole driving it. He's on the phone and doesn't give a fuck what you think. Why drive one? To show everyone you can. There's no practical need for one of these things, it's just resource destroying bravado.

So, what, just let it be? Hell no. What about making Hummer driving a pain in the ass? Find certain traffic intersections that are easy to get away from, arm yourself with some eggs, wait until you see that single driver Hummer come rolling by—attack! And then run like hell. I think these guys would fucking kill you if they ever caught you. They have no other choice. They are genetically pre-disposed to kick your ass when you destabilize their position of dominance. Come on! It's just an egg . . . or ten! Or if you find an Hummer parked, say at night, you can always high-contrast color spray paint the side with something like "Republican Party Staff Car" "J-Lo and Ben 4-ever!!!" "USA in Iraq!" "Will Change Regime for Gas" "Save the Environment—Blow Me Up!" "I'm Thirsty" "I Heart P-Diddy!" It would be great to see Hummers all over Amerika dented, spray painted, thoroughly abused. They could re-name it "The Pariah." "Drive at your own risk!" Imagine waiting outside the car wash with eggs! You know how things are, one thing leads to another. Beer, cocaine and draft dodging lead Bush to run for president, eggs and spray paint will eventually lead to Hummer torchings, Hummer dynamiting and hopefully the discontinuance of the model altogether. Is there a gig around here I can play?

06-15-03 Boston MA: 11:53 p.m. Now that was a good time. There was no opening band. I don't understand that. What, it was a detail that was overlooked? It's like telling a band that there's no PA because no one got around to getting it. There's apathy on a lot of levels on this tour. Not from our end, of course. What the fuck, you can't expect anyone to care about this stuff as much as we do but when the promoters and the agents are giving it the mighty whatever, it's hard on the morale.

I had a disturbing incident earlier in the day. I was backstage working online on business stuff and the one and only Springa from SS Decontrol came in and started talking a mile a minute. He looked totally insane. He seemed to be talking to himself or something. Oblivious that I am working, he goes into this thing about coming out from Chicago to bury his father who never did anything more for him than chain him up in the basement. He repeated that about three times and then said he was thinking of auditioning for some kind of acting troupe that was going to tour in the summer. He went on and on, it was nuts. Finally someone from the venue came up to him and tried to throw him out because they thought he was some guy off the street. Springa asked me if he could come to the show and pulled out a few crumbled one dollar bills and said that's all the money he had. I nodded to the guy to ok it and told Springa I would see him later. He went on about some other spacey shit and then the guy said he had to leave and he just shuffled out. I never saw him again. The backstage manager told me that earlier Springa had come up to him and told him that I said it was alright for him to have a ticket and if he didn't get one, "Henry was going to be very angry." This is long before I saw him. The last time I saw Springa was years ago in Chicago and he came barreling backstage walking around the room, sweating like he was on something, going off on some insane tangent. I don't know what's up with the guy. We used to play with his band and they were good.

Anyway, the show was good and the audience was fantastic. I think it did ok even though WBCN didn't help out at all. I guess they play only lame music now and can't play the great stuff because it might upset the listeners.

On our website, there's one of those post your message boards and someone posted that when I was here on the talking tour a few months ago, I took young boys to the back of the bus, luring them in with jazz music. Huh? Who writes this stuff? This is worse writing than in *CMJ*! I get these letters, hey man what's this asshole saying about you and little boys?! I have to actually sit there and answer this shit. No, I wasn't molesting little boys that night. Little boy molesting is only on Sunday nights. Oh fuck it, let's go to Philadelphia and rock the fuck out.

06-16-03 Philadelphia PA: 11:44 Back on the bus. Another good night in Philadelphia. I was here in the same venue a few months ago on the talking tour. This place, the Theater for Living Arts always has it together, good lights, good sound. It's a great place to play. The audience was into it from the start. It's so cool to see Keith up there singing this stuff. People are loving it. Tonight was the 6th show in a row and it felt fine. The opening band was really cool, the singer was a guy in drag, they played all covers as far as I could tell. They covered an Eno song, that's class. At one point, he took his wig off and finished the set without it, it was great. The last time I was here, I talked to a dominatrix and she told me what an overwhelming rush it was to fist a man. Doesn't that make you want to do it too? It's now at the top of my to-do list. I've met several doms. Some of them have offered me their services. I can't muster the interest. Tie me up and fuck with me and I'll just "go with the experience." Hello, have a life? I would rather work at fucking McDonalds than tie someone up and beat them—talk about boring. Piss on me! No, me! No, me!! the men cried out, as they waved their thick stacks of twenties.

06-17-03 Cleveland OH: 11:31 p.m. A night off in Cleveland. Got in a good 6.25+ mile run in a few hours ago. Been watching the news for some hours now. I watched Joe Scarborough on MSNBC and at the beginning of his show, there's shots of him in some kind of military uniform. I wrote him at his e-mail address, Joe@MSNBC.com, and asked him what branch of the Military he was in. I told him that I looked at a few website biographies on him and there's no information as to his involvement in the Military. If he wasn't in the Military, isn't the imagery he puts forth a bit misleading? I got this reply back almost immediately:

Thanks for dropping us a line...The show gets a ton of e-mail and we can't always send you a personal reply (sometimes we do though!) but we read all of it so keep your comments and sugges-tions coming in...we want your input! In the meantime, check out our website http://www.joe.msnbc.com and sign up for our free daily newsletter for all the latest news and guest lineup for each night's show!

Maybe I'll get an answer to my question someday.

I did an interview with a guy named Waleed Rashidi from *Alternative Press* today. He tried to turn the thing we are doing out here into some kind of us versus Greg Ginn thing. *AP* has a long record of crap writing and writers who lie and this just another exam-ple. I told him the straight facts, but who knows what he'll write. *Alternative Press* is no place to expect real writing. Still, I fielded his questions. His main thrust seemed to be all about Greg's upcoming Black Flag show and what he has been saying about what we're doing and what's my response to this and to that. Wow, how dramatic. I told Waleed that since he was attempting to drag the interview down into that shit talk thing, my respect for him was rapidly evaporating. He backtracked and said that he was sorry or something. I told him I was sorry for him. He asked me, "How are you characterizing these shows? Are you calling it Black Flag?" I told him that we were calling it exactly what it is: The Rollins Band playing the songs of Black Flag with Keith Morris as a guest singer. That is what it is. I also told him that every night, Keith tells the crowd, "We are the Rollins Band, my name is Keith." As always, I am honest with these fuckers. I told him that being in a band with Greg Ginn was like being in a band with Ornette Coleman. Greg is easily a genius. There is nothing like Greg's playing anywhere. In my opinion, he is the one of the most amazing guitar players ever, full stop. What a sorry excuse for a journalist. I guess you can't really attach that moniker on a writer for a corny magazine like *Alternative Press*. You can't match me on any level, bitch. Next time bring me someone with an intellect.

What Greg Ginn does with Black Flag, the name, the band, what-ever—it's his to do. I was the 4th singer in the band. I never considered myself much of a member—just the 4th singer. Whenever people tell me how much they like the songs, I tell them the same thing, that's it's Greg Ginn and Chuck Dukowski's work they're talking about because that's exactly what it is. I hope his show at the Palladium is good. I can't think it's going to be easy to pull off. I think it's a heavy thing to play under the name Black Flag. You're messing with a serious piece of history there. I wouldn't touch it with a ten foot pole. It's like Page and Plant going out and calling it Led Zeppelin. Those are big shoes to fill and Greg built the shoes! I could never be part of that thing. I can't think of anything more depressing. An intense letter came in tonight:

Henry -

I wanted to give you your props on the West Memphis Three show. Kudos to you for keeping the Flag name alive in the best possible way, by treating the songs and your performances with total respect! The Amoeba show was incredible and the Glass House show was even better. The Glass House show was as good if not better than some of the Flag shows I saw! It was absolutely inspiring. You rocked the house so completely and convincingly.

The reason I bring this up at this moment is that I just saw Greg Ginn play Flag songs and it was the polar opposite of your show. Ginn and company were HORRIBLE. Atrocious. Whereas your band was tight as hell and you delivered the tunes with precision and all of their original fire and emotion, Ginn's band was sloppy, his singing lousy, and the show came off like a bad joke. It was embarrassing. To make matters worse, this girl ran up to grab the mic during "Gimmie, Gimmie, Gimmie" and he kind of slapped her, openhanded, in the face. What was he afraid of? That she'd sing better than him? No doubt she would have. His whole performance, or lack thereof, was like a huge slap in all of our faces. Disgusting. He is really doing Black Flag's legacy a huge disservice.

Which brings me to his "First Four Years", or should I say "Cat Flag" show in September. This is a terribly ill-conceived function. I feel bad for Keith doing this thing. I guess cats are a good cause (though it's probable only his cats will reap the rewards), but I'm personally a little more concerned about my fellow human beings. Speaking of, he should do a benefit for all the musicians he has neglected to pay royalties to from the SST catalog over the years. Now that's a benefit I can get behind. I had so much admiration for him in the old days when the SST thing was collective. Everyone broke their back for the label and to see him disrespect so many of my heroes sickens me. He is just a one man show now, and a bad one at that. Thank you again for doing the Flag songs right.

A lot of drama. I am on the road playing songs of two of the great masters of music, Greg Ginn and Chuck Dukowski. The resulting rabble is not of great concern to me considering the reason we're out here doing this show 5-6 nights a week.

06-18-03 Cleveland OH: 11:31 p.m. On the bus. No opening band again tonight. Luckily a guy from a band called Disengage turned up around soundcheck to talk to Keith. They met at South by Southwest. Keith found out that there was no opening band so he asked Disengage man if they wanted to play. The band members all got off work, ran over to the venue with their gear and played. They were good. I don't understand this no opening band thing. It's like no one's looking out on this tour. I know it's not coming from our camp. We always tell the promoter to put on whoever he thinks will help out the bill the most. I don't know where the fuck up is coming from. So many of these venues are Clear Channel, which means they don't really care about the acts, they just want to have everything. It's like when you're on Sanctuary Records, they aren't a label really, they're just a company that buys catalog and puts out records of already established bands and reaps the rewards but it's not like they really get into the bands. Clear Channel will soon have almost every venue in Amerika and you can tell their momma's don't dance and their daddy's don't rock and roll.

We had a great time playing. This crowd never disappoints and the Odeon is a great venue. I was here a few months ago with the talking show and that was cool too.

06-19-03 Columbus OH: 11:54 p.m. Another show with no opening bands. Thankfully Disengage happened to call the venue and ask what the opening slot situation was and found out there wasn't one so they drove over from Cleveland and opened the show. This kind of thing used to insult me but I know it's nothing personal, they're just businessmen. It's the Clear Channel way.

Anyway, the Disengage boys were good again and people liked them. They finished their set with 'Damaged II,' what a song! The backstage at the Newport is at an all time low. The bathroom door is broken, the whole area is filthy. It's interesting that so many of these venues have such demolished backstages. Isn't it the bands that bring people into the venue? I wonder what these places will be like a few years from now? Sometimes it feels like the owners go the extra mile to show their contempt for the bands. Oh, you're playing our venue? Fuck you. Why bother? Isn't it easier just being cool to people? Doesn't matter, it's not as if they're your friends but it would be better if they were a bit more professional.

The sound in the place is hard to deal with. It's an echoing racket onstage and if you're not careful, you start singing along with the slap back bouncing off the wall and you're way off. Still, it was a good time. It's always a great audience here.

06-20-03 Detroit MI: 5:19 p.m. In an Amerikan ghetto. I was told that this was a tough neighborhood. I got several letters from people asking why we are playing Harpo's instead of the St. Andrews Hall. Seeing that this show is unlikely to sell out either venue, we went with this one because they offered more money and money is what we need to make on this tour. A man was killed here awhile ago, after a show I think. I don't know much about it but I got a lot of mail on the topic. It seems that the venue is in a bad neighborhood. Hello? Isn't Detroit a bad neighborhood? I'm not putting the place down but you can't be here and think you're somewhere else. For that matter, Amerika is a bad neighborhood.

Soon after four, soundcheck was done. I went outside to set up the weights and met three heavily tattooed men who told me they were going to be hanging out all afternoon and asked me who should they give ticket money to since they weren't going to be buying tickets to get in. I told them they should just go get tickets like anyone else. They told me that they don't buy tickets and they don't stand in line and that was that. Well ok! We get the same guarantee no matter how many people show up so it's not interesting to me to get into it with three skinheads about anything. As soon as I met them they started in with the nonstop questions just to be talking. I knew how all this was going to end. I've been there so many times. Let's see, they'll hang out all afternoon and drink steadily until show time when they will be very drunk and in that silent/violent phase. After the show, they will have found some bone to pick with me as I will have somehow offended them and there will be some bullshit drama to deal with.

I set up the rack and got in four sets of squats and that felt good even though I know that my legs will be feeling like they were caned in forty-eight hours. These guys talked to me almost the whole time I was working out. They started drinking and switched into lurk mode. All this shit takes me back. This was part and parcel Black Flag pre-show antics. The local hard heads hanging out and getting loaded, their mood getting darker as the sun set. I think tonight will be one of those nights with many slow talking drunks who take great offense to just about everything. If I had a dollar for every time I've had to deal with that confused, fucked up, angry drunk who needs help being lead out of his own mind like a lost child, I'd own this venue.

If you are a drunk, then I am talking to you—you fucking waste of my time. You are fucked up and thinking 65% slower than your usual entry-level pedestrian moronic mode. You think that everything is normal and you wonder why someone like me gets impatient when you launch into the third slurred version of your rambling story that you think is so interesting and something I can't live without hearing. You get into that "Hey, what's YOUR problem?" thing. It's such a fucking boring story. Fuck you. Are we clear? Has anyone cut the crap and picked up something blunt and hit you in the face with it? They should.

Post show on the bus: That was one for the books. One of the opening bands singers told the crowd that they were going to play a Misfits song and if the audience yelled really loud, I would come out and sing it with them. Sure, that's going to happen. They played a fair version of either '20 Eyes' or 'Skulls,' I forget.

Finally it's time to play and Keith and the lads clamber onto the stage and set it off to great fanfare. I'm standing on the side, near the load in door. Large, drunken men are coming in and out like it's a public building. I'm getting ready to go out there and they want to talk and shake my hand and they're not all that happy when I wave them off as I focus myself for a set that will at the least be all uphill due to the intense heat and humidity that's coming from the stage in hot, wet blasts. This one's going to hurt. I've done so many of these shows where a few songs in, you know it's going to be brutal. I'm getting ready to hit it but the drunks are all over the place and they want to hang out and socialize. It's hard for me to be around people who are not intense and professional when it's time to do a show. If you're not part of the production you have no business anywhere near the backstage area. One of the hang out all day guys whose eyes are almost shut he's so fucked up, walks up and proceeds to the stage. I go to the guy with "staff" on his shirt and tell him to move that guy and I am told that he's one of the stage security guys. I guess the guy forgot his duties because he soon wandered off and re-appeared with two drunk girls and staggered off.

Keith finishes his set and I hit stage. It's going to be one of those nights. The sound is all over the place and it's hot as hell. This is why you train and focus. This is why you don't get drunk. This is why you don't fuck around. This is why you don't waste time talking to fucked up losers.

Played hard and it hurt but I'm in shape for it. There's only these shows and the pain that comes with them. That's all I need to know. The audience was great and totally into it.

We went offstage and were coming up with songs for the encore when one of the all day drinker guys stumbles into the room and sticks his hand out for me to shake. I kind of shake his hand but I'm thinking more about the bottle of water in my hand, the fact that I'm out of breath and that we still have five songs to deliver. He starts complaining that all he wants to do is shake my hand and what's my problem? Funny he should ask that. My problem is that there's a drunk piece of shit backstage who wants to talk to me while we are still playing a show and he's worse than the most nagging girlfriend you've ever had. Why is it that so many of you tough guys get drunk and then act like such bitches? You should work on that or take it on the road and be a group of needy alcoholics who get their asses kicked instead of just going home and knocking your moron girlfriends around. Please don't breed.

We finished the encore and it was a great time. I remembered to tell them that the last ever Black Flag show was played in Detroit in 1986. I went back to the dressing room and put a towel on the floor and kind of fell on it. My legs were shot from the show and the leg workout.

After awhile I got it together and dressed and walked out towards the bus and encountered all the post-show people. I signed all their stuff and did photos until they were all gone. Very cool people at these shows. Homemade WM3 shirts, people who drove hours to the show, the real thing. It's great that we're making a difference out here and people are digging it. Makes it all worth it. I met up with one of the all day drinking guys, he invited me to come over and . . . . have a drink! I had to pass but thanked him. Now we roll to Chicago. Hopefully people will show up. We asked to get an interview on Mancow's morning show. Mancow is a very popular radio personality in Chicago but he wasn't interested so I got a very short interview with someone else at the station and she told me that she sees me all the time on MTV, I think she meant VH-1, but I didn't bother to correct her because by golly, I just don't care. Let's go to Chicago and see if anyone wants to see two old men sing a lot of old songs.

06-21-03 Chicago IL: 11:29 p.m. On the bus. It was a good show and the audience was into it. This tour is proving to be a low priority with the promoters though. Rarely is there an opening band and when there is, it's just whoever they could get for cheap. Tonight, no opening band. It's Chicago! This place is crawling with bands who would have loved to play. You can't make one phone call? I know, it's business and it doesn't bother me. I'm here to play. The venue is going to pay us the same price no matter what they do so I guess some of them want to do as little as possible. We're on a mission. I'm not in prison. Whoever shows up, shows up and they get what they get. It's why I am very business like when I meet people after the shows. I would feel lame for taking any credit for the songs they tell me they enjoyed hearing so much that night or luxuriating in the praise they bestow upon me. I had nothing to do with the creation of the songs. My bandmates and I are just taking them out for a walk around the world to help out some guys who got the short end of the stick. I truly wish I didn't have to go to such extreme measures to help Damien, Jason and Jessie get a fair day in court but this is what we're doing because the powers that be are pissing me off and they're not getting away with it on my watch.

Doing this tour makes me see even more clearly than before, how weak a lot of the people in the music industry are. We have been watching for some reason, a top 100 songs of all time thing on VH1 over the last two days. It always seems to be on. I watch *Rolling Stone* and *Spin* "music journalists" talk about some of these songs. Listening to the *Spin* moron talk about Public Enemy with her mindless up-speak is hard to take. To paraphrase: "Public Enemy were really good? Because they had a social consciousness that other rap acts didn't have?" Are you asking me or are you telling me, you dunce? The idiot from *Rolling Stone,* the spore-like barely male sub-human extolling the virtues of the lamest music in his smiley, dreamy way of speaking caused me to have a revelation. Yes, you weakened bitch! Now I know. Now that I've had a chance to see what these people look and talk like, I see why shitty records get five-star reviews. Now I see that there's nothing to be concerned with when they open their mouths or write. One less to thing to concern myself with.

Back to the show. It was a major change from the night before where it was a hot festival of pain. Tonight was a good one. I never know what to expect with this music, what people will think. Besides the one guy who felt the need to pat me on the head every few songs like I was his dog, it was a good night. After the show some of the crew guys said they were expecting me to clip the guy in the face but reckoned the reach would have been awkward with the distance of the stage to the barricade. It did occur to me. I figured the guy meant no harm and he did stop when I told him to. So it wasn't an eventful night as far as drama but another good night on the road and off we go to Milwaukee.

06-22-03 Milwaukee WI: 11:44 p.m. Post show and post hang out with the people at the bus. I was here a few months ago on the talking tour. One drunk girl had to be hauled away by security when I was signing stuff out in the cold. I think my grandmother lives here. I don't know if she's alive though. Soundcheck in this place is always bad because it's nothing but echo and sound knocking around but it tightens up pretty good when people show up. I didn't think anyone would care about this show here but the place looked great when we got out there. People really dig on Keith. Nothing to remark on about the show, 5th in a row and it felt fine. It's such a blast playing these songs.

06-23-03 Minneapolis MN: 11:19 p.m. A night off. A waste of time. It would have been better to have played. I guess it's good to give the body a rest seeing how hard it was to get out my bunk today. It all hurt.

Watched a lot of news today and it was good to see *The Nation's* editor, Katrina vanden Heuvel, knock heads with Pat Buchanan about the Affirmative Action rankling going on with Michigan University and the Supreme Court. I've seen her on a few different shows. The male host always tries to shut her down because she comes at them so fast and hard—like Ariana Huffington without the comfort layer. I have always been impressed by anyone who can articulate themselves on live TV like that. It's not easy to do. She's a Princeton graduate, so

I guess she's got some ammo up there. Buchanan and other soft white loaves say that to give a handful of non-whites a shot at a good education is a bad idea and makes the Civil Rights Movement a farce and that it discriminates against whites and all that other shit that keeps everything the way it is year after maddening year. She pointed out that it was a version of Affirmative Action that got George W. Bush into Yale. BAM! It's alright when it's in the white male country club. Perhaps some aspects of Affirmative Action are slightly out of skew with the Constitution—so what? Corny whites would say that to let someone into a university to give the student body more racial diversity and get Amerikaaners on a more level playing field is in itself racist. Let's get the playing field level and watch the white right freak the fuck out! Pat Buchanan and his corny ilk couldn't handle racial equality. Maybe they're afraid their maids and gardeners might possibly end up being their contemporaries. Certain aspects of this country are so repellent and cowardly and the people who back it are so lame and see-through. I hate pseudo-intellectuals. Book smart but not road tested. What's knowledge without mileage? It's sterility with attitude. There's aspects of Affirmative Action that have drawbacks, of course, like the smart black guy who's seen as "pretty smart for a black guy." There's no one cure, but you have to want to make things better and the resistance to that by some of the agencies in Amerika frustrate me. If it doesn't change, then we have failed. Everyone knows this. So come up with something, don't come up with nothing and say that everything's fine. The mistake that the Buchanan types make is that they think they're treating everyone as equal when they're just treating them like they're white. It's not equal yet. That might not be racist but it's not the way to look at it with an eye towards making things better, and if you're not going to try and make things better, fuck you.

This tour has been good for me. Moving against the grain. It's like jumping into cold water. It's something at first and then it feels like home. All the corny drama with Greg Ginn and his effeminate, bloated, weepy promoter friend Rick Van Santen, the Memphis TN drama, the apathy of the record label and the rest are just grist for my mill. It's food. It feels good. It makes me train harder. It makes me play harder. It makes everything better.

So fuck it, let's turn it up louder and do more shows in a row. Let's hit it harder and turn over more rocks and bring the cowards out and thrash 'em. More vampires to sink stakes into. Repetition as religion. Higher consciousness through harder contact is better than what doesn't kill you makes you stronger. To draw your borders via conflict and define yourself by that which you confront allows you to always know where you are and where it's at. It's why Palestine will never quit. It's why Amerika will always be attacked by cultures that define themselves in this manner. A Hezbollah warrior will die for his cause right now. What would soft drunks like Cheney and Bush do for theirs? Send you out to die for their cause right now. I'm not talking about right and wrong, just about commitment. Drinkin' and Drivin' Dick Cheney's pals are getting great business opportunities with all this war and terrorism going around. Halliburton's Kellogg Brown & Root subsidiary has made well over 600 million USD in troop services in Iraq and Afghanistan. They'll make plenty more before it's all over—if it's ever over. Smell a little like Vietnam? You bet. Isn't it intense that for some people, all these horrible events of the last couple of years are the best thing that ever happened to them? Can you imagine a man buying a new house with the money he made selling the US Government 200,000 gas masks? He'll tell you it was good business. If the companies who made the bullets, planes, tanks and other equipment used in war had to give it up for free in times of war, there wouldn't be as much fighting and if there was, the conflict would be over really fast. If Amerikans had to pay monthly for the war in Iraq, as in a bill sent to their residence, with late or non payment resulting in stiff fines, there would be no war. If a "War Tariff" were imposed on tobacco products, alcohol and fast food items at point of purchase, there would be no war. The companies would boycott, and millions of tobacco addicted, alcoholic, fast-food fanatics would storm the houses of government and shut down the whole system. What would the Pentagon do against millions of berserk-fat-bastard-drunk-chain-smoking-maniacs who can't afford their fix storming their doors and going nic-fit apeshit crazy? Cool!

Like every other human, sometimes I don't want to do any of this shit. Work hard and keep breaking myself and pushing myself brutally forward until I am a new species and for what? To die eventually. Just bugs flitting around a light bulb at night. I don't worry about death. Seneca said it's stupid to put so much thought into something that's eventual and so brief. He said that a horse dying of thirst will lick flames but will die as quickly as any other living thing dies, so why waste time thinking about it? I'm fine as long as I remember the truth that there's only the work and the application and the duty to it. What someone thinks of it is quite peripheral and totally inessential to the work itself and to let any of their puny squeaks divert the shot is to filthify what is initially pure. It is as pure as you are willing to stay true to it. Life is too short to listen to much else except the roar in your ears. That's the soundtrack. If your soundtrack happens to be all the people around you then it's your problem when you end up gutted at the end of the line.

Seven more shows in Amerika and then I am out of this obese piece of real estate for a few weeks.

06-24-03 Minneapolis MN: 11:49 p.m. On the bus. We are supposed to be hitting the road about now but I don't know when we'll be getting out of here. There's a fairly raging storm outside. Thunder and lightning is rockin' and the rain is coming down so hard on the roof you can't hear yourself think. The sky broke open about forty minutes ago and it hasn't let up at all. There were tornado warnings a little earlier.

Tonight's show was one for the books. I walked out onstage and when I grabbed my mic, it was almost too hot to pick up, heated up from the lights. A few songs in, I knew it was going to be one of those shows that you don't enjoy playing at all, you just try and get through it in one piece. The heat and the intensity of the lights was amazing. I thought I was going to pass out during 'Black Coffee.' I hung in there and made it to the end of the set somehow. I went backstage and wondered if I was going to make it through the encore. I am in shape but that one nearly broke me. We played fine though and the audience was fantastic. I have done a lot of shows with intense stage temps. This was in the top five.

After the show was over, I sat there and watched my body drain itself on the floor. I kept drinking gatorade and kept sweating out. It took me about an hour for my body to regulate its temperature. It's better now. All the training I do, all the thresholds of pain and endurance I push myself through are for nights like this one. Good thing I have been working this way, I don't know if I would have gotten through it otherwise.

06-25-03 Lincoln NE: 11:30 p.m. A day off comes to a close. We pulled in here from Minneapolis. We're hitting the road in half an hour to drive to Denver. I found a book of Kafka's letters for pretty cheap and am looking forward to reading some of the letters he wrote to see the differences between the way he was with his friends and the way he was with his stories. I have been reading Kafka on and off for many years. He's a hard nut for me to crack. I dig him, but it's hard going. I wonder about anyone who says they "understand" Kafka. I don't know if his work is to be understood as much as it's to be, I don't know, tripped on? There's so many instances in his writing that I see happen around me all the time. If you read *The Castle,* especially the newer translation by Mark Harman, there's so many insane and illogical moments, it's like those days you have when nothing seems to be right. Whenever I'm trying to find the hotel room and they have the rooms sequenced in some order that only makes sense to the hotel, #113, #114 and the exit door, my room # is 115. This happens to me all the time. This is a Kafkaesque moment. The newer translation of *The Castle* has a lot more humor and bite than the Muir translation. Kafka is a funny man. When I read a passage that makes me laugh, I can look at a picture of him and it will look totally different to me than if I just looked at it and thought of the Kafka who wrote *The Penal Colony.* If you think of him having a sense of humor, then pictures of his face reveal what looks like a man with a wicked sense of humor. I don't know, there's something in the corners of his mouth that have smart ass all over them. Or is it that I don't get out enough?

I watched a lot of news today and as it does so often now, it makes me mad. Got in a pretty good workout at the local YMCA. It would have been better if people didn't start conversations with me while I was running on the treadmill.

We are parked across the street from a small club and little by little I think I met almost everyone who was in there as they came over in groups having heard that I was sitting on the sidewalk next to the the bus. All of them were very friendly. So now we start six straight tomorrow night in Denver.

06-26-03 Denver CO: 5:10 p.m. On the bus. This town has so many homeless people. At least this neighborhood does. I first came here in 1982 and it was like this but now there seems to be more folks on the streets. Saw a drunk couple a block down from the venue almost punch each other out. Amerika is drunk and fat and stupid and easy to kill and ready to be overthrown.

11:54 p.m. Good crowd and a good show. I was surprised how many people showed up and how into it they were. Not always the friendliest or most responsive audience around but tonight they were great.

I went out front and signed all the stuff, did the pictures. The drunk factor made it a drag. I don't handle drunks well. Being polite and patient doesn't work. Unfortunately, only one thing works but I can't afford to get sued by one of these fucks so I have to be cool. I dealt with the first one who asked the same question over and over and wouldn't leave. He grabbed my hand and wouldn't let go and that kind of thing sets me off and I broke out of his hold and that was almost enough for me to fire on him but I can't be doing that kind of shit. Then there's the asshole youth who do that thing where they keep up this line of patter trying to be cute. They keep asking questions like they're teasing me but only kidding but really but only kidding and it's late and I just played and I don't understand what the upshot of this is. "Mr. Rollins, will you come to our house and bake cookies with us?" "Ok, then will you come out here on Halloween and we can go trick or treating?" There were a few of these guys and they're all about one hundred and forty pounds so you can't touch them and they make it impossible to be anything but hostile. What's the point of trying to be cool to people? I should just walk through them, get on the bus and get to the next place and do the thing that I came there to do: play the fucking show as hard as I can and leave. So finally they leave and I do all the other signing stuff including the drunk girl who had me sign her underwear on both sides. I was almost to the bus but there were a few more people and I was signing their stuff and then another drunk starts up and I realized that if I didn't walk away at that point, I would have worked out on the guy and I can't be doing shit like that. Denver has its share of fuckheads. Always has.

I wish young people weren't so weak as they seem to be these days. It's not good to generalize but so many youths are soft and already ruined. There might be a time when I'll have to move out of Amerika. I love this place but I think about moving all the time. I don't know where exactly but I get so tired of so many people living on borrowed money, cheap calories and wasted time.

06-27-03 Salt Lake City UT: 6:29 p.m. It was either the basement of DV8 or a night off so of course we took the show. Above us in the regular venue is a band called Trapt. I guess they're very big right now. We saw their video on MTV. How embarrassing. Some lyric about making a girl's fantasy a reality and then the money chorus with this bony guy saying he's headstrong and he'll take on anyone. I have a road manager you can take on. I think there's a kid half your size in Baghdad who might want a piece of you. It's that MTV music, these bands sound the same. It's not my problem.

Past midnight: Now that was a show. It's a basement. It's packed, there's no stage really and people are all over the place. It was great. It was a steamer but it was awesome. I was walking to the stage area and some guy grabbed me by the shoulder and he wouldn't let go and before I knew it, I had punched him. Oops, I did it again. Anyway, the gig was nuts, the PA was almost falling over from people banging into it. There was no air, nowhere to move, a pillar in front of me and I couldn't hear anything. You can't lose in a situation like this because all you can do is rock. Now it's quiet outside and we will be rolling for Boise soon.

06-28-03 Boise ID: 9:29 p.m. On the bus. It was an early show tonight. Boise is in the middle of some multi-day music and culture fest. We were one of many bands who played. I have to think we played for at least forty-five people today. The stand out pair were the two guys up front dressed in prison orange, complete with inmate numbers and dirt on their face I guess to show evidence of their escape to come and see us perform? I thought they weren't digging the show because they just stared at us all comatose but they were just wasted and came alive towards the end of the set.

After the show was over, I went back to the bus and the crew had put all the lawn chairs around the side and were lounging out. Hilarious. Why in hell would you ever want to leave this? You get to play music almost every night, there's plenty of weights and a squat rack in the side bay, the coffee's free and you get your own bunk. I hung outside until the sun was gone and came back in here.

06-29-03 Seattle WA: 11:29 p.m. On the bus. Earlier today I was walking from the venue to the bus and two guys walk by and one of them says hello so I say hello back. He says something about me look-ing old and then said, "Partying too hard, huh?" I don't mind being called old. I don't even mind being told I look tired and old at the same time, that's like a two-for-one sale but the party reference, I did-n't have a come back for that one. I just kind of stood there looking at the guy, he must have thought I was stoned. Actually I was con-sidering how insane it would be to just crack him one and I was pick-ing out what part of his face to punch but then I realized that wasn't cool. I signed some pieces of paper they handed me and they walked away.

We have been in this place before. It's a good venue, the Show Box. People were into it. Sometimes they are a little laid back here but they were into tonight. Played hard and no one got in our way.

I put myself in a better mood today by not watching the news. Right now, the e-mail I get from Marines in Iraq and the mail I get from wives and girlfriends who have people over there just pisses me off. I feel if I don't watch the news, I am copping out somehow. I watched the movie *Bottle Rocket* instead. I liked it a lot.

In two shows we lose Keith. I can't believe how fast this all went by. Tempe feels like a week ago. I wish Keith could be on the rest of this tour with us. People would get off on him in Europe and Australia big time! It's been great hanging out with him every day.

06-30-03 Portland OR: Late. Show over. Got in a good chest work-out today. A good workout usually means a good show. Always a great audience here. Last time I played this venue with a band was 1997, the day Timothy McVeigh was given the Death Penalty™ instead of life in prison. About four years later he was murdered. I don't like the Death Penalty™. I saw interviews with people who had lost friends and family in the Federal Building bombing after the execution, and none of them seemed all that much happier now that McVeigh was dead. I know it's impossible to not hate someone who killed 168 innocent people. I hate him. He killed people, his trial cost the Amerikan people almost fourteen million dollars. Who knows how much the Lethal Injection™ that killed him cost us. He's the worst. It's just that I don't think you can pretend to lead the world and still have sanctioned murder. I know, I want to kill the guy who kills the kid too, I just don't think it's the long range high road. The Death Penalty™ doesn't do a damn thing to the stats. Don't get me started. Disagree with me? I know where you're coming from, believe me. Richard Allen Davis, the killer of Polly Klaas, flips off her father on his way out of the court room? On some days I disagree with me too.

It's always great to go to Powell's Books which is right up the street from the venue. I found a book today called *Bits of Paradise: Twenty-one Uncollected Stories*. It's all the remaining F. Scott Fitzgerald stories that aren't in the two large volumes of his short stories. There's some stories by his wife Zelda in there as well. I knew there were some that I hadn't read. I have found so many great books in this place, going to Powell's is one of my most anticipated rituals of a tour.

The show was fun. I like the way that venue sounds and the audience was totally into it. Black Flag used to have some pretty wild shows up here. It's so cool to play these songs and have people get off on them so hard. Some of the facial expressions I see out there every night are intense. People are just going for it. People are cool to us here, we have played here twice before with this line-up and the place was packed both times. We're lucky here.

This town is like Denver in that there's a lot of homeless on the streets near the venue. They were outside all day, all over the place. Mikal Gilmore, states in his absolutely-must-read book, *Shot in the Heart* that he has a brother who's in and out of homeless shelters living here.

07-01-03 San Francisco CA: 7:01 p.m. A night at the Fillmore. One of the great venues in Amerika. I first played here 10-31-82 when it was called The Elite Club. Apparently, Bill Graham had the place for awhile and then lost it but it became the Fillmore again in 1994. I have played here many times and it's always great. I am very glad I was fortunate enough to meet Mr. Graham in 1991, shortly before he died.

Tonight Jello Biafra is going to sing with us. Yesterday, I wrote one of the staff at Alternative Tentacles and asked if Jello wanted to pick the winning raffle ticket for the guitar prize and sing 'Jealous Again' with us. She wrote back and said that he would do it. He came to soundcheck a few hours ago and sang 'Jealous Again' a couple of times. The first time he sang it, it sounded great. He asked to sing it again and on the second pass, he killed it. Amazing. He's such a great singer. So, for our last show in Amerika, we'll have some star power up there. This place is so intense. When I think of all the bands who have been on that stage, it's hard to believe that I get to be up there as well.

07-02-03 On the plane en route to Austria: 8:20 p.m. About an hour into a ten hour flight to Frankfurt and then onto Austria. We have a day off there and then we play a festival. These songs on jet lag will be a trip.

Last night was a great time. It's hard to have a bad show at the Fillmore. Six shows straight seemed ok. The real test is coming up with a run of eight straight plus the added bonus of singing all the songs that Keith isn't here to do now. It was so cool touring with him. He's off on a Circle Jerks tour starting in a couple of days. I don't know how those guys travel. I know they're going out with GBH for at least some of their shows and they are playing a lot of the same places we just played. Shows with GBH, how fucking dismal. At least Keith and company can leave after they play and get away from the sound and the hairspray. But anyway, back to last night. After the set, I came out with the box of raffle tickets and told the audience about the signed guitar that we had been raffling off and announced that Jello Biafra would come out pick the winning ticket and everyone cheered. He came out and picked the winning ticket, a fellow by the name of Mark Philips from San Clemente, CA who was actually at the show. Pretty intense when you consider there were over three thousand tickets in there and Jesse shook and shuffled those tickets for quite awhile to make sure they were really mixed up and when Jello pulled the ticket out, it was only after he shook it up as well. After he pulled the ticket and announced the winner, he talked about the Death Penalty™ and Ashcroft and Bush and the audience was really into it. Then the boys walked onstage and played 'Jealous Again.' Jello sang great and when the song was over, he dove into the crowd. I came back on and we played 'Modern Man,' 'Shock Treatment' and 'Rockaway Beach' and that was the night.

I talked to Jello after the show He said that Wesley Willis is having major health problems. They are going to release the *Wesley Willis Greatest Hits Vol. 3* CD soon and he asked if I would write some liner notes. I'll send them in from Europe. I'm sorry to hear that WW is doing so bad. He's had a hard life. He rocks like hell.

Jello also told me the latest news on the court battle he's having with the rest of the Dead Kennedys about the band's catalog and royalties. The rest of the band are suing him and from the reports I get from his newsletter and the man himself, he's getting his ass kicked. I urged him to consider letting go of the whole thing before he loses his house and his record collection. He seemed adamant about hanging in there and fighting them. I can't see the good in it. I know he has an emotional connection to the whole thing and the fact that the band are trying to gut and clean him is harsh but still I urged him to consider cutting his losses and walking away from it all. I can't see the court case all of a sudden turning in his favor. I don't know the insides of the case and for the life of me, I can't understand why the rest of the band feel so compelled to destroy the guy. What a fuckin' bunch of deadbeats they are. What have they done with themselves since the DKs broke up? There are so many weaklings in the world. Society's weak hold down the strong. The weak can't handle the strong and that's why there are lawyers. You can get cleaned out by some motherfucker suing you. You can get sold out by a weakling at almost any time. There's so much of it in the music business. You see the lamest bands perpetrating the worst shit and not only do they get away with it, they prosper. Those MTV bands are the weakest shit. So glad I'm not a part of it. It's been great playing Black Flag songs, they make you see the truth. They are the bottom line bullshit annihilating ordinance. It will be so hard to let them go at the end of the month. I wish I could keep playing them. They feel so right, it's a great place to go every night.

I am grateful that we have at least another month of shows. Last night in my bunk I thought how hard it would be at my house tonight if the tour had wrapped. What an empty night. With all the training I've been doing and the intensity of the shows, I don't know what to do with myself on a night off much less the end of a tour. I think at the end of this tour, I will set up some insane training schedules and see how hard I can push myself. It will take me a while to come down from this one.

I get so wrapped up in the music and the shows every night that I sometimes forget to think about why we're out here doing these shows. It's not that I don't care but there's a point in the day where nothing matters but the stage and the set and that's all there is in life is that night and getting through it.

07-03-03 Frankfurt Germany: 8:56 p.m. We're here for a little while longer to give the bus driver a rest. We're right near the main shopping street. I went out walking and at one point heard some voices speaking English at me. I turned and saw two guys who called out to me and I waved at them and kept moving. One of them yelled out, "I want my money back!" the tone of his voice had me running at them, measuring up the first one to see where I'm going to hit him. I get there and pull out a large wad of Euros and tell them if they want it, come and get it. They backed down and told me that they were from Ireland or Scotland and whatever. So what is it, stress? Don't know, don't care.

07-04-03 Weisen Austria: Evening. The Cardigans are playing and you can't escape the sound. The gal can sing but it's all in one key and the songs are all mid-tempo and weepy and low energy and you really wonder how they can even get it up for band practice much less a show. Can you imagine touring with drippy music like that?

Have you ever seen Lemmy smile? He has such a great "fuck this!" expression. It's exactly how I feel right now. Fuck this. Fuck lightweight music and popstars. Fuck good looking people onstage. Fuck slick lighting and bands who use backing tape. Fuck music critics and their corny writing. It's bullshit. No, fuck you. I'm right. These bands—no intellect. No chops. When you come to Europe, you can't take any of this shit seriously. I mean, come on, they buy Super Grass records.

Good show today. It was good to get the first one happening with all the extra songs. I can do it. I felt it but I was ready. Two weeks on the suffer bus. Live in your own sweat and get used to the smell of the fuckin' bog, mate.

07-05-03 Novi Sad Serbia: 3:28 p.m. We pulled out of Weisen last night with the strains of the Cardigans polluting the air. What a numbing set of music that was to endure.

We drove for awhile and crossed into Hungary and parked the bus for the night. This morning we crossed into Serbia. I looked out the window of my coffin-like bunk to see the pre-Wall fall inspection stations now standing lonely, windows broken out, walls spray painted and weeds pushing up through the pavement. The exact scene I witnessed years ago passing through Hungary had a very different appearance. When those stations were up and running—what an operation they had going. You would go in, get in line for the photo booth, pay, get your strip of photos and get back in line to hand them in and buy a visa. They staple your photo to a piece of paper with some hastily scrawled information on it and then throw it out. Welcome to Hungary. It was so cool to drive right past that place.

We drove for about an hour and arrived here where we'll be playing outside tonight. It's an old fortress. Sloping brick walls, tunnels, turrets. Sting could come here and feel the pain of the ghosts of the prisoners who died here and write songs about other people's pain.

The Eastern Block is my favorite part of Europe. The architecture, the history and especially the people. I was looking at an old woman today as she sat outside a hotel with her broom and dust pan in her right hand. She didn't even bother to put them down even though she wasn't using them. They were part of her. I looked at her hard face and tough hands. She had most likely worked too hard for way too long for way too little. She was way into grandmother age and still working. You see a lot of that out here.

Thirteen club wielding soldier cops just walked past the bus. Their uniforms were dark blue, the clubs were white. I wonder if they ever get the clubs bloody. The scenery around here is beautiful. Huge, ancient trees everywhere. The sky is clear and the weather is mild. It's hard to look at all this and think about what has gone down here. Every time someone walks by, I wonder what stories they have to tell.

My body is feeling the shows and the jet lag. The first half hour upon waking up in the dank, unmoving air, rich with the stench of the toilet chemicals, I spend making an inventory of the trifling aches and pains that plague me daily. It's small stuff, a lot of them have been with me for years, they've become old friends. An eye doctor once told me that I have shaken my head so much that I've knocked the pigment all over my eyeballs. He showed me a picture. It looked pretty cool. He said it wouldn't do anything to my sight but he had never seen that before. I have basically done that to my entire body and at this late date, it's all coming back to get me. I've been on the road since January so an aching and slightly buzzed, disoriented state is the norm. Take two aspirin, smile.

I have come to the conclusion that I don't like playing festivals anymore. I hate having to endure the music of pop bands and watch them walk around the site with their stupid outfits and entourages. It always reminds me of someone walking around in their pajamas. So much bullshit and pretense. I have also come to the conclusion that I don't like being around bands and musicians. Not all of them are bad, I don't mind being with the guys in my band but in general, band types and actors make me want to jump out a window. It's the hardest part of doing a movie. It's like when someone asks if you want to meet that model right over there and you don't because there's not one damn thing you want to know about that person. You don't care about one thing they think. That's how it is when I am around musicians, they are some of the dullest, most self-involved morons I have ever met. For me, playing is all about discipline, focus and concentration. Hard to achieve any of this in the festival setting.

I watched the festival crowd walk by the bus yesterday as they made their way to the field. I am about twice their age. We can't have much in common at this point. The ones I met yesterday were friendly, drunk and boring.

Later: It's late. What a show. What a crowd. Nuts. That was awesome. Why can't they be like that every night? Thousands of people, totally into it. I don't think I've ever done an encore at a festival before, that was a first. It's that lack of jaded seen-it-all attitude that one encounters in this part of the world that makes playing here so great. I have seen it in Russia, Poland, Czech, Slovak, Hungary, Slovenia and now here. People just go off like there's no tomorrow. Considering what they've been through, it makes sense. Such a difference from yesterday's tame, Euro-soft experience. Whoa. Is that a new genre?

07-06-03 Hungary: 0847 hrs. On the bus at the Hungarian-Austrian border. We camped out here in Hungary last night after crossing out of Serbia.

We finished the show last night and took a van ride down to the bus and dropped our stuff and then walked back up the hill to a hotel where we were promised some dinner. Someone assigned two large soldier cops to "escort" me to the hotel. Huh? These two large men got on either side of me and we started walking. They were literally squeezing me between them and grabbing my arm to steer me through the crowds walking up the hill. Anywhere they wanted to go, they just shoved people out of the way. The rest of the band were behind me and these bone heads. I asked them to cool it and told them I can walk on my own. One of them said, "It's our job," and we pushed on. As we got closer to all the different stages, it only got worse as these guys were both holding me with one hand and sweeping people out of the way with the other. I asked them again to cool it and that no one cares who I am and no one's going to bother me. They nod and keep shoving people. Part way there, they lost the members of the band and then they got lost and we're just wandering around. When a skinny girl came up to get an autograph, they nearly knocked her over. That's when I lost my temper and went off on them. They just looked at me stupidly, waited for me to finish and then we pressed on. They reminded me of K's two assistants in Kafka's *The Castle*. Finally I got to the hotel and was rid of them. The guys in the band showed up minutes later having somehow found the place on their own. We ate our crap food and wandered back down the hill to the bus. By this time the festival was packed with people. They estimated about seventy-thousand were there. We got on the bus and got out.

The afterburn of Totalitarian oppression is all over that place. I had to go up the hill right before show time and do one of those silly press conferences that Eastern European countries insist on having at the worst time, like right before you go on stage, like you have nothing else to do. Mike and I get in the van with driver guy and festival girl and we get up to the gate and they won't let us by. Cel phones are yelled into and hands wave and we are past the security who have no doubt seen this woman all day but are still compelled to use their temporary authority to oppress and be a pain in the ass. I thought we were on our way but then the soldier cops just stood in front of the van and we had to stop again. They want to search the van. We are one city block from where we got in the van and about two blocks away from where the press conference waste of time is being perpetrated and they want to search the van. Mike and I just get out and walk by them leaving these people to their bullshit. We find the press conference on our own.

The "press conference" was just like I thought it would be. A bunch of people sitting in chairs with walkmans and no questions. It starts and they all sit silently. Finally a few of them ask meager questions. Do I like Serbia? Did I know that Serbia is on planet Earth? What were my first impressions of Serbia? Soon it's all over. We have to be onstage in less than an hour. It's always this same wacky bullshit in places like this. Good show and a great crowd so it was all worth it.

After almost two hours of waiting in line, we are now in Austria and hurtling down some really bad road under gray skies towards our semi-day off. We are thirty-five kilometers out of Vienna at the moment.

07-07-03 Koln Germany: 0852 hrs. Outside the venue. The side doors are open and three people slowly sweep out the plastic cups and cigarette butts and push the chairs to the side. Two men and a woman, all elderly with that worked hard all my life look in their eyes. Done some good shows in this place. Listening to Generation X. The song '100 Punks Rule' always reminds me of an old friend Dave

Byers who died on February 9th of this year. I remember him yelling the lyrics of that song outside a club one night and it stuck in my head. I can still hear him yelling them out. I had not seen him for years but always think of him when I hear the song.

Almost everyone has songs they associate with certain times in their lives. For me, songs are the major reference points to instances in my life. The way the sky looks right now out the window, gray and about-to-rain reminds me of walking to work in DC and I hear Generation X immediately. I put the tunes on and I'm back there instantly. Some songs, damn—I play them and I have to sit down. Sometimes I put a record on and I don't know if I'm even hearing it, I just stare at nothing, I'm off somewhere. A lot of the time, records are way better company than people.

Like a lot of people, I have a lot of records but there's a solid few that get played more than all the others combined. I should try and make a list of the 100 Albums to grab when the house is burning down. That would be hard. Living the way I have over half of my life now, music means so much to me. I do most of my listening on headphones and boom boxes on the road. There's some records I have traveled with for almost twenty years. The music of The Rites of Spring on Dischord Records has been on the road with me in one form or another for nineteen years. Sometimes when I get off the road, the only music I can listen to is the songs I had out with me on tour because they make me feel like I am still out here. How lame.

11:32 p.m. Show over. Sitting in the suffer bus, breathing fumes, waiting to go. Show started badly tonight. Well, it started fairly well, the opening band Aerogramme was really cool and I enjoyed listening to them and was looking forward to playing. We get out there and start in on 'Rise Above' and I get hit with two cups of beer. I hadn't done anything to them and I get beer all over me. It fucked the mic up, I'm drenched and stenching of beer. I did what I always do in this situation. You have to let them know how it is immediately and in the most direct manner. I took my bottles of water and threw them as hard as I could at the largest amount of heads. Three bottles, three hits. Does it matter who I hit? No. You must hit someone though and

broken summers
195

then everybody will clearly understand what time it is and your position on this matter and then you can get on with things. I would much rather make it personal and just punch the guy but the stage and barricade didn't allow this to happen. A pity. I was told later that I hit one of the perpetrators. A bonus.

After that, the audience no longer mattered to me, only the music did so I just got deep into the music and played my ass off and twenty-five songs later we were done. It was good playing and we didn't take much time between songs, we just pounded them. The set is a real test. I have eight straight coming up and it won't be easy.

I think I am getting over jet lag fairly quickly. It's almost midnight and I'm feeling alright. I might even be able to take on a few pages of Kafka before I sleep.

I usually don't allow myself to think this way but it hit me before we went out tonight: What if all this work we are doing for Damien, Jessie and Jason actually helps? What if the DNA results come back as something that can be used as evidence and there's a new trial and the tide turns in this case? I have been in the mindset that this is all for nothing, that we will raise a ton of money and their lawyers will do something stupid with it or the DNA evidence won't come back as conclusive and this was all a wash and that Damien will be executed and the other two will spend the rest of their lives in prison without ever getting a fair day in court. I know this isn't the most positive light to look at this situation in but that's how I see it. I just think that at the end of the day, ignorance, fear and basic stupidity win in the end. Look at the president we elected, the guy's probably going to get elected again. We will let this happen. Three guys go to jail with no evidence tying them to the crime and I get static from Arkansas and Tennessee locals for trying to help finance evidence testing? I don't know, I don't see this amounting to anything more than a damned good try. Worth it, yes but I am not expecting a Hollywood ending. Three boys in the ground and three boys in prison. It's like getting hit in the stomach. And they throw beer.

The weak run things. The soft handed, never worked cowards seem to win more than they lose. Sometimes it's hard to take but it keeps me mean and ramming my shoulder into it.

07-08-03 Amsterdam Holland: 11:49 p.m. Early show for the Paradiso. For the millionth time, this is the venue I turned twenty-two in. I love playing this place. Not much to remark upon besides the Amsterdamers were pretty lively tonight. Usually they are into it but a bit reserved. Tonight they cut loose a little more than usual. Nothing to remark on about the gig itself. They showed up, we played and it was cool.

I walked around on some familiar streets before bus call and all the stuff I saw when I was first here in the 80's remains for the most part unchanged. There's all the student age types walking around, they gather in packs and don't seem to do much but stand around and smoke. There's a lot of tourists in this town. I always feel strange around tourists. I am in these cities so often, I feel like an employee of the venue on break walking around. Sometimes someone from Amerika recognizes me and they trip out. "What are you doing all the way out HERE?!" Pal, Amsterdam isn't all the way out anywhere. Look, there's a Starbucks! It's a small world! Didn't used to be.

Day off in London coming up.

07-09-03 London UK: 5:45 p.m. Just fuckin' lock me up. I got here several hours ago. At one point I was walking around and I see this small pack of guys walking around, they're junkies going from place to place doing their fuck up thing. An hour later I am walking back from dropping my clothes at the wash and I see this roving pack of scum again and they're walking towards me. One of them, who looks like the Stereo MCs guy, looks at me, spreads his hands wide and says, "I'm all ears." I started walking at him and winding up to take him out, I'm so fuckin' happy he's serving himself up to me like this and I only hope one of his friends wants some too. This is how fucked I am right now. Forty-two. I'm going to get so killed one of these days. Anyway, the dirtbag walks way around me and lives to shoot up another day. Too much 'My War.' Other frustrations work on me as well. Let's just say that male/female relationships can sometimes be stressful and make one feel vulnerable and foolish. Yes, that's right, male/female relationships, as in, I'm in one, although, that might be over as of a couple of hours ago. Contrary to urban legend, I am not a homosexual, just a low-key heterosexual. So far, today has been in the key of E.

07-10-03 London UK: 11:50 p.m. I'm always glad when the London show is done. It's not that I don't like playing here, it's more that it's such a hassle to do anything gig-wise in this city. Can't park the bus, can't make noise until this time, has to be over by that time, etc.

Today I was walking around, waiting for the show to start. The weather was hot and the streets were packed with people. So many tourists.

But, the show, the show, the show. The show was good. Aerogramme opened again and they were really good again. That's a good band. We played well and the audience was into it. There's not a lot anyone can do about it at this point. We cannot be stopped. The fact that we're going to kill it every night is a given. As lame as London audiences can be at times with their hilarious lightweight attitude, they didn't stand a chance against this stuff. And at the end of the day, that's what this is all about. Confront and deliver as promised. Unity? Fuck unity. Fuck you. Fuck these press shitheads. I was told earlier today that I had an interview with some magazine about the WM3 so of course I did it. I was told that this was a big deal magazine and I was really lucky to be in it and they were doing an article on the WM3 anyway and the press agent managed to get them to talk to me and they told him that they would, " . . . send over an interviewer to record any utterances of Henry Rollins." I couldn't wait to meet this fuckin' guy. I did, finally. We went to the dressing room and I asked him if he was the guy who was sent to record my utterances. I then asked him if I looked like a fucking barnyard animal to him. I then reminded him that I was between him and the door. He was cool and we had a nice little chat and then he went on his little way. I looked at the copy of this great magazine that he left me and it was a bunch of models dressed up in shitty clothes. Can you imagine being so lame that you will buy a shirt for half a week's paycheck that says "Sean John" on it? I know what you are. You're a bitch and you deserve all the beatings you have coming your way.

It was great to see TV Smith and Gaye Advert after the show. They are one half of the legendary band, The Adverts. Can't say enough about TV Smith. What a man, what a songwriter. Almost thirty years in and he's still writing great songs you don't have to be embarrassed to listen to like so many of these fucks. Have you heard what passes for music these days? "From writers to scientists, it's all the same, their facts to twist. I've been hit by passing fists, but this is where I'll stay. Here it is, all around me, my place." –TV Smith 'My Place.' Now that's a lyric. Been listening to that song for at least twenty-three years.

Never lose your anger. Never lose your will to confront. This town always pisses me off.

07-11-03 Liverpool UK: 11:44 p.m. On the ground floor of the good ol' suffer bus. Tonight's show was good. The audience was a bit more lively than the London crowd. A lot of hard heads out there. We had one of those annoying drunks in attendance. He gets onstage and gets tossed off. He goes up to the front of the stage and punches Brian a couple of times. Bad move. Brian is off the stage in a flash and pounding the guy. Brian was actually able to punch the guy while he was in the air after diving off the stage after the guy. It's a bird. It's a plane. It's Brian Blumeyer punching your lights out! Brian gets pulled off the guy. Brian's so not the guy to mess with. A few songs later, the guy is back and pulling me into the crowd by my leg so I punch him in the face and drop him. The rest of the night he's pointing at me like we're going to have some business later. That's how insane this bitch is. I begged him to stay after the show. Besides this loser, and the people who couldn't seem to stop putting their fingers in my eyes all night, it was a good time anyway. I went out to the bus after the show and there were some people there and they were all totally cool but the guy with the death wish was nowhere to be found. We could have had fun! You on the ground coughing up all that beer mixed with blood. Oh well. All in all, a good time was had by all. By my count, thirteen more shows to go on this thing and then it's over. I think what will be best for me is to forget about this tour as fast as I can and get on with things. This is the best music there is but it's not mine and it's from a different time. Somehow, I feel closer to the songs now than the first time around. Be that as it may, it's the past and I sang these songs when I was young and I'm not young anymore so I shouldn't be singing them.

I have been getting the kindest, most enthusiastic e-mails from people every day. They are so into the shows and why we're doing it and it gives me a lot of strength. It's a heavy thing to tour with. I get a short break from it onstage every night, getting to rock out. The rest of the thing is three boys in graves and three young men in prison and a whole lot of bullshit and apathy to hack through. I got a letter from a guy who told me to check out an item on E-bay. It's a DVD of our Seattle show. The initial bid price is fifty bucks! I go to the ask the seller a question box and asked him if he'd like to get sued. The guy writes me back and gives me attitude like I'm out of line. Aren't people great? This is what comes with trying to do the right thing. The weaklings come out. The ones who should have been put in pails of warm water at birth, do nothings, music journalists, they would be better off as alligator food. So now, on to Nottingham.

07-12-03 Nottingham UK: 11:33 p.m. On the wonderful suffer bus. I love this venue, Rock City. It's what all these other fucked up venues should be. Great PA, crew guys who know what they're doing, a great production office and catering. We had a good time last year when we played here and tonight was even better. The two women groping me and chewing on my stomach were intense but the show was good nonetheless. I like intense audiences who get into the music. Too many nights there's the personality parade. The guy who has to come over the barricade seven times, the dramatic drunks, it's all display. Some nights you wonder if you could have played better if they were more committed. Some nights, the only thing that got in the way of a good show was the audience. I've heard movie crew people say that making movies would be so cool if it weren't for these actors all over the set. It's the only reason I'm in their town. I have been waiting all day and part of the night to play the show. It's hard when it gets treated like it's nothing. There's a lot of that in this business.

Can't think about that part of the music world too much. There's so much disappointment and time wasted, incredible effort squandered like it didn't matter. It's not easy to fight off the bitterness. First thing you have to remember is that you're owed nothing, you will meet a lot of people and hardly any of them will ever be your friends. If you can keep that one up front, you can get through this stuff with relative ease. No one's asking you to do any of this and you can quit any time you want and no one will notice or care. It's not a matter of poor little me, fuck that—it just means you have to have your fun and not worry about any of it too much.

Last night's venue was the last place Joe Strummer played. I think they said he died soon after. It was strange sitting in the dressing room thinking that he had been in there months ago. I miss that guy. He was still playing at fifty. I'll never be able to pull that off. Imagine how many people would be at that show. About as many as who live on this bus!

07-13-03 Dour Belgium: 1121 hrs. This is classic Euro-fest hell. We go on in about twelve hours and ten minutes. It's hot out and we are conveniently parked next to the "Last Arena" stage. It will be a day of relentless ska bands and then for my sins, we'll have to suffer through the very excruciating Stereo MC's. At least Therapy? is playing so there will be something to look forward to. We are on the same stage. They have the prime slot and we have the asshole slot late at night when no one will be interested in live music anymore. Can it get any better?

6:12 p.m.: Still here. I just finished JH Hatfield's very fine book on George Walker Bush called *Fortunate Son*. What a read! George W Bush, way to be a draft dodging-cokehead-richboy-drunk who won't cop to it! Here's a guy who got his dad to get him off a felony cocaine bust in 1974 and get his record expunged. He also got his dad to get him out of going to Vietnam. He's no dead beat. He's the president! The offenses and self-serving obscenity of this coward pile high as the clouds. The other day, a US Marine went into a market in Baghdad and got his brains blown out by an Iraqi man. Meanwhile, Bush is in Africa. The paper ran a photo of him with one of his daughters, he was smiling and patting an elephant. You just got an Amerikan soldier shot for nothing because you sent him into harm's way and you're hanging out with an elephant? You should be at that Marine's mother's house begging for forgiveness. Obscene. If that's not the most let them eat cake shit you've ever seen. Even in Africa, he's having to avoid questions about Iraq. If he doesn't like the question, he just doesn't answer. How about that?! Are you allowed to do that? Certainly isn't the most confrontational of people. Still hours to go before we get to rock.

07-14-03 Hamburg Germany: 2:36 p.m. Sitting on the bus. Last night was pretty cool. Before we went on, that Stereo MCs crap played on a different stage. I watched it to get inspired. That is the lamest shit. Smoke, lights, canned music, some background singers and that fucking guy. So weak. Finally we get to play and it was a great time. The audience was into it and we played really hard. It was good to play outside in cool air. It allows me to play harder. We've got these songs down and our playing is incredibly tight now.

All too soon we were back at the bus. I was standing outside with Mack and I hear a guy with an Amerikan accent around the corner from us talking about how much he liked that I said, "Turn on the fucking lights, there's a band onstage who wants to play," when we hit stage. And then he continued, "And then it went downhill from there," and I heard someone laugh. As I remember, being only a few moments over, the show was a good. I figured I better go over and see if this bitch might need a clip in the teeth. I ran over there and got in the first face I found. It was the lumpy little men from Yo La Tengo. Sacks of oatmeal in t-shirts. You punch one of them and they all die. I asked them what the fuck they were saying and they all started talking at once. They're nice guys, aren't they swell?! I asked them if they could play music that tight and they said they couldn't. I know. Anyone whose ever heard you knows.

Their agent Bob used to be my agent. He would always tell us that he hated our band but really liked us as people. That got old after a while. Once he called me begging me to put in a good word about him to Sonic Youth and I did. I wouldn't be so presumptuous to think I had anything to do with the Youth hiring him but I can't think it hurt. I imagine he does well for them, he's a good agent. Around then, I signed the band to a better, more together agent who wasn't a pot head and who even liked our little band! I called Bob to fire him and he was a little surprised but when I reminded him about all the times he gave us the rap about how he didn't like the music when he just could have kept his mouth shut and gotten paid, his surprise wore off a little didn't it, yes, it did. That was over ten years ago. Bob, you fucked up! 15% of over 100 shows a year, every year? 15% of of a have-no-life touring machine? You would have made so much money!

Then the rave started with a roar and all of a sudden it was that fake music pounding through the PA. There was a "DJ" onstage and the entire field was full of people, more than who showed up to see any of the bands. Obvious conclusions: This isn't music. This sucks. These people are idiots. It was time to leave. We did.

07-15-03 Malmo Sweden: 7:48 p.m. Backstage. Moist and unmoving, but the air is cool and it's quiet here for now. We have been here since early morning. I woke up a little past dawn and looked out the small window of my bunk and stared at a broken bicycle leaning against the wall of the venue. In my half asleep/half awake state, I started reading way too much into the image of a broken and forgotten useless hunk of metal once depended on and utilized frequently now thrown away no longer needed.

Last night was pretty insane. There were over 1100 people in that place. It was a frenetic sweatbox. I couldn't believe how hard those people were going off. They never quit the whole night. It was hard for me onstage. The monitors were such that the louder I yelled, the quieter they got so I had to sing underneath them somehow. The stage was hard and smooth so when they threw their beer from the balcony onto the stage, it covered me and the stage making it impossible to get a place to stand without patching out. Pounded through the songs anyway and had a good time. They always save the best for last. As I am leaving someone dumped beer on my back. It's hard to be cool to these people who would freak out if anyone did anything like that to them. After the show, they were all there waiting to get their stuff signed and they were cool and I was cool to them. There was a young homosexual man who told me that he loved me with such sincerity, it actually put me at a loss for words. I said, "Thanks." That's what you say, right? Kinda trite though, isn't it? It sounded a little lame coming back with thanks but I didn't know what else to say. Perhaps, "Way to go!" "Awesome!" "That's killer!" would have been better but thanks will have to do. Soon after we were on the bus and heading toward the ferry.

We go on in slightly more than an hour and fifteen. I am listening to The Fall. I went down to the stage a moment ago to get the set time and heard someone butchering 'Commando' by the Ramones. The Red Hot Chili Peppers. Damn, they sure took the balls out of that song. I guess it was part of that major label white wash CD of Ramones covers that came out awhile ago. I don't know why Flea went with such a tired sounding version. Then again, who cares? Best thing to do is not pay attention to most things in the music world.

The semi-retarded guy I met last time I was here was at the same door again today. I signed another piece of paper for him.

11:49 p.m.: On the bus. Walked out of the venue and met some people from the show. Are they all drunks or was it only just the drunks who stuck around after the show? They ask the damndest questions. The most open ended I-am-fucked-up-or-I-wouldn't-bother-asking-such-a-dumb-ass-question questions. "What are you thinking for the West Memphis Three?" Then there was the killer non-sequitor, "We want the rug!" What, the rug on the stage? "Yes!" Cool. I signed all their things and then got crushed by the embrace of the big breasted woman, said thank you and went on my way.

The show was fine. Not as dramatic as last night's sweat fest. We were basically left to our own devices as the audience kind of witnessed us from a safe distance. Still, they were into it and they didn't throw anything or spit so you have to like that. I remember being in the middle of 'Depression' during the encore and looking to the side to see a girl against the barricade scrolling through messages on her phone. This is why I don't really enjoy being near young people much. It's those little things. I like being around animals a lot.

Right now, I am listening to the Damned's *Black Album* for the millionth time. Twenty-three years I have been playing this record and it still holds up. Two days ago, when we were in Hamburg was twenty-three years to the day that the great Malcom Owen of the Ruts passed away. He was only twenty-six. Virgin has recently re-released their amazing album *The Crack* along with a collection of singles, sessions and live tracks that came out after Malcom Owen's death called *Grin and Bear It.* All on one CD, what a package. Perfection. I listen to *The Crack* often, it never disappoints.

I am feeling these shows now. One hundred and twenty-four so far this year. I come offstage now, put a towel on the ground, lie down and just stare at the ceiling for several minutes. These European shows have been intense since I do all of Keith's songs now. I get through it fine but I feel it after the show and sometimes on the last song of the encore.

Some records I have been listening to for so many years that I guess they're no longer records, they are a way into myself, a way to check in. I don't know if they're any good, all I know is that as soon as I put them on, I am there. People are ok but records are better. I put on the *Black Album* and I am back in DC.

We have been rolling down the road for some time now. We have a long haul to Stockholm. The bus is very quiet tonight. Only Mack and myself are up. The bus has a lot of sway because it's so tall and the driver isn't all that smooth so it's a choppy ride. Time for a little aspirin and a trip to the bunk to pound through some Kafka, my nightly ritual. This is the last night on the bus. We are hotel guys after tonight.

07-16-03 Malmo Sweden: 3:29 p.m. Backstage waiting for sound-check to start. Watched the news today. More dead Amerikans in Iraq. Isn't Bush's capacity for not dealing with a situation amazing? What is it, thirty dead Marines since the "war" was "won" and he tells Amerika to be patient. Patient? Patient for what? It's not a matter of patience. He gets nailed for spouting false information to the Amerikan people about Iraq seeking nuclear materials from Africa. He cops to it, kind of, he blames CIA director George Tenet and then says, "I've got confidence in George Tenet. I've got confidence in the men and women who work at the CIA and I look forward to working with them as we win this war on terror." Tenet swallows hard, dives on the grenade and takes the blame. You know that was a security adviser telling him exactly how it was going to play. Bush refuses to take responsibility for anything that isn't going his way. When asked to follow up on this, Bush sends White House spokesman Ari Fleischer out there to tell Amerika "The president has moved on." How easy is that? Got a problem? Just move on! Oh, ok.

I know I probably don't understand this stuff all that well but it seems to me that Bush is a coward and has no thoughts of his own. He sent brave men and women in to do a coward's job and now all those troops are sitting ducks hanging out in Baghdad waiting to get shot. Be patient?

07-17-03 Tampere Finland: 7:10 p.m. The Finnish are a weird bunch. I can't put my finger on it, they're just strange. We always have a good time here but I can't figure them out. There's all these drunk, emaciated punk rock guys outside, sitting with their alcohol and their dogs and they're hanging out with the emaciated hippies and they all look like they were chipped out of some ice block. What's Finnish? What is distinctively Finnish? There's the famous Tom of Finland and the great band Hanoi Rocks and that's about all I know of this place. We played here with Iggy a few years ago and it was one of the best shows I've ever seen. I met Mike Monroe of Hanoi Rocks after the show that night and he was totally cool. Iggy is going to be out doing some dates calling it the Stooges. It's the Ashton brothers and Mike Watt on bass. Sonic Youth opening. Perfect opener. A low energy band with no frontman. Iggy goes on after and it's all you remember.

The venue is a long way from Helsinki so we have another drive to look forward to after this show. We have been falling asleep here and there on the floors backstage. I managed to get some sleep on the floor of a room I found in back and feel fairly normal.

Oh, and then there's this: After soundcheck, there was a man hanging out around the backstage area. He mumbled something about an interview and it was hard to understand him so I said that I couldn't help him and left him on his own. I kept coming out and he kept being there so it was easy to see that he wasn't leaving. I asked him why he was still hanging around and he went into his hard to understand, mumbling ramble and I managed to decipher that he wanted to talk to me about Joey Ramone. He pulled out a book he had done on the Ramones and showed it to me. It was pretty cool, actually. He asked if I would tell him what I thought about the Ramones. It was hard to understand him and the whole thing was over in a few minutes. He gave me the book and shuffled out talking the whole time. His name is Jari-Pekka Laitio-Ramone, that's what it says on the cover. The name of the book is *Heaven Needed a Lead Singer: Fans Remember Joey Ramone*. It's got a lot of interviews and pictures and it's not always easy to follow but it's really cool. It also says on the cover "Also featuring the Ramoniac life of Jari-Pekka and his Homepage since 1995 (www.kauhajoki.fi)." I don't know what that site is like but it has to be worth checking out because the guy was intense. A Ramones fan for sure.

07-18-03 Copenhagen Denmark: 3:42 p.m. Sitting in the plane, getting ready to fly to Bangkok, Thailand. We'll be breaking up the flights by taking a layover in Bangkok. I am looking forward to being there again. We hang out there for several hours and then go back to the airport and head on to Melbourne, Australia. Today starts four days off.

We just finished eight straight and I knew we could do it but I'm glad it's done. I was wondering if my voice was going to get through it. With all the extra songs night after night, I thought I was going to blow out at least one of them but I kept it together and last night we did an eight song encore. We played everything we had except for 'Damaged I' which I just now remembered. Damn.

The show last night was great. For the two opening bands, there was no one out there. I thought that we would be playing in a cave. That doesn't bother me. It used to when I was younger. Now I am happy to play in front of anyone who shows up. So we walk out there to play and the scene had changed dramatically. There was a ton of people out there and they went off as soon as the music started and didn't stop until we did.

Those two dopey girls who were backstage last year in Helsinki turned up again. I was trying to come up with more insane shit to yell at them but couldn't be bothered.

I felt that last run of shows in my legs big time. They always take a beating on band tours.

And what about that? This tour is almost done. I'm not ready for it to be over. I wish we had another month in Amerika to go. The other night in San Francisco was the last US date and even though it was twenty-five shows, it didn't feel like enough. I know, it's not my music to play and it's dangerous to live in the past but it was great to be out there doing it night after night. Six shows and it's over. I think about getting back to LA with only workouts to help me de-compress. I have a lot of things to do at the office so maybe that will take up some time. Until what?

07-19-03 Bangkok Thailand: 7:16 p.m. Now this is a day off. We'll be here for another couple of hours and then off to the airport and on to Melbourne. I don't know how many times I have been to Bangkok. I love this city. We got in early this morning and got some day rooms at a hotel.

First thing that hits you when you walk out of the plane is that wall of wet heat. I've never encountered anything like it. The cab ride into town was eventful. Most places you look, there's some interesting street action. The best thing I saw was a young man kneeling on a sidewalk, hands closed in front of his face, praying in front of a monk. People were opening their market stalls situated under huge sheets of corroded metal. Everything looks like it's about to fall apart, the walls of a lot of the buildings are crumbling, not showing poverty as much as humans trying to battle the climate of this place with varying degrees of success. Pretty much everything melts, rots or otherwise falls apart in this kind of heat and humidity. The whine of small motorbikes is ever present. Old people sitting on wooden fruit crates. The heat, the noise, the smell—I love it. It was not even 0700 hrs. and already it was hot and wet.

Now it's night and it's still hot and wet. I'm sitting on a balcony outside the room and there are bats everywhere. The roar of traffic that sounds like a motorcycle rally is all around me. I only wish I had another day here. I don't know why but when I'm here, I am able to shut off to a certain degree.

I've been trying to figure out what the smell of this place reminds me of and it just came to me: India. It's the smell I remember from the streets of Calcutta. Car exhaust, burning rubber, the smell of everything that can disintegrate, breaking down. It's the smell of civilization and death and human eventuality. I think I've attached the image of people I saw burning at the funeral home in India to that smell. I like it. It snaps me out of time and makes me feel like I am in the yellowed pages of a Jim Corbett book.

Obscure reference? Ok. Jim Corbett was a tiger and leopard hunter in India in the early part of the last century. Villages would lose literally hundreds of people due to man-eating tigers and leopards. They would call for Jim Corbett to bring the animal down. He wrote books about his adventures and it's some of the most intense stuff you'll ever read. He didn't enjoy hunting the animals. He states several times in the books that he would rather be photographing them but when these beasts keep dragging farmers and their families off to the woods and eating them, he's got to stop it. The books are not all that easy to find but worth it when you do. Check out: *Leopard of Rudrapryag* or *Man-Eaters of Kumaon*. The guy would tie himself on a tree branch as bait! Thirty mile walks, living in deep woods for weeks; these are real deal adventure stories.

I don't know what the pull of this place is for me. Every time I am here, it feels like the place to end up. A small room and no possessions. A few years and no contact with anyone who might know me.

07-20-03 Melbourne Australia: 7:10 p.m. Trying to stay awake. How intense was that? Walk off the plane in Bangkok where you get bucketed by the air and then walk out of the plane here and it's cool and dry. Same planet?

It's great to be here at this time of the year. It's Australian autumn and it's very much like October on the east coast of Amerika. It gets dark early and there's a good snap in the air. I walked around the streets here in St. Kilda trying to stay awake but am too wiped out to do anything. I was going to try to hit the gym today and force my body into the new time zone but I can't do it. Some day off.

07-21-03 Melbourne Australia: 11:55 p.m. Hung out with my good pal Mick Geyer and picked up the conversation from where it left off a few months ago. Tonight it was Ralph Waldo Emerson, Ralph Ellison, the recent re-release of many Ranier Fassbinder films and all his great work. He mentioned a title of his that I never heard of, *Bolweiser* from 1977. I don't know that one but I looked it up and it came out right after his movie *Satan's Brew* which is totally nuts. I should see that one again. I can't imagine what *Bolweiser* is like. Of course the one you can't find is the first one out of Mick's mouth. We talked about Wire and some of the band member's side projects like Dome and He Said. I know, I know—as interesting as mold growing to most people but if you're like me and want to see interesting documentaries and read and listen to interesting stuff, you might find yourself hard pressed to know anyone with similar fascinations. As always, the time flew by. I wish I could hang out with Mick more often.

07-22-03 Melbourne Australia: It's late. It was good to get the first show done. I always have a bad time with jet lag when I come here. I am always dead tired about half an hour before the show starts. I was almost asleep while the opening band was playing tonight. I just sat on the couch backstage with my toothbrush in my hand, spaced, looking at the wall. The show was good though. There was the annoying fat skinhead guy up front who talked at me the entire night like he's got something to say that anyone would care about. Mildly distracting but not all that bad. Show slightly blurry in the memory because of the jet lag but a good one. When I am jet lagging hard onstage, there's always the sensation that I am falling. Now I'm back in the room. Wish I had the energy to walk around a little but I just don't have it tonight.

07-23-03 Melbourne Australia: Late. Before the show tonight, I went to an art gallery with Mick to check out the work of a painter from New Zealand whose name I forget. I thought the guy's work sucked. I'm so uninterested in one hundred paintings of Christ. There was also an exhibit of Aboriginal work and that was incredible. Talk about tripped out. The Aboriginal mind space is amazing. Many of the paintings looked like aerial photography. Strange for people who hadn't been in planes. It was cool to see Mick one last time because I didn't think I'd be seeing him after the show and I was right. I liked tonight's show a little better because I was more on the ball. The audience was a little more into the music and not as into rolling over other audience member's heads as much as last night. I have been exchanging e-mails with Nikki Sixx. He wants me to sing on a project he's doing called The Brides of Destruction. He sent me a sound file of a song called 'Shut the Fuck Up.' It sounds pretty cool. I never thought I would be writing letters to Nikki Sixx but as Sheryl says, "Every day is a winding road." Does she ever ask about me? She's into me big time, and one day, we're gonna duet. Why don't we duet in the road? Hello!

07-24-03 Adelaide Australia: 11:29 p.m. I don't know what it is about this place but I always have a great time playing in Adelaide. The show always seems to go down well and the people are always cool. Tonight's PA was cheap and the monitors were bullshit because the promoter is cheap but I have come to expect this kind of thing from this guy. I'll never forget the time he was supposed to pick the road manager and I up and take us to the airport early in the morning a few years ago up in Darwin and we nearly missed the flight because he was too fucked up from the night before to drive and couldn't be bothered to tell us. We figured it out before it was too late and just got a taxi. You waste your time when you trust these people. It's a shitty business. I always let the road manager deal with this guy, because to me he's not even in the room. I apologized to the crowd tonight and recommended that next time they swing him from his feet and beat him like Mussolini. In spite of the obstacles thrown our way by the lightweight promoter and his venue, we still managed to have a great time playing and the audience was great as usual. We have to get up early and fly to Brisbane so there's no time to read or think. I have to try and sleep and get my throat patched up to hit it tomorrow night.

07-25-03 Brisbane Australia: It's past midnight, we went on late. A good opening band tonight, The Giants of Science. Those guys were cool. I love playing this town. I don't think I had been in that venue since 1997. Anyway, the audience was totally into it and we pounded them. I am so deep into the thing now. I just play and play. It takes a lot of shows to get into that mode where you're just a gig machine. I pull open my gig bag and there's my small world inside. I see the bag and its contents almost every night. I have the pre-show down to a system. I can do it in my sleep. It's instinct. I don't want to leave it. I don't want to get off tour. There's nothing for me back in LA. There's no one I want to see. There's nothing but the office and traffic and trying to figure out what to do with the nights. Try to sleep. Try to not break stuff. Try not to mouth off to people when they look at me too long in the supermarket. I try to be cool but it's so hard.

07-26-03 Sydney Australia: 11:50 p.m. Back from the show. Had a good time playing and the audience was cool. I couldn't hear myself onstage at all and I think I did a real number on my voice. It's been three straight shows of dodgy monitors. The usual amount of punters rolling over people's heads over and over again. There was a guy up front trying to hand me a card all night. It's strange that someone will pay to come into the show and not even get to the music but just stand there waving a card in my face knowing full well that it's just an annoyance. Why are people so lightweight? You're trying to play some songs in front of over a thousand people and someone wants to have a little chat, isn't that just precious? Past that, it was a good time. It's great when the barricade is far away from the stage so I don't have to watch out for people's legs hitting me as they flip over. I got clocked good a few times in the last few days. A band called Mass Appeal opened the show, I think they're on the bill again tomorrow night. Apparently they reformed for these shows on request from our agent Tim Pittman. We played our first ever shows here with them in 1989. They were really good and people were getting off on them big time.

It's good to be alone in this room. Listening to the Damned's *Black Album.* Only two more shows on this tour. It's been the fastest tour I can remember. The first month went by like nothing. It was strange only being onstage for forty-five minutes or so every night. The sets we're doing now feel more like they're beating the hell out of me like usual. I think that's also the exhaustion kicking in. We are doing a thirty song set. It's a blast but not easy. More and more I dread the bottomless blank time that happens after tours. I have been outlining things to do in my mind for when I get back to LA. I will try to do a full day in the office as soon as I get back from Tokyo. I'll be getting in early enough. I'll be jet lagging and will be able to get to sleep early and be back in the office around 0500 hrs. on Thursday. Anything to keep going until I can forget where I just was and the go go go of it. It's hard the first few nights away from it. It's all I want to do. I want to hear Mike tell me when doors are and when set time is. I want to stretch and get ready to engage but there's nothing. Just me in my room. The boys in the band, they go from Japan to Belgium to do shows with Daniel Lanois.

07-27-03 Sydney Australia: 11:10 p.m. Back in the room. I liked tonight's show better than last night's. It's weird when you play the same place two nights. Always leads to comparison. Tonight there was less of the corny people over the barricade thing and I didn't have to watch out and hope that I didn't get clobbered. Mass Appeal was really good again.

So that's it for Australia. Good shows. I wish I remembered more of it. I remember the shows well enough, it's all the time in between I don't. The travel and show in Japan will be challenging. There won't be a lot of sleep before we hit stage there.

07-28-03 Sydney Australia en route to Tokyo Japan: 6:11 p.m. On the plane. Have been up for about two hours with about five more to go before we get to our layover in Singapore. If you look on the map, it seems that we are basically doubling our flight time to Japan. It's the only flight we could get.

Read this in the July 08 issue of *Newsweek* in the Perspectives section.

"He said 'bring it on'. Well, they brought it on and now my nephew's dead." This is a quote of Mary Kewatt, whose 20-year-old nephew was killed by a sniper in Baghdad in July. The "he" she is referring to is George W. Bush and his response to Iraqi resistance in the region. Here's a guy who's never been in a war. A draft dodger sending men into war and talking that macho bullshit. Here's another quote from Bush referring to the faulty information that he barked out in his State of the Union Address, the information he let George Tenet hang out to dry for: "I think the intelligence I get is darn good intelligence." Darn good! You betcha! You're going to vote for this guy? You need your head examined.

I hate to admit it but I didn't remember much of Australia. I played well and hit it hard every night without fail but the falling asleep twenty minutes before show time and the irregular and infrequent sleep made it hard to be on top of much more than the actual shows.

It was great to see Mick Geyer again. It's always great. I went online after I hung out with him the other night and got a book of Emerson's essays. Looking forward to checking that one out. I had just finished reading *Waiting for the Barbarians* by J.M. Coetzee before he and I got together and I recommended Coetzee to him with some reservation. Coetzee is a brilliant writer but it's hard going. The stories are set in South Africa. Lots of racial conflict, depravity, struggle. There's one particularly disturbing image he utilizes in the book where captured tribesmen are brought back into the settlement. All the men are in line and all have their hands on their cheeks like they have a toothache Coetzee writes. It's because there's a wire going through their hands and cheeks and it makes for a very meek and easily lead captured tribesman. I have been reading Coetzee on and off for about sixteen years, his book *The Life and Times of Michael K* is an excellent but harrowing read. I recently found a book that looked interesting called *Country of My Skull: Guilt, Sorrow and the Limits of Forgiveness in the New South Africa* by Antjie Krog so I got it along with another book that looked interesting called *A Human Being Died That Night: A South African Story of Forgiveness* by Pumla Gobodo Midikizela. I can't say that it's interesting to me, like I'm fascinated that people get tortured and fucked over but I definitely need to know more about this aspect of Africa. Reading those Ryszard Kapuscinski books last year made me want to know more about Africa and post-Czarist Russian history. Someday it would be interesting to learn more about Nicholas II, Rasputin and Czarist Russia, there's got to be some good stories to be found. Back at the house, I am a good way through Antony Beevor's book on *The Fall of Berlin 1945*, it's great and I just ordered his book *Stalingrad: The Fateful Siege, 1942-1943*. I can't call myself an enthusiast of WWII stuff but reading these books gets one into Russia's story and the Stalingrad siege was so brutal. I saw a documentary on it this year, people walking over dead bodies lying frozen in the streets, dogs chewing on them. Insane. Hitler must have lost his mind in the end, or his denial got the better of him. That's the idea you get when you read about the fall of Berlin. He just didn't want to hear bad news and sent his soldiers out to get slaughtered. Stalin did it too when the Germans invaded. He had a policy where any recovered Russian P.O.W. was considered a traitor because during capture, they must have leaked information, making them a traitor to the country. When the soldiers got back to

Russia, they weren't treated as heroes, they were thrown in gulags! Stalin left one of his sons to die in a German camp. After the smoke cleared from WWII the final death toll of the Russian-German conflict was astronomical. Apparently, there's not a lot written in Russian history books about this stuff. Makes me want to know more about it. My curiosity will be my downfall.

11:05 p.m. Singapore Airport. Hot and crowded tonight. Seems like a lot of Europeans this time around. I can't think they're vacationing here, it must be a stop over from Thailand or Bali or somewhere. I can't see Singapore being all that interesting to tourists. I played here many years ago. The mens room had instructions on how to use the urinal. Don't wet the floor was the first command. Remember to flush, wash your hands and don't litter. Got it, thanks. I have to try and get some sleep on this flight. When we hit Tokyo, it's no sleep until after the show. We'll get in at the crack of dawn and have the hour plus ride to the hotel, we'll have a couple of hours to get it together and then we'll meet up with a pal of mine named Mark Rappaport at noon and he'll take us from Roppongi where we are staying down to the Shinjuku to hit all the record stores and then it's soundcheck and an early show. I think we'll have a great one but we'll be knocked out by the end of it all.

The record stores in Shinjuku are not to be believed. Some stores have no legit CDs at all. Another great tour ritual.

07-29-03 Tokyo Japan: 1110 hrs. I wish I could have slept a little but I couldn't. Today into tonight will be a stretch but I'll make it. I slept about an hour out of the fourteen we were in the air and feel pretty beat. I am keeping myself awake with protein bars and momentum. I figure I can haul myself through one more show and then get some sleep tonight and maybe some more on the plane. I wish I was more aware of where I am and could have more fun with it but I'm too burnt. It's Japan and Tokyo is an amazing city but the way we're hitting it this time, it just feels like a strange rush. We'll be out of here in the morning. I've stayed in this hotel before in 1994 and 1997. I met Rob Halford in this hotel. He was playing with his band Fight. I can't think clearly. I want to see some cool record stores and get to the venue and start thinking about this show. It's been a strange week of distance and blur, the only thing in focus being the shows.

07-30-03 En route to Los Angeles CA: 9:56 p.m. Have been on the plane for about five hours. I don't know how long the flight is. I slept some last night but kept waking up and staring out the window as the room got light.

Met up with Mark. We hopped on a train down to Shinjuku and did a high speed raid on the record stores. One of my targets was some 1974 King Crimson shows. It's one of the years of Crim that I don't have well covered. I have recordings from Hamilton, Ontario, Toronto, somewhere in Italy and Heidleberg, Germany but that's all. I'm always on the lookout for too many bands but I remember every time I've hit these stores, there's always been a generous amount of Crimson and I don't think you can ever have too much live Crimson.

The expedition was fairly fruitful. The shops don't seem to be as well stocked as they used to be but I did find some cool stuff. J Mascis live in Japan 2-13-01, Sabbath at the Fillmore, Funkadelic live Amsterdam 1978, Van Halen live 1982, some King Crimson from the 1974 tour.

We went from there, back to the hotel, grabbed our gear, met the van and went to the venue for soundcheck and the show.

Before the show Brian came in and said that there were Amerikans or Brits up front and they were drunk and yelling. I could hear them all the way down the hall and knew it was going to be one of those nights. How many times have I played outside of Amerika with a group of Amerikans up front making the whole show a pain in the ass? Happens a lot in Germany. You're playing and you see four guys up front who are trying to get your attention, they HAVE to talk to you, even though you're in the middle of a song. Finally the song ends and they start talking to me like there's no one else there. Usually it's about how all the other people there are assholes and don't know what's going on. Everyone around them can understand them, of course, and all you want to do is get these idiots out of there so you can play your show. But no, they stay and talk to you the entire time like there's no show at all and it's get to know each other time, like you just want to hang around with four drunk, oppressive idiots. These are the most vibe killing agents of anti-cool imaginable. They are the death of what could be a good show.

After all these miles and hard work, all the way over in Japan, was I going to have to endure the wrath of a bunch of drunk, round eye fuckheads? I figured I was. I was right.

We hit stage a little after 7:30 p.m. First thing I remember is beer flying through the air hitting the smooth floor, making it impossible to stand without slipping. What a way to start your last show. I move to the side and Brian comes out with a towel, nearly wipes out just getting to my spot. I move to the side, wipe the beer off my face and get through the song. Immediately the generic fuckheads at the front follow their genetic imperative to be a pain in my ass. The one main fuckhead is talking to me and waving his hands in my face when he's not shoving people around and laughing with his friends. I concentrate on the songs. This is the last night of my life I get to sing these songs. This is it. The last time I get to sing 'My War.' This show means a lot to me. They all do but this is the last show of the tour.

The songs go on and the audience is just tremendous, so into it, so full-on, except for the fuckheads up front who just talk at me between songs. It is so annoying and they are so light weight. If you don't want to rock then don't come to a show. If you want to talk to someone, get a girlfriend. Don't fucking talk to me. I got a good laugh out of the crowd when I said to the guy between songs, "Eat dick round eye." He didn't like that but everyone else did.

We're now about four songs from the end of the set and the stage is dry and the band sounds great and I've moved away from the center of the stage so I can see a real audience and not those poser assholes and it's going great. I return to the center of the stage to see that the fuckheads are now policing the area in front of the stage, throwing people over the barricade and laughing and following that preordained path to their future as oppressive assholes who will hopefully blow their brains out before they waste more natural resources or breed. One boy is overhead, being passed towards the barricade and one of the fuckheads starts twisting his ankle, looks like it hurts. He takes the kid's shoe off as he falls over the barricade and as the boy is lead off to the side, he manages to hit the kid in the back with the shoe and gets a laugh out of his friends. Seconds after, two kids come over the barricade, the fuckhead proceeds to punch both of them several times in the face. The kids have no defense and take the shots fully. Then there was a curious turn of events. Seconds later, as if the heavens opened and divine retribution interceded, a full and tightly capped bottle of water flew with alarming speed in an angry, spiked, downward trajectory and caught the puncher fuckhead behind the ear. This water-filled vessel turned missile hit the guy with such force that it actually broke open upon his shorn skull. Judging from the way the fuckhead disappeared from view and came back up holding his head and grimacing, it must have hurt. It must have hurt a lot. He looked around to see who could have done such a thing. He held his head for a while and didn't seem as active as he had before this water bottle scudded him. Folks, I am not coordinated nor am I graceful, can't sink the ball into the net, can't even get the balled sheet of paper to go into the trashcan from more than five feet away so I guess my throw was just pure damn luck. I was amazed that I hit him that cleanly with that much velocity. It was a truly beautiful thing to behold. By that time there was a break in the music and I told the fuckheads that there were eight hundred people there who knew they were a bunch cowardly bitches and they all wanted them to fuck off and why didn't they? The place went off loudly and solidly and the fuckheads actually walked away with everyone cheering and waving goodbye. Then I asked everyone if they were ready to rock and we went back to playing and the place went apeshit. What a great night. What a great crowd.

After the show, I could hear one of those guys out in front whining to our crew guys about how they were sorry and they had respect and blah blah blah. It's always the same with these guys. It's never about the music, it's always about them. Finally the voices faded and

Brian came in and told me about their drunken apologies. He's seen this shit a million times. As far as gigs go, there's not much Brian hasn't seen a million times. I was about to tell my story about how I had a momentary attack of coordination when Brian said, "Nice shot with that bottle. Did you see how it exploded?! That must have stung." I had a witness! What a great night.

Mark came back with his wife to say hello and then Hiro Arashima came back to say hi. He's one of the better people I have met in this industry that is so chock-full of pussy ass phonies. When we did the *End of Silence* record, BMG Japan heard it and passed on releasing it. Hiro, who at the time had spots on radio and local music channels, as he does now, heard it and went to the BMG offices himself and laid into them, telling them to pull their heads out of their asses and put the record out. They listened to him and did it and that's why and how we got our first release in Japan. Without Hiro, this man none of us had ever met at the time, we wouldn't have had a record out or a chance to tour in Japan. This is the real stuff. He's the real thing. Every time I see him, my heart swells up. He's still great and busier than ever. He introduced me to one of his new staffers and I took him aside and told him to listen to everything Hiro tells him and he said he does.

Eventually we went out to the van and there was a ton of people out there. Some of the friendliest people you will ever meet. We did photos and signed everything. The level of gratitude took me aback. This music meant a lot to them. These songs are important. I wish Greg was there for that. I wonder if he or Chuck have any idea how far and wide their music has reached. It's quite something. Some of these people were just trembling. It was very intense but very cool and a great way to finish it all off. Finally, after everyone had their stuff signed and had used their cameras and cel phones to take pictures, they all stood there as the van pulled away and waved and cheered and we waved back until they were out of sight. We went to a restaurant and had some great sushi and called it a night.

I got back to my small room and packed. I tried to sleep but it was hard. The reality that the tour was over hit me, all the training and the preparation, the focus and mental toughness needed to get through this music and deliver it the way it should be delivered—all of that was now over with. The idea that we weren't going to be playing the next night made me feel lonely and small. It happens after tours. I have spent many nights alone in hotel rooms, waiting for the sun to come up so I can go to the airport and leave the tour behind me. It's never easy, no matter how tired I am, I always want another one. What now? It's dangerous to define your life by such fleeting instances. You can't hold onto to them, it would be like trapping bugs in a jar—they just die. It's the quiet that's hard. The time. It's the silent and solitary sorrow of a sailor with no boat who dreams of the sea. Until the next voyage, I wait.

Disintegration:

I have been here a few days and I am aware. I am aware of every particle of pollution I breathe in. In traffic, I count H2's and drivers who don't use their turn signals. I inventory all the plastic surgeries at the grocery store. I am unable to sleep for more than a couple of hours at a time. It's my post tour heartbreak. It's my one hundred and thirty-three show momentum hung up on a hook in a dark closet rendered expended and past tense. Purposeless, I wander through the no life of my life. Earlier this morning, I sat in my closet with all the old photos and momentos of over two decades of tours past. I do it every time. I sit with the old stories, all the miles, the voices. The workouts are adequate but there's no fire in them, just putting in the reps because it's what I do when the sun goes down. But there's nothing to train for, it's just flatline time. There's no duty here. No mission. No standard. Do what you want. Show up, don't show up. I'm not tied to anything. The woman I was going out with flew in here a couple of days ago. She was back at the airport fourteen hours later. We broke up. It's sad. It's just two people, why things can't work out? I said have a nice flight, she said I'm dead sorry. I returned to my car and slipped back into traffic.

It's been a few days of approximation and distraction. I've been sleeping at the office, avoiding myself, hiding from myself in books and music. Velemir Khlebnikov, Alfred Jarry, Hubert Selby Jr., Antony Beevor, The Fall, Johnny Thunders. The hours pass like the water comes from a bucket not carried carefully—wasted, unnoticed. Coming back from the living, breathing world into this dead, dry veined, toxic, killing field of vampire fucks feels like waking up in a Joan Didion novel. The California she writes about is the Killafornia I see all around me. The other night, one of my agents asked me if I wanted to go to dinner. Sure. We did. We did dinner. I just done did doing dinner with someone. Do alliteration? Do sushi? Done did dat. Got a letter from the agent the next day. "It's great to have you as a client." Mr. McVeigh, I'm going to put a needle into this vein here, there'll be a small stick. There you go. It's really great to have you as a client. I saw a group of people leave the table to my left. When the man got up I could see the handgun sticking out of his pants. He looked right at me until I looked back down. I know what he was thinking. You know what he was thinking? What the fuck are you looking at? Eat your food, bitch. That's what he was thinking.

My house is situated on a piece of road that seems to be the last place that drivers can use their cel phones before they climb the hill and lose signal. Sometimes I can hear the conversations of these movers and shakers. The guy today walked from his truck to my driveway, back across the street talking and making circular movements with his free hand as he worked his client. "When you go in there, you show them that the way you want to express yourself to the world is through acting and that's the gift you want to give to them. This is infectious and everyone there will be swept up by it and that will make them want to get shit happening for you. Yes, of course I know you're freaking out, and you're welcome to come over any time. Yes, I am totally devoted to you and I think you have a lot to give. I think you have THE thing to give. Ok. Gotta go. HANG IN THERE!! YOU ARE DOING GREAT OUT HERE!! GREAT STUFF!! TALK SOON." He checks his watch, looks around, gets back in his SUV and he's gone.

I've been languaging with the locals and it's been going pretty good. At the grocery store the checkout guy asked me how my weekend was. Fine I guess. Then he asked me if I was going out on the town tonight. Nope, just back to the office. The last question woke me up. Are you a dancer? My answer: "Do I look like a fuckin' dancer to you?" Everyone in line stops what they're doing. We're the show now. I'm alive again and completely focused on him. Just trying to put a smile on my face? Oh.

Oh. And lonely somehow. For what? Who can answer the questions? Who can know? Who can slip through the tree line into the clearing? The one who stayed fourteen hours and left? Can relationships be more than approximation and compromise to avoid the darkness beyond the fire light? Is it ever real or just desired into fact inside a sliver of grace pulled from a wave of sorrow and disgust?

In these polluted Killafornia nights I have put my arms around a naked woman and felt the distance between us set by the outcrop of her implants and knew that we both knew that everything we were going to say and do was going to be one calorie, artificially flavored and sealed in a scratch resistant easy to wash coating. I have looked for poetry in these nights and found only sirens and coyote howls bouncing off the walls of the canyon. Only found whitey fear melodrama and bleached teeth, stillborn intellect, blood turning beige and small rooms in stucco slapped apartment buildings, slow horror, darkness.

Only a few days ago, my legs took me places worthwhile. Vocabulary was utilized and the brain processed real world information. There was air to breathe and somewhere to be the next day. My mind strained at the leash, teeth snapping at everything, perpetually demanding and open throated. Now here, now this.

Never tell, never cling, never confide, never beg. Not here. They will surround you like predators. Neck first—they snap it and as you lie paralyzed, you witness your evisceration. You can hear the neighbor's laughter and their glasses clinking a few doors away. Never relax, never exhale, never release, never reveal. Not here. They will ignore you like the dead. Mind first—they kill it and as you relax catatonic, you witness your decline. The neighbor hands you a glass of wine and gives you his card. Great stuff. Drop dead. Talk soon!

I ignored memories that had became defining lessons in shame to come from the cool shadows of the tree line to the clearing because you put your hand out to me. I stopped thinking that need was danger disguised as desperation because you said my name. I stopped thinking that desire was violence disguised as mutual disgust because you kissed me. I stopped thinking that life was fear disguised as mere existence because I could feel you breathing when I held you in my arms. And when I was finally standing at my full height, emboldened by the sheer power of wanting and being wanted, of calling out and being heard, this is when you chose to show me that I am invisible to the eye unless viewed under the spotlight of rejection, that I am voiceless in the howling storm of your indifference. Time passes in a vacuum and then suddenly you summon me like a siren to the fatal shore of your heart. But there's no shore, no heart. Just vast desert expanse where the weary and bewildered wander lost, wishing for the cool shadows and the darkness behind the tree line.

So now that the sun has set on this failed city, let us not raise our voices above a whisper, let us not look into each other's eyes. Let us be safe in darkness and silence and still our hearts for a moment, or many moments. But most importantly, let us forget. Until this land is reclaimed by the desert, until denial and greed have finally dried up all that once flowed, until the lie has perished, until all is as it should be, until next time.

Albatross!

8-23-03 LA CA: 4:28 p.m. At the office proof reading this book and need to take a break.

Yesterday I got a press release from Alternative Tentacles. Wesley Willis passed away in the hospital on the 21st. The exact cause was not specified but apparently he had just been in surgery. Jello told me that Wesley had been having bad health problems as of late.

Wesley was an amazing guy. One of his portraits of the Dan Ryan Expressway is here at the office. I sat in front of it for a little while yesterday. I also listened to his great song 'Rock and Roll Macdonald's' and his version of Thin Lizzy's 'Jail Break.' He came over here once years ago. He sold every one of the staff some of his CDs. I bought ones I already had, I figure you can't have enough Wesley Willis around. I just got his new DVD but haven't seen it yet. Damn, that's bad news.

Nostradamus Dept. This off the internet today:

West Covina CA: Two young men shown in a surveillance video-tape released by the FBI are the prime suspects in a $2.5 million vandalism and arson spree that targeted sports utility vehicles parked at car dealerships and on city streets, officials said.

Slogans such as "Fat, Lazy Americans" and "I (heart) pollution" were painted on vehicles during the early Friday attacks concentrated in Los Angeles' eastern suburbs in the San Gabriel Valley.

The radical Earth Liberation Front stated in an unsigned e-mail Friday that the incidents were "ELF actions" but added it had not be in contact with those responsible.

The underground group has taken responsibility for vandalizing sport utility vehicles at dealerships in Santa Cruz, Erie, Pa., Seattle and Eugene, Ore., and earlier this month claimed responsi-

bility for burning a San Diego area apartment building that was under construction.

About 20 vehicles, mostly Hummers, were torched about 5 a.m. at the Clippinger Chevrolet in West Covina and other vehicles were badly damaged, said Rick Genovese, West Covina's assistant fire chief.

The ELF has claimed responsibility for a slew of arson attacks against commercial entities that members say threaten or damage the environment. It is suspected in a $50 million arson Aug. 1 fire that destroyed a five-story housing complex under construction in San Diego's fast-growing northern edge.

ELF tends to distance itself from criminal acts but urges others to commit them, said Randy Parsons, assistant special agent in charge of the counterterrorism branch of the Los Angeles FBI office.

Yeah! That's so cool. Hummers beware. Every time I see one of those in traffic, which in this town is every few minutes, I think of my fantasies of the spraypaint and egg attacks. Torching the vehicles, that's intense. That sends a message out. Hummer drivers beware . . . The ELF is in effect!

I got an e-mail from Lorri Davis several hours ago:

Henry:
I write with some bad news. Damien and all of death row were moved in the middle of the night with no advance notice to a facility called the "super max". It's a set-up that is designed for the utmost in punishment. Inmates have no access to other inmates, they are held in solitary confinement - even the showers are in their cells, meaning they don't even come out for a shower. If they have to see a doctor, the doctor comes to their cell. They can still have visitors, however. There is no radio reception and TV's are controlled by the prison. The "yard" consists of cinderblock pens that are covered by block on top and bars on the front, allowing no contact with other prisoners. Phones are still a mystery, we don't know how much access he will have. It's sensory deprivation. I managed to see Damien yesterday - he's in a tough place, but seems to be

holding up. I have been in such distress since yesterday morning, but am trying to stay strong for him, it's what he needs.

I write not to upset you, but to tell you Damien needs your support. By that I mean please keep him in your thoughts, Henry. I know you care about him - I just wanted you to know. It just makes me want to fight harder.

This thing is so uphill. I can't imagine what Damien or Lorri go through. I wrote her back and told her that I think of the both of them every day, which is true. I guess I can't write Damien now. I can't see them forwarding his mail.

A hot topic in e-mail to me has been the Black Flag shows that are booked for September 12th and 13th at the Palladium here in Los Angeles. It has been advertised as "The First Four Years" with all original members. All proceeds will be going to cat rescue agencies, although none have been specified and in the advertisements, it says that the agencies will be picked at a later time.

Since the first show was booked and sold out immediately, much speculation has been made as to who is really showing up to this thing to share the stage with Greg Ginn. In the best case scenario it's all three singers: Keith Morris, Ron Reyes (Chavo) and Dez Cadena with Robo on drums and Chuck Dukowski on bass. That's the real First Four Years if you ignore the fact that Robo, although credited on the *Nervous Breakdown* EP, does not actually play on it. Drums were done by a man named Brian Migdol. That being said, if you had the above five guys and Greg Ginn, you would have the First Four Years as advertised.

While we were on tour, I asked Keith about it and he said that he's into it as long as it's the above line up. He said if he went to practice and didn't see Robo or Chuck, he would bail. A few weeks after Keith told me that, I wrote Chuck Dukowski and asked him what he was going to do and he replied that he didn't think he was going to do it. I told Keith with some reservation, as it's really none of my business, but I thought it would be better if Keith at least knew what was up from Chuck's end.

So, everyone's just a'speculatin' away and then came this statement from one Keith Morris:

"I need to let everybody that's interested in knowing that I WILL NOT BE A PART of the Black Flag reunion show at the Hollywood Palladium on Sept.12th and 13th as I was told that my presence or services were not necessary! At the very beginning of what's turned into a complete mess I made a commitment to do the shows based on the word of one of the main players that Ron Reyes (Chavo), Roberto Valverde (Robo), Dez Cadena and Chuck Dukowski (The Duke) were all going to be a part of this and as of last week Dez is doing it for sure and Robo might show up.....I've apparently been spreading vicious and damaging rumors and the story gets even more stupid the further we get into it. The bummer is that a large amount of people have already purchased tickets based on the fact that these shows have been advertised as "The 1st Four Years" but if there is no appearance of Ron Reyes, Chuck Dukowski or myself I guess that would make it the last year of the 1st 4 or some silly stupid such thing. Thanks, Keith."

Ok, so there's no Keith. No Chuck. Then another interesting twist comes from the website of Mike Vallely, the famous professional skateboarder. Mike V issues the following:

"Founding member of Black Flag Greg Ginn has reunited the band. The only reason why this Black Flag reunion is taking place is because Greg Ginn is able to take out the greed factor of doing a reunion. How? He will be giving the money made at the Reunion shows to fuel Southern California Cat Rescues. Both reunion shows will take place in Los Angeles at the Hollywood Palladium. Dates for the Black Flag Reunion are September 12 and 13, 2003. Direct support for Black Flag both nights will be a new band that Greg Ginn is putting together which will devote their set to playing the My War album in its entirety. The Band will consist of Greg Ginn

(Guitar), Dez Cadena (Guitar), My War Bassist Dale Nixon (Bass), Drummer Ducket (Drums) and Mike Vallely of Mike V And The Rats (Vocals). Additional support acts are as follows. Friday September 12, 2003 will include Epitaph Recording artists 1208 and Mike V And The Rats. Saturday September 13, 2003 date will include Fu Manchu and Good Riddance."

So, if one is to understand this, the opening bands will play, then Black Flag will play with the line up consisting of Greg's drummer, Drummer Ducket, Dez on vocals, Dale Nixon (who is Greg Ginn playing bass on tape), and then this other line up with Dez and Greg Ginn on guitar, Greg Ginn-on-tape and Drummer Ducket will play the songs from *My War*.

If this is correct, I wonder what people will think when they see Greg Ginn, Dez, Drummer Ducket and the invisible bass player who will have to be triggered somehow. Do you think that people will care that Keith, Robo and Chuck and perhaps Ron Reyes will not be there? At this time, I have not heard anything about whether Ron will be part of this. What do you think? Do you think people will not care or even notice?

I have received some intense letters about all this. One person wants to have a MAGG (Musicians Against Greg Ginn) Benefit for all the musicians Greg Ginn has allegedly not paid. A lot of other people say that they don't think that Greg Ginn will be giving the money to cat rescue agencies since none are specified in the advertisements.

Well, it will be two interesting evenings to say the least. I have heard a CD of a radio broadcast of Greg Ginn on guitar, vocal and bass-on-tape and Drummer Ducket playing Black Flag songs and, well—I guess Greg Ginn knows what he's doing.

Ok, play time over, back to work.

08-24-03 LA CA: 2:51 p.m. Taking a break from typo chasing and reading the incoming e-mail. A letter from someone who's a mutual friend of Keith and myself encountered Keith yesterday and Keith said that he has been re-invited back to the Cat show! Greg Ginn eats crow? Back against wall? Hello! Keith said he'll probably do it since he committed to it before he was dis-invited. Well, it's Keith's call and he is the man and we can't call him on it but if it were me, I think I would stay dis-invited. It's one thing to be kicked out but then to be un-kicked out, no doubt by pressure from the promoter who is easily shitting bricks at this point—it can't be all that happy of an environment. Glad it's not my show! If it were, it would be running a little differently. What is it with grown men?!

09-06-03 LA CA: 11:58 p.m. Been living at this desk. Book this, book that. Auditioned for some movies. I am a laughing stock. *Alien VS Predator*, oh yes, they're making that one. I went over to Fox, walked through their New York City set to building 12, room 201. Stood in front of the camera and acted out! I did a voice over session for a cartoon called *Teen Titans,* I was Johnny Rancid, a bully. I wrapped, I walked out and left a message for someone on their answering machine per the receptionist's request. Macy Gray walked by me. I knew I was in LA.

Meanwhile the Black Flag Palladium shows grow closer and since no one's talkin', speculation is all. Silly internet squawk drops into my mail box. Here's one allegedly from Raymond Pettibon, in all its typo-riddled glory:

> *Black Flag is my name, concept and logo. I changed my name from Ginn to Pettibon to distance myself from my fucked up brother. I created countless album art for his band and label-mates, including the bars! and I've never received a fucking penny. I watched my brother fuck over 25 memebers of his own band and the hundreds of artists that he signed and screwed. The fact that he's still alive, baffles me, especially since the Bad Brains had a hit out on him in the early 90's. He hasn't spoken to my mom & dad in 20 yrs. whom funded his band and started his label. Would someone please kill my brother now. --Ray*

If that's written by Ray, then I'm your mother. I'm not your mother. I got a call today from someone I've known for twenty-two years and he told me he just saw Greg Ginn on a cable access show and when asked who the hell will be onstage with him at these shows, he said that whichever members choose to come to practice and be involved will be at the show. Wow! That leaves things pretty wide open. Sounds like it's going to be "a wastey one," as we used to say. Sounds like someone didn't call certain individuals and invite them to band practice. My pal who has his ticket for the second show wonders if there's going to be anything left of the Palladium after everyone gets done wrecking it after the first night. Well, I guess we'll know soon enough. I drove by the Palladium the other day and seeing the words Black Flag on the marquee tripped me out and took me back. Hail the mighty Black Flag.

09-15-03 LA CA: 12:25 p.m. Well, it's Monday and the reports of the Black Flag show are coming in. So far, they have not been all that charitable. Actually the reports have been pretty brutal. The one below, from Ben Edge, is in the journalistic vein and makes for interesting reading. There might be some typos in the following. I am leaving them in:

> I'll start with the purchase of the tickets. They were set at $27.50, but with Ticket Master "service charges" the total came to $41.10. This is by far the most I've ever paid for a concert ticket, but hey, it's Black Flag we're talking about, right? Well . . .
>
> September 12, 2003, Judgment Day. At this point I've heard all kinds of rumors about who will be up on stage. A month earlier I was told by Chuck Dukowski that he wasn't even asked to perform. A few weeks ago, Keith Morris sent out an e-mail to let everyone know that he was told his "services aren't needed." So I'm expecting to be let down.
>
> I arrive at 6 pm and there is already a massive line outside. I see people I know from as far as Detroit and New Jersey waiting to

get in. Most of these people have Black Flag tattoos, some of them
have never been to California before. I am informed that Robo will
be playing. I am also told that HR will be a guest vocalist. I don't
know what to believe.

The audience has its share of sketchiness, a few LADS shirts,
a swastika tattoo here and there, but nothing to the degree that I
expected. The lobbies are full of booths set up by animal rescue
organizations. Most people are indifferent. The first band goes on
at 7:30. They are called Mike V. & the Rats, and they are okay at
best. The guitarist walks out waving a Johnny Cash poster. Cash
had died the day before. Some people cheer. The Rats are basically
imitating the Damaged/My War era Black Flag sound, and Mike V.
is doing his best Rollins impression. Mike V. says something like,
"Years from now when they talk about Dylan, Springsteen, Cobain,
Neil Young, and Cash, I'll feel honored to have shared the stage
with one of these legends. And that is Greg Ginn. His tireless atti-
tude and perseverance have paved the way for so many, and he will
go down as one of the greatest songwriters and guitarists ever."
They get some clapping in between songs. Most people are indiffer-
ent.

The second band is called 1208. They are a pop-punk band on
Epitaph who have only two things in common with Flag: Raymond
Pettibon did the art for their album cover, and they are from the
South Bay. 1208 try to have as little silence in between songs as
possible, but when the band does stop to tune, they are met by a
sea of booing. No one wants to hear them.

Finally Ginn is on stage setting up. On the opposite side of the
stage is Dez Cadena, whose hair is half way down his back. Ginn's
drummer, named Drummer, is setting up his kit which looks and
sounds like it was salvaged from a junk yard. There is no bass play-
er, but instead an SVT cabinet crowned with a head and some kind
of sampler. On top of the sampler is a cardboard face with a huge
mustache wearing a real sombrero. This is "Dale Nixon," a com-
puter that will play bass lines laid down by Ginn earlier.

Dez grabs the mike and says something to the extent of, "There have been a lot of rumors flying around about this show. I want everyone to know that anyone who is not on this stage tonight has been given the opportunity to perform. Now we're going to do the entire My War album, and Mike V. is going to come out and sing."

Mike V. comes out again, and this time he is literally getting a chance to do this best Rollins impersonation, which isn't that great, but not terrible. The whole band is keeping up with "Dale Nixon," which only allots 2-3 seconds before automatically going into the next song. There is no time to tune. A few songs into it, there is a group of men towards the front who are shooing away and flipping off what they see on stage. One of them crowd surfs and gives two middle fingers to the band while yelling obscenities. Someone holds up a sign that reads "Bait Flag." A large plastic garbage can is tossed towards the stage, but only makes it to the front of the audience. When the entire My War album is played, there is a 10 second pause. 1/3 of the audience is clapping, 2/3 is booing. I'm just standing there scratching my head. Then Dale kicks back in and they're playing "Black Coffee." The second that song ends, Drummer's set is broken down.

For the next 15 minutes stage hands are setting up Robo's kit. Robo is helping. A bassist who I am told is C'el, the last bassist for Flag, is on stage with an actual bass. Dez has his guitar in hand, and says, "This song is called Life of Pain." The band plays and Dez is singing now. I still don't know what to think, nor do most people. Half way through the song, Robo totally forgets his part, and it crumbles. Dez just starts the next song, "Thirsty and Miserable." After this, Dez takes off his guitar and grabs the mike. Alright, this is it. They play "Wasted," and the place goes nuts. Bodies are jumping and swirling around. There is a huge, scary slam pit. Robo sounds like he's rushing the songs, and screws another one up. Dez says, "This next song is called You Bet That I Don't Care, which is a hybrid song containing the verses of "I Don't Care" and the choruses of "You've Bet I've Got Something

Personal Against You." The song feels like a real attack on it's orig-
inal vocalist, Dukowski, and its original target, Morris. They play
"Louie Louie" and Robo goes into an extended drum break. The rest
of the band leaves the stage. People are getting uptight. Is this it?
The band comes back and finishes the song. They were doing a
John Bonham "Moby Dick" thing I guess. Somewhere around this
time, Dez says, "After all these years, it's good to know who your
real enemies are." My friend and I look at each other and shake our
heads. What the fuck is Dez talking about? After about 10 songs
from the first four years era, Dez says, "We'll be back in 10 min-
utes. Don't go anywhere." What now?

Robo's kit is torn down, and Drummer's kit is set back up.
Great. Sal leaves the stage, and the building. Now the line up is
Drummer, Ginn, Dale Nixon, and Dez on vocals only. They blast
through another 15 or so first four years songs, with the computer
pausing only 3 seconds in between songs. Another plastic garbage
can is thrown towards the stage, and misses again. The band
butchers "T.V. Party," and "Revenge." Dez comes in late on most of
the songs, because he doesn't know when the robot/computer/Dale
thing is going to hit it's first note. Everyone's timing is off. The
machine begins the legendary opening for "Six Pack," but does it
twice as fast as it's supposed to be. Ginn can't keep up on the open-
ing guitar part. He has trouble playing along to his own recording.
The band does some new Ginn jam song, and Dez has everyone
singing along "FUCKED . . . UP!" Fucked up is right. After a few
more early numbers, I look at my watch, and it is 10:59 pm. The
lights in the whole building turn on. The band is still playing. They
are doing "Depression" I think. A stagehand informs Dez that they
have to stop. Dez tells the other guys to stop. Dale goes into the
next song, and drummer turns him/it off. We all file out.

I saw the Rollins Band do all Black Flag songs just a year pre-
vious, and it was incredible. Every song was played slower than on
the records, but the energy and the spirit were there. What I saw on
Sept 12 was not cool. It wasn't bad enough to incite a riot, but I
couldn't get into it. I just kept wondering when the band was going

to screw up next. Plus, there was this aura of backstabbing and negativity surrounding the whole event. It didn't feel right. What I saw on that stage was not Black Flag.

Wow! Intense. I got a call yesterday from an old pal who went to the second night and said there was nonstop projectiles being thrown and so much liquid hitting the stage that they had to mop it up and it made one stage diver fellow patch out and fall while onstage. He also said at one point, the bass on tape thing broke and Greg had to fix it. My friend said it was a "Mili Vanilli moment."

Today's incoming mail on the topic has been constant. Kira and Chuck wrote me today, asking if I knew anything about what had happened. A few people wrote me, irate that I had not shown up as they were told I would. Finally, something around here that's not my fault!

So, it's over. Our little tour and Greg's thing are history now and it's September, the summer's over, school's in and it's time to get to work on the next thing. Of course, our involvement with the West Memphis Three will continue.

I put in some pictures I hope you will like. Darrell will kill me when he sees I've put in the picture of him and Mike with the grapes. He doesn't see things the way I do. I think Darrell is very photogenic and natural in front of the camera. Hey, it's a gift. Darrell has that "it" thing, don't you think? I do too. I think he should stop fighting it, get an agent, go for some modeling jobs and see where it takes him. The shot of Darrell and Jesse in their J. Crew day off attire is a testament to his star power. Don't fight it Darrell—you are the power. I tried to include everyone in the band and crew to give you a better picture of who we are and how it was.

I must relinquish this manuscript to Carol, the woman who runs things around here. If you got this far, if you came to one of the shows this year, if you wrote in, if you gave a damn about any of this—I thank you and thank you.

Your faithful correspondent,
Henry